THEATRELAND

Theatreland

*A journey through the heart
of London's theatre*

Paul Ibell

continuum

Continuum International Publishing Group

The Tower Building	80 Maiden Lane
11 York Road	Suite 704
London SE1 7NX	New York, NY 10038

www.continuumbooks.com

First published 2009
Reprinted 2011

British Library Cataloguing-in-Publication Data
A catalogue record for this book is available from the British Library.

ISBN 978 1 84725 003 2

Typeset by Pindar NZ, Auckland, New Zealand
Printed and bound in Great Britain

Contents

Illustrations

Map courtesy of The Society of London Theatre; pictures 2, 3, 4, 6, 7, 8, 10 and 11 courtesy of the Mander and Mitchenson Theatre Collection; picture 5 courtesy of the Donmar Warehouse; pictures 9 and 12 courtesy of Oleksander Putrov.

To Dolores,
with love

Acknowledgements

I would like to thank all those who have helped with my research on this book or with their general enthusiasm for and interest in it.

I would particularly like to thank Richard Pulford of the Society of London Theatre, Rosemary Squire of ATG, Geoffrey Marsh of the Theatre Museum, Richard Mangan of the Mander and Mitchenson Theatre Collection, James Bierman of the Donmar Warehouse, Malcolm Sinclair of Equity (and as an actor), David Dell, John Causebrook, Tony Field, Tom Erhardt, Charles Brown, Paul Hackney (who keeps the spirit of Lord Harewood's Coliseum alive) and also, of course, Ben Hayes of Continuum for his support, advice and cheerfully provided professional expertise.

In addition I would like to thank Adrian Poole for his friendship and hospitality, his cousin Tony and wife Sylvia, and John Fanagan for his informed and cheerful encouragement over late-night glasses of wine. Gabrielle Djanogly for a calming hand and soothing – though lively – presence and Pip Pickering and his family for their affectionate efforts in helping keep my particular show on the road.

My aunt Dolores, to whom the book is dedicated, provided my earliest introduction to the world of theatre, for which I am immensely grateful, as I am for her support of my various ventures in Theatreland.

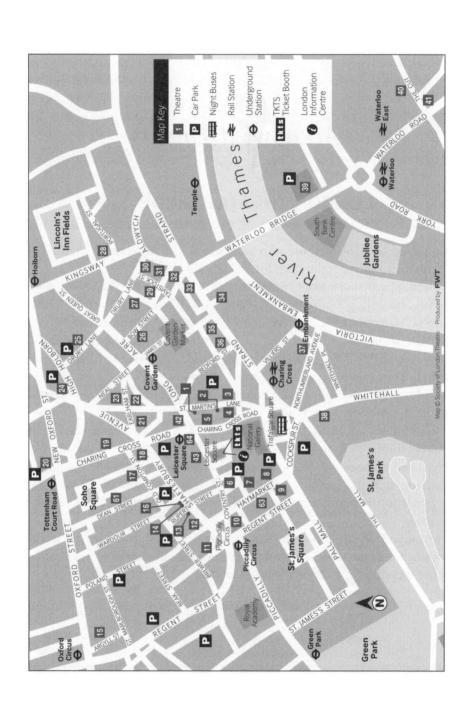

LONDON THEATRE GUIDE

SOLT member theatres by map reference number

1. Noël Coward
2. Duke Of York's
3. London Coliseum
4. Garrick
5. Wyndham's
6. Prince Of Wales
7. Comedy
8. Haymarket
9. Her Majesty's
10. Criterion
11. Piccadilly
12. Lyric
13. Apollo
14. Gielgud
15. London Palladium
16. Queen's
17. Prince Edward
18. Palace
19. Phoenix
20. Dominion
21. St Martin's
21. New Ambassadors
22. Cambridge
23. Donmar Warehouse
24. Shaftesbury
25. New London
26. Royal Opera House
27. Fortune
28. Peacock
29. Drury Lane
30. Aldwych
31. Novello
32. Duchess
33. Lyceum
34. Savoy
35. Vaudeville
36. Adelphi
37. Playhouse
38. Trafalgar Studios
39. National Theatre
40. Young Vic
41. Old Vic
42. Arts
43. Leicester Square Theatre
44. Greenwich
45. Shakespeare's Globe
46. Royal Court
47. Victoria Palace
48. Apollo Victoria
49. Apollo Hammersmith
50. Lyric Hammersmith
51. Open Air Theatre
52. Tricycle
53. Almeida
54. Hampstead
55. Sadler's Wells
56. Barbican
57. UCL Bloomsbury
58. Hackney Empire
59. Theatre Royal Stratford East
60. Unicorn
61. Soho
62. Roundhouse
63. Cinema Haymarket
64. Hippodrome, Leicester Square

Introduction

London has been the theatre capital of the world for five centuries, since the explosion of writing talent headed by the works of William Shakespeare, in the later years of the reign of Elizabeth I.

Elizabeth's rule (1558–1603) was unique in many ways and when later generations have thought of it, the images that they have conjured up are of Drake's ships, Raleigh's cloak on the puddle, Elizabeth's pearls, her mass of auburn hair, her gutsy, rousing speech to the troops at Tilbury at the time of the Spanish Armada ('I know I have the body of a weak and feeble woman; but I have the heart and stomach of a king, and of a king of England, too . . .'), of Shakespeare's theatre, the Globe on Bankside, of the raucous crowds standing in front of the stage, of the astonishing range of unforgettable characters created for them – of Hamlet, Othello, Romeo and Juliet, Lady Macbeth – and of the soaring, majestic poetry of the lines that the first generation of Shakespearean actors spoke, and which have entranced theatregoers ever since.

In a context where eras are traditionally seen in terms of princes and politicians rather than actors and playwrights, this is an extraordinary testimony to the enduring power of the stage and its place at the heart not just of England's cultural history but of how the nation sees itself and is seen by others.

That power continues to be a defining part of London's cityscape five centuries later, with Theatreland still a distinct area which is dominated, in an un-showy way, not only by the theatres and opera houses that are its *raison d'être*, but also by the restaurants, bars and hotels that are testimony to the continuing commercial as well as cultural power that theatre produces in the early twenty-first century. For if the export of the English language is one of the most enduring legacies of the British Empire, then the range, depth and richness of English theatre remains one of the main attractions for visitors to the capital, long after the Empire has vanished.

Just as Elizabethan London is conjured up by royalty and theatre – through images of the Virgin Queen and the rumbustious world of the sixteenth-century playhouses – so today's London is for many visitors the State Opening of Parliament, the Changing of Guard, Trooping the Colour – and the Royal Shakespeare Company, the Donmar Warehouse, musicals at Drury Lane, stylish comedies in Shaftesbury Avenue and the world's longest-running play, *The Mousetrap*.

For though the tourists, who are a vital part of the economy of the world's greatest city, still come to London to see the present Queen Elizabeth, and to enjoy the living legacy of London's history, they also come in astonishing numbers to see plays and musicals, to share the centuries-old experience of being part of English theatre, whether in the replica of Shakespeare's Globe, the Victorian and Edwardian playhouses that make up most of London's theatre stock, or the vast modern edifice of the National Theatre.

London's only competition is New York, which has an energy, exuberance and talent pool that makes it an undoubted rival of the older city, but which cannot ever quite topple it from its throne.

It has, since the 1960s at least, been fashionable in some English circles to run the country down; to assume that everyone else does everything better. There have been elements of this when it comes to theatre, too, with an assumption being made about the energy and pace of the Great White Way compared with the relative dowdiness of Shaftesbury Avenue.

Yet although, as with most criticism, there has been an element of truth to it, it is undeniable that London's Theatreland continues not just to have an extraordinary vibrancy, but also a class that cannot be matched. It is for this reason – a continuing standard of excellence as well as sense of history – that American actors, whether they have grown up on Broadway or in Hollywood, continue to see the London stage as the pinnacle of any serious acting career, whether in drama or comedy. It is for this reason that Dustin Hoffman appeared as Shylock in *The Merchant of Venice*, and why younger stars like Christian Slater, Josh Hartnett, Macaulay Culkin, Kim Cattrall and Brendan Fraser have also made the pilgrimage to Theatreland.

Americans undeniably do great musical theatre – though so do the British, whether Ivor Novello's *The Dancing Years* or Julian Slade's *Salad Days* in the past, or Willy Russell's *Blood Brothers*, Lionel Bart's *Oliver!* and Andrew Lloyd Webber's *The Phantom of the Opera* today. It is London, rather than New York, however, that does the world's best Shakespeare – and Rattigan and Coward and Pinter and Wilde and Stoppard . . .

In celebration of this, and of the history that gave it birth and continues to nourish and inform it, *Theatreland* is a journey through London's theatre district. It is an exploration of the streets, squares, alleyways and stage doors, hotel foyers and dressing rooms, restaurant tables and cabaret rooms of today's West End, taking in some of its characters and many of its characteristics.

It also looks at the experience of theatre in twentieth-century London: from the point of view of the public, of actors and the range of people who together create a production, and gives a brief idea of the process that takes a project from page (and occasionally screen) to stage.

Theatre is a resilient art form as well as an enchanting one, but it is also a business that makes a massive contribution to London's economy. Unlike most businesses it tends to prosper in times of economic or political crisis, so it is better placed than most to deal with the credit crunch and whatever other disasters are in store.

The one requirement for theatre to flourish is a space in which to perform in front of an audience. As this book examines, the open-air theatres we associate with Shakespeare's London gradually gave way to indoor playhouses – initially converted from other buildings but later purpose-built.

The Globe continues to provide as authentically Shakespearean an experience as possible, while those who want a cross between the Globe and a Greek theatre can brave the English weather and watch a performance at the Open Air Theatre in Regent's Park.

While mentioning these, this book concentrates on the theatres and opera houses that make up London's unique theatre stock. For anyone who loves theatre, Theatreland itself – centred on Covent Garden and Soho, but also including the small but perfectly formed upper-class enclave of St James's – is a magical cityscape where theatre's past and present mingle and mutually support each other, to the delight of audiences, performers, creatives and critics alike.

Above all, this book is a personal take on Theatreland. As such it is partial, in both senses of the words. Books larger than this one have been written on individual theatres, actors and playwrights, let alone Theatreland as a whole, so the writing within these pages can only give my angle on the subject. A comprehensive study of the subject would be far too heavy to lift, let alone to read.

If some theatres, some productions and some playwrights have been concentrated on rather than others that is because they speak to me, so it is through the prism of their experience that I chose to look at the world that they helped or are helping to shape.

This book was largely written in a wine bar in Covent Garden, in an alley that runs alongside a West End theatre and overlooks the courtyard where two stage doors face each other. I like it as a wine bar and restaurant but most of all because the very bricks of the theatre wall that it faces seem permeated with history, while the stage doors see today's actors, directors, choreographers and lighting designers come and go. Theatre may love, and be shaped by, its past, as is this book, but, like this book, it is always about the present: about today's cast, this evening's audience, tonight's after-show bottle of wine when performances and patrons are discussed before they dissolve in claret and laughter.

Theatreland's aim is to conjure up today's London theatre area, both for those who have lived, worked or visited here and have fond memories of it, and for those who have not yet been here but who hope that, when they arrive, they will, like so many of us who have made our way here over the last five centuries, feel that they belong.

1

A River Runs Through It

London was built on the banks of the Thames. Its docks were, until the 1960s, the biggest and busiest in the world, and the river was a highway, a working stretch of water that teemed with boats – from great ocean-going cargo ships to small tugs, police patrol boats and ferries.

Winston Churchill liked to refer to the river as the silver ribbon that ran through the heart of London, and though his sense of poetry as well as history informed his choice of words, his description was as accurate as it was elegant. The Thames was the one geographic feature that linked the various parts of London as the city grew up along its shores, and it was on the south bank of the river that theatre, in the form of Elizabethan playhouses and the works of Marlowe and Shakespeare, became London's great cultural gift to the world.

Today the river is largely ignored by Londoners, who will occasionally stroll along the South Bank (the route from the National Theatre to Tower Bridge is a favourite), or perhaps use one of the ferry services that link Docklands with the West End, but by and large it is left to the seagulls and tourists.

Although south Londoners will deny this, 'proper' London is north of the Thames. This is where the city, as Londinium, was first settled by the Romans, who laid the foundations of today's City of London – the square mile that was, as its name implies, the original London, but which is now the financial centre as well as a repository of historic churches, the Guildhall, various livery companies, the College of Arms (where the Queen's heralds still work, as they have for centuries, researching and drawing up coats of arms for individuals, corporations and companies) and other historic institutions.

There are no ancient theatres here, however, as Elizabethan theatre developed outside the City and on the southern shore of the Thames, away from the jurisdiction of the City authorities.

There were two reasons for the City's dislike of theatre. The first was on grounds of morality. An essentially Puritan ruling class found the performance of plays to be ungodly: an affront to morality. Plays touched on passions best left unspoken or, if mentioned at all, to be condemned from the pulpit.

Playhouses also encouraged noise and traffic – albeit mostly pedestrian. Plays, it was argued, therefore blocked the streets and created a public nuisance. In a place as crowded and busy as the City of London there was simply no space for a playhouse, and even if there were, the congestion it would cause would be intolerable.

Most importantly, however, was the worry about the potential political, rather than moral, danger that could be caused by gathering large numbers of people (some 1,500 it is estimated) together and then addressing them from a stage. This concern was to be justified in 1601 when, in the dying days of Elizabeth I's reign, one of her ex-favourites, the Earl of Essex, tried to raise London in revolt against her. The night before this attempt to overthrow her, he commissioned a performance of Shakespeare's *Richard II*, a play that is all about the overthrow of an out-of-touch and unpopular monarch by someone more ruthless and dynamic.

The analogy was obvious to everyone, and confirmed the City authorities (who remained loyal to Elizabeth) in their fear of the use to which theatre might be put by the unscrupulous. In the event, the attempted revolt failed, and it was Essex rather than Elizabeth who paid with his life.

Londoners may have had to leave the City to enjoy their plays, but although there was only one main foot crossing from the north to the south side of the river, the Thames was packed with ferrymen who would row customers across to the playhouses. River traffic was busy, and the river itself celebrated as part of London life in a way that has been sadly lost today. Elaborate barges for river transport were owned by the Lord Mayor of London and all the livery companies (grand trade associations that were initially established by merchants in the Middle Ages and which have continued to survive, often with their ancient livery halls, where they meet and dine).

In the winter, the Thames, which was shallower and wider in Shakespeare's day than it is now (following the embankment of the river in Victorian times), used to freeze over in very cold weather. The result was a popular feature of London life called Frost Fairs, when Londoners would, as the name implies, hold fairs, go ice skating, sell goods and even make meals on the ice that covered the Thames.

So whether it was a case of taking a small boat or of simply walking across the ice, theatres were accessible, despite being outside the City walls and across the water. What were those early theatres like? We have a number of engravings that give us a visual idea of the outsides, and these, along with contemporary references were used when constructing Shakespeare's Globe, the twentieth-century reconstruction of the theatre that some of Shakespeare's plays were originally performed in.

Thanks to the imagination and energy of an American actor and film director, Sam Wanamaker, the Globe stands on the South Bank today, across the Thames from St Paul's Cathedral. Set amidst the concrete and glass of twenty-first-century London, and overshadowed by the tower of the old Bankside power station, now the Tate Modern, where modern works of art are displayed in a highly fashionable gallery, the Globe may be far smaller than its neighbours but it has an extraordinary presence, not least because it looks as if a part of the river bank has somehow been frozen in time, and that the sixteenth century co-exists with the twenty-first.

The modern building was created as much like its sixteenth-century original as possible, using the materials and techniques that would have been available to Tudor craftsmen. The exact lay-out of the interior was, inevitably, the subject of some debate, especially the stage area. Some modifications to what was known of the design of the original were necessary on modern health and safety grounds, which require that a building the size of Shakespeare's Globe be capable of evacuation, in case of fire, within a maximum of three minutes. This was tried and achieved by an audience of volunteers before the building opened to public use. Fire finished the first Globe, when a canon, used as part of the pageantry associated with the theatre's production of Shakespeare's *Henry VIII*, set fire to the thatched roof.

Fire was a constant danger in Theatreland from the very first. Few theatres have escaped it, which is one of the reasons why older theatre sites have generally had several playhouses on the site. In Covent Garden, both the Theatre Royal, Drury Lane and the Royal Opera House were built to replace earlier versions that were engulfed in flames. The amount of wood used in the construction of theatres and the use of candles and other unreliable sources of light all contributed to the propensity of theatres to catch fire.

Other than the flames unleashed by the Luftwaffe's incendiary bombs, Theatreland was relatively unscathed in the twentieth century, though the example of the Savoy, which was gutted by fire in 1990, showed that it was a hazard that required constant vigilance. For this reason the larger theatres like Drury Lane and the Coliseum don't rely merely on alarms and sprinkler systems, but have firemen who man the building 24 hours a day.

This is why extra exits were incorporated into the design for Shakespeare's Globe, a reconstruction of that famous 'wooden O' referred to in Chorus' opening speech in *Henry V* when he asks audiences to suspend disbelief and to imagine that instead of seeing a stage they see the fields and castles where the action of the play takes place:

> . . . can this cockpit hold
> The vasty fields of France? Or may we cram
> Within this wooden O the very casques
> That did affright the air at Agincourt? . . .
> Suppose within the girdle of these walls
> Are now confin'd two mighty monarchies . . .

Under Mark Rylance, its first artistic director, who trod those boards as Cleopatra and turned the South Bank stage into the banks of Nile, Shakespeare's Globe became an international success story, attracting support and theatregoers from around the world, keen to partake in the experience of enjoying Shakespeare in the nearest way possible to original audiences.

One of the most popular ways of doing this, for the young and the strong, is to be a 'groundling': one of the customers who stand in the space into which the stage thrusts forward. Tickets for this experience are cheap, but the enjoyment gained is out of all proportion to the cost. With the mass of groundlings, the actors on stage in Elizabethan costume, the tiers of seats and thatched roof above them, it is almost possible to believe that you have indeed gone back in time to Shakespeare's days.

The illusion is broken from time to time when an airplane or perhaps a helicopter passes overhead, evoking the occasional droll look or ad lib from whichever actor is speaking when the distraction occurs. Far from ruining the event it adds to the overall sense of fun – because even when the tragedies are being performed, there is a sense not just of occasion but of celebration of England's theatrical heritage.

There was a risk, when the Globe opened, that this aspect of the experience, the sense of travelling back into the past, could turn the whole thing into a glorified theme park, but despite some carpers the theatre has escaped this, thanks to the strength of the productions that have been staged here, under the oversight first of Mark Rylance and subsequently of Dominic Dromgoole.

A short walk along the Thames, upriver towards Westminster, brings you to a very different theatre complex; one that also attracts theatregoers from over the river and across the Atlantic, but which could not be a greater contrast with the Globe's gentle nostalgia.

There is nothing gentle about the National Theatre. The epithet that most comes to mind when describing its South Bank home is 'brutal'. An unlovely bulk, it has the threatening atmosphere of a squat fortress that stands at the south of Waterloo Bridge like something a modern-day William the Conqueror might have established to ensure that the local populace stood no chance of sweeping across the bridge and storming the West End.

Not so much Theatreland's hand of friendship as a mailed fist, even the National's outdoor terraces are bleak, uninviting areas. However, the river frontage, at ground level is far more attractive. Theatre Square, between the National and the Thames, is a welcoming performance space that, in the summer months is full of activity, from theatre to music, with all ages encouraged and involved in the numerous activities that supplement whatever is happening in the three auditoria within the walls.

Similarly, the glass walls of the ground floor invite theatregoers in, in direct contrast to the overall effect of the concrete architecture, which looks like bomb-proof armour cladding designed to keep people out. Much of the Thames frontage is taken up by the walls of the Lyttleton foyer, full of seats, with its own bar and café area – and another café set slightly apart and entered directly from Theatre Square.

The foyer also includes a piano and performance area, where pre-show jazz groups and other performers entertain audiences and anyone who happens to walk in and wants to enjoy some free music.

The foyer areas on all levels are similarly open to the public, and among the recent displays has been one of the photographs of Simon Annand, which have been collected into a large and very dippable-into book called *The Half*, produced by Faber & Faber, one of London's most prestigious publishers, specialising in poetry, fiction and plays.

The Half is a collection of photographs, many from the 1980s but most seemingly from the 2000s, of actors and actresses in and around their dressing rooms (with a few lurking in stage doorways) during 'the half' – the half hour before a play is due to start. The photographs cover a wide range of moods as exhibited by their subjects, from weariness to joy, through the inevitable pensiveness as make-up is applied, to the playfulness of actors revelling in their roles and their sometimes outrageous costumes. One of the most memorable (on page 87) is of Sara Kestelman, dressed like Queen Elizabeth I, enjoying a cigarette.

Although the National is a modern building, opened in 1975, it has some long-standing theatrical traditions of its own, including the banging on dressing-room windows, by cast members, before going on stage. The dressing rooms at the National all front onto a central well, so the noise when this ritual is carried on is very impressive – a variation on the traditional thunder sound effect essential to the storm scene in *King Lear*.

As well as staging classic plays, the National has the luxury of being able to take risks with new ones, and to import some of the best from America and further abroad. One such example was *Jitney*, August Wilson's play about black American taxi drivers, which was a surprise (but fully justified) hit in 2001.

In more than 30 years of plays, everyone will have a favourite, but one of the best that the National has produced was the drama – with music – *Ghetto*, about a Jewish ghetto during the Second World War and the moral questions that faced the leadership of the Jewish community in dealing with the Nazis. The young actor playing the SS officer who memorably embodied the evil of that regime was Alex Jennings who, like a number of others, has spent much of his professional career at that theatre.

Jennings, who later went on to play a memorable Profesor Higgins in *My Fair Lady*, is thought of primarily as a stage actor, despite successes in other media – rather like another National stalwart, Simon Russell Beale. Widely regarded as one of the best and most consistently intelligent performers of his generation, Russell Beale has, despite excursions outside the stage door in various acting roles, mainly carved out his full and enviable career inside Theatreland.

Russell Beale was rewarded for his devotion to the stage in general and the National in particular with a production of *Hamlet* in which the portly and almost middle-aged actor was cast against type as the Prince of Denmark. The casting decision was spectacularly justified by rave reviews, packed houses and an international tour.

Although the National does serious plays very well – like Sir Antony Sher in a stage version of Primo Levi's *If This Were A Man* – it can also do sheer fun, too. Trevor Nunn's production of *Anything Goes* was a major hit that transferred to the Theatre Royal, Drury Lane, where it continued its early momentum, with a cast headed by Sally Ann Triplett and John Barrowman.

Anything Goes seemed to work even better at the Lane than the National, but that was as much due to the Lane's sheer theatricality and sense of occasion as much as anything else. The first night of *Anything Goes* had an excitement and a glamour to it (it is after all set on a 1930s transatlantic liner) that has been matched, in recent years, only by the next first night at the Lane – that of Mel Brooks's *The Producers*.

This section is on the National rather than the Lane, though, so some final words about the experience of going to the theatre there. There are two major auditoria: the Lyttleton (named after the first Chairman of the National Theatre Board), which is a traditional proscenium-arched theatre space, and the Olivier, named after the National's founder, Lord Olivier. This is a semi-circular shaped auditorium with a thrust stage and a versatile drum revolve, which can create extraordinary effects, as it did especially in *The Shaugraun* and in Alan Bennett's stage adaptation of Kenneth Grahame's children's classic *The Wind in the Willows*. The Cottesloe (named after a Chairman of the Arts Council) is a small studio theatre, but is very far from being an also-ran in terms of artistic achievement.

There is a 'National Theatre audience' which tends to be different from that in West End theatres, even though there is of course a cross-over between the two. Audiences at the National give the impression, whatever their age, of being rather more cerebral, more serious about theatre, than West End theatregoers.

There is also a real sense of community at this theatre, something that is indefinably encouraged by the architecture of the building itself. Once safely inside the glass walls, patrons are faced with the bar, the café, or the National's bookshop: any of the three make an ideal way to kill time while waiting to meet friends to see a show. The ground floor also hosts an information desk and box office.

The 1970s public spaces may be dated in terms of style, but there is a warmth to it (a combination perhaps of a red colour scheme and plenty of brass) that somehow envelops you once you arrive. The Thames always looks better at night, and the views of it from inside the theatre are strangely comforting: glamour at a safe distance. An added attraction, especially in the Lyttleton bar, used to be the availability of bourbon chocolate biscuits, but these delicious snacks (which have also inexplicably disappeared from the stalls bar of the Donmar Warehouse) seem to have been discontinued: one of the few National traditions that have been allowed to wither away.

2

The First West End

Shakespeare's Globe may be a reconstruction rather than the original, but it carries on the work of the Elizabethan theatre on which it is modelled and it is at least there, a living reminder of the heyday of the South Bank playhouses.

Sadly, all that is left of the next generation of theatres, which together formed what was in effect London's first West End, is a couple of plaques and a street name.

While everyone is aware of the Wooden O, which Shakespeare himself referred to in *Henry V*, few realize that his later plays were performed in indoor theatres, on the north side of the Thames, in today's Blackfriars and Fleet Street area, on either side of the north end of Blackfriars Bridge.

These indoor theatres – the Blackfriars, the Whitefriars and the Salisbury Court – were Elizabethan and Stuart constructions, beginning with the Blackfriars, which was built in the remains of the Blackfriars monastery, dissolved on the orders of King Henry VIII following his break with Rome over his divorce from his first wife, Catherine of Aragon.

Indoor theatres, which became fashionable in the first decades of the seventeenth century, allowed better stage effects (ideal for *The Tempest*, for example) and appealed to a more upmarket audience than did the wooden theatres south of the river.

The Whitefriars monastery was similarly dissolved, allowing for partial conversion to a theatre, while the Salisbury Court, situated between the two monasteries, near St Bride's Church, Fleet Street, was on land that had been part of the London palace of the Bishop of Salisbury – hence its name.

The Civil War led to these theatres' closure, and the Whitefriars was deliberately wrecked by Cromwell's soldiers. After the Restoration, a new theatre, designed by Sir Christopher Wren, was built on the banks of the Thames, south of Fleet Street.

This was called the Dorset Garden Theatre, though it was also for a while known as the Duke of York's, in honour of Charles II's brother and heir, James.

This theatre was, initially, very popular; partly because of its beauty, but largely thanks to its location. At a time when London's streets were narrow, noisy, dirty and dangerous, especially after dark, it was much cleaner, safer and swifter to travel to the theatre by boat than by coach or foot, and the Dorset Garden benefited from this.

Despite this natural advantage the centre of Theatreland was moving again. Having crossed north of the river and into indoor playhouses, it was now moving Westwards, to the new centre of Covent Garden, where a central piazza in the fashionable Italian style was being laid out, with superb new houses that, with their modern architecture, spacious size and relative closeness to the Court at Whitehall and St James's – an area also being developed in the 1660s – were far more desirable as residences than the ancient houses in the crowded medieval streets of the city.

As a result the Dorset Garden eventually lost out to the Theatre Royal, Drury Lane. As Drury Lane flourished, the Dorset Garden decayed from being a fashionable playhouse into a place of mixed and populist entertainments, like fencing tournaments.

The City is an area where memories linger in the stones, and over the two thousand years of its existence the various areas that make it up tend to revert to the uses they had centuries before. This is as true of the first Theatreland, in and around Fleet Street, as it is of other districts.

Standing near Ludgate Circus looking south, a visitor to St Bride's Church (on whose spire, by Sir Christopher Wren, the first of several billion tiered wedding cakes was modelled by an eighteenth century cook, Thomas Rich) will see that along the side of the church runs a quaint-looking lane called, appropriately enough, Bride Lane.

This is not named after all the brides who have, without realizing it, helped their new husbands cut into a slice of Wren's spire. It is, instead, named after the sixth-century Irish Saint Bride, to whom a holy well, probably worshipped as such in pre-Christian times, was dedicated when her missionaries arrived in London and established themselves in an earlier church on the site of Wren's masterpiece.

St Bride's and its surrounding streets deserve a separate book in themselves. The theatrical connection, however, is found by walking down Bride Lane, past the site of the well (now located under the rector of St Bride's garage, itself tastefully set into the ancient wall of the churchyard) and standing before the impressive Queen Anne style frontage of the St Bride Institute.

The Dorset Garden Theatre, built by Christopher Wren in 1671

As you stand there, you can see a set of doors, which lead from the Institute's basement up onto the lane, which at this point turns in right angles towards New Bridge Street, the road which, leading to Blackfriars Bridge, covers the Fleet River that runs underneath it and into the Thames.

The Institute is a Victorian charitable foundation, established in 1894, that was set up to provide education and recreation for the workers and residents of the parish of St Bride. The basement included the City's first purpose-built indoor public swimming pool, which was still being used in the 1960s.

In the Institute's heyday, from the 1890s to the 1930s, the swimming pool would be boarded over in the winter and used as a theatre. Only a couple of minutes' walk from Salisbury Square and plaques to the Salisbury Court and Dorset Garden theatres, the spirit of Shakespeare and subsequent playwrights was kept alive on the swimming-pool boards.

This theatrical tradition fell into disuse after the Second World War, when the Institute began a slow decline that was not halted until the late 1980s. In 1993 a theatre director, Carol Metcalfe, was engaged by the Institute to convert the swimming-pool hall into a fringe theatre – for a Shakespeare play. The pool's boards were at that time permanently in place, hosting not thespians but a row of table tennis tables.

Under Metcalfe the 'new' theatre space, named the Bridewell, became a lively and innovative hive of activity, with an increasing reputation for staging musical theatre – so much so that Stephen Sondheim became a patron, and a number of his works were staged there. Thanks to the shell of the swimming pool, under the stage, the Bridewell is the only fringe theatre to have its own orchestra pit.

The Bridewell also has two very attractive balconies with wrought iron banisters that lead down to the performance area, and which were incorporated into the staging of several productions at the theatre in the 1990s. The larger, north-facing balcony (a few yards from St Bride's Well) contained a number of changing cubicles for the swimmers to use. Some of these were removed when the table tennis room was converted into a theatre, while others were adapted to house the lighting and sound desks.

Similarly, what had been the ladies' changing rooms were converted into well-equipped dressing rooms that put some West End theatres to shame. This area had apparently been known as the 'coffin room' for some years, as a cardboard coffin from a student demonstration (itself a rarity in the City) about the death of democracy had been taken in from Bride Lane and left in the then derelict changing room.

The theatre's name, the Bridewell, came from Henry VIII's Bridewell Palace (now long since demolished) that stood between the Thames and the Institute. It was in this palace that Henry and Catherine of Aragon met before crossing the Fleet River that marked its eastern boundary, over a footbridge to the Blackfriars monastery, where the court was to hear Henry's case for a divorce against the Queen whom he liked well enough, but who could not give him the male heir he so longed for.

Shakespeare accordingly set some of his play *Henry VIII* in Bridewell Palace. Henry later turned it over to the French government as an embassy, and it was here that Holbein painted his portrait of two French diplomats, *The Ambassadors*.

Later still, the palace was given to the City of London by his heir, Edward VI, whom Henry did finally produce, but who was to die in his mid-teens only six years after his father. A stone portrait of Edward, set above a plaque recording his gift of the palace to the City, is the only physical reminder that this part of the City was once an important Tudor palace – apart, that is, from the Bridewell.

Bridewell Palace became, bizarrely, a school and a prison – within the walls of the one palace – and in Elizabeth I's time the prison became a mini Tower of

London, being used to imprison and torture political prisoners. One such was a playwright, Thomas Kyd, whose reputation rests largely on his play *The Spanish Tragedy*. This was a revenge tragedy that strongly influenced Shakespeare and other contemporaries, with its theme of gory revenge for terrible injustice – as with Hamlet's avenging of his father's murder. Kyd was also the author of what has been called, by theatre historians, the *Ur-Hamlet*, meaning an early version of the story that Shakespeare was to turn into a masterpiece.

Kyd had his own share of injustice and gore when he was arrested on a charge of blasphemy. He had shared rooms with Christopher Marlowe, the playwright and atheist. Marlowe proving difficult to catch, Kyd was hauled off to the Bridewell, in a case of guilt by association, and brutally tortured until it was decided that he was not, after all, guilty of anything much. He was released, a free but now broken man, whose health and career never recovered.

Playwrights, as mentioned earlier, were seen as a potential threat by the City authorities, which is why Marlowe, and through him, Kyd, were targeted by them. This distrust is a feature of all authoritarian regimes, as the Czech playwright Vaclav Havel was to find to his cost several centuries later, but at least in his case his story had a happy ending, with the extraordinary volte-face, years after he was first imprisoned, of Communism collapsing and the playwright being elevated to the position of President.

The Bridewell's period as a political prison came to an end, but it remained as a place where vagrants and especially prostitutes were imprisoned and beaten: part of Hogarth's *The Harlot's Progress* is set there, and the name Bridewell became synonymous with prison, just as did another gaol, on the other side of the Thames – the Clink.

The name Bridewell now lives on in the theatre, which has in the last few years been used extensively by the Stock Exchange Drama and Opera Society and by Tower Theatre, both leading amateur companies – Carol Metcalfe having moved on in 2003.

The Bridewell, a converted theatre space that is named after a converted palace, is the true heir to the Blackfriars, Whitefriars and Salisbury Court theatres that stood nearby. Bride Lane is a remarkable little street, especially when seen from the Fleet Street end. The lane itself, the Institute, the Church with its quaint churchyard and trees, the plaque on the Institute wall commemorating Henry VIII's palace – all create a very old-world feel amidst the rush, noise and modern buildings that dominate and define the rest of Fleet Street, and it is entirely appropriate that at the end of the view should be a theatre.

A footnote to the Bridewell Theatre is that if you turn away from the view down Bride Lane and cross Fleet Street to its north side where it becomes Ludgate

Circus, you will see another plaque. This is a large, rectangular one, with the profile of an intelligent, elegant and amused-looking man incorporated into it. That man is Edgar Wallace, a rags-to-riches Victorian character who went on – among other achievements – to be one of Fleet Street's most popular journalists. He was also a highly prolific and popular author, churning out so many thrillers and detective novels that a cartoon once, in a play on the several editions of newspapers that were then common, showed a customer asking a newsagent whether he had the midday Wallace.

Wallace's life would make a wonderful Hollywood film, which is why it is fitting that this Londoner, born in poverty in the East End, should actually have died, in February 1932, in Hollywood. He had gone there to write the screenplay of one of the many of his stories inspired by his own time in Africa: an extraordinary tale about a giant gorilla called *King Kong*.

Wallace's other accomplishment was as a playwright, and from the 1920s until his death he was not only a Fleet Street columnist and novelist but also a very popular author of West End thrillers, a venture in which he went into management with the matinee idol Gerald Du Maurier – father of the novelist and playwright Daphne Du Maurier.

The theatre with which Wallace is most associated is Wyndham's, which he took a lease on, and where he left his second wife (a much younger and very ambitious woman, who was to die from cancer not that long after her husband) in charge of his literary and theatrical empire when he went to Hollywood.

Wallace loved theatre. His first performed work, written while he was a young soldier in Victoria's army, was a music hall song. He took great pleasure in his theatrical successes, and loved a good first night. His plaque is at the Ludgate Circus end of Fleet Street for a poetic reason: it was here that, as a young boy, he skipped school in order to make some money as a newspaper boy, selling papers to passers-by.

This makes his posthumous memorial there so fitting, but the presence of a theatre a few dozen yards away makes it doubly so, and if his ghost visits the Circus where his newspaper career began, it undoubtedly then strolls down Bride Lane, with his trademark cigarette holder clamped between its lips, and takes a seat in the balcony of the Bridewell to watch that evening's show.

3

The Theatre Royal, Drury Lane

The Restoration, as the return of the monarchy is known, took place in May 1660.

Charles II, the eldest son of Charles I and sometime Prince of Wales, was officially recognized by Parliament as King – a title that until then had been acknowledged only by his Court-in-exile on the Continent and by a handful of die-hard supporters in England, who kept their spirits up during the long years of the Commonwealth by singing the Cavalier Song 'When the King Enjoys His Own Again'.

Charles's return saw the re-opening of theatres in London, with a royal charter being given to Drury Lane as well as to its ultimately unsuccessful rival the Dorset Garden, on the banks on the Thames. The legalization of theatre performances saw a return to royal and aristocratic patronage of the stage. The plays that defined his reign were to be 'Restoration Comedies' – a genre that was quick-witted, highly sexed and astonishingly cynical, just like the King. The crucial difference between theatre in the reign of Charles II and that of his father, grandfather and Elizabeth I was that when Charles finally did enjoy his own, he insisted on the cultural revolution of having girls on stage played by girls, rather than by teenage boys.

Charles, known as 'The Merry Monarch', was very much a ladies' man. Unlike Henry VIII, he refused to divorce his wife, a Portuguese princess called Catherine of Braganza, when she proved unable to produce an heir. Charles's virility was not in question. He sired several illegitimate children, including his favourite, the ill-fated Duke of Monmouth, who after Charles' death was to lead an unsuccessful rebellion against the new King, Charles's younger brother James. Monmouth paid for the revolt with his head.

Charles chose, rather than divorce and try again, to keep his wife, whom he liked and respected, but to indulge himself in numerous affairs. He combined his interest in women and the theatre not only by insisting that girls appear on stage, but in having a long-term relationship with one of the leading members of the new profession of actress – a 19-year-old girl called Nell Gwynne.

Nell has often been dismissed as simply an orange seller at the Theatre Royal, Drury Lane, given her career as a royal mistress, and the fact that orange sellers sold not only refreshment (oranges being the seventeenth-century equivalent of an interval ice cream) but also themselves: most were prostitutes.

Although the confusion is understandable, she was in fact a highly accomplished actress, specializing in light comedy, which suited her natural wit and an exuberant disposition that matched her sensuous good looks. Samuel Pepys records going to Drury Lane to see 'pretty witty Nell'. Her career was to be the subject of a 1930s film *Nell Gwynne*, starring Anna Neagle. Neagle is more often associated with saintly or at least dignified roles, especially that of Queen Victoria, but she made a very lively and effective Nell Gwynne.

Nell not only gave Charles a lively time and several children – whom he ennobled – she also inspired a much-treasured London institution: the Royal Hospital, Chelsea. This is, in effect, a retirement home for ex-servicemen, founded by Charles II, whose statue is to be seen in the grounds in the front of the imposing structure.

Chelsea Pensioners can often be seen in the West End, often in pairs (comradely habits carry on long after active service), and are distinguished by their scarlet costumes, rows of medals, and tall hats. They owe their home and their costume to Nell Gwynne's kind-heartedness. Spotting some homeless and clearly destitute old soldiers on the street as she drove past in a carriage with Charles, she is said to have asked whether something could not be done for such men. Charles agreed, and the Royal Hospital was the ultimate result.

A carriage was the setting for another favourite anecdote about Nell. She was always very popular, but another of Charles's (concurrent) mistresses was Louise de Kerouaille, who upset the English lower classes by being both French and a Catholic. One day, Nell's carriage, spotted in the street, was attacked by a mob, who thought it was the Frenchwoman's – and tried to overturn it.

Realizing the mistake, Nell leaned out of the window, showed her face – and bosom – and shouted 'Good folks, desist! I am the *Protestant* whore!' The mob were delighted to see her rather than her rival and let the carriage pass on its way, unmolested.

Nell should have a statue at Drury Lane, along with the other various theatrical figures commemorated there, but instead she is commemorated by the name of a pub opposite the theatre, called Nell of Old Drury, and by the Nell Gwynne pub in an old and atmospheric alleyway off the Strand called Bull Inn Court. This latter pub has a sign with an engaging portrait of Nell in her prime, and some quotes about the actress on the adjoining wall, by Samuel Pepys.

Although the tiny pub has a very modern television, the picture of Nell, the words about her and the narrowness and quaintness of the alleyway with its gas lights and old brick walls, combine to give a sense of an older London. Walking south past the pub into the noise and bustle of The Strand, with its incessant traffic and the roar of bus engines, is like suddenly stepping forward several centuries.

Nell's own time was very limited. When Charles II was on his deathbed, in 1685, among his last recorded words were 'Let not poor Nelly starve!'– for he knew that the career of an ex-mistress of a dead King was not a lucrative one. His brother honoured the dying King's request by granting Nell a pension.

Despite the intense Catholicism that was to cost him his throne only three years later, James himself had slept with a number of women outside wedlock – though his seeming preference for relatively plain ones caused King Charles to quip that his brother's mistresses were acts of penance rather than pleasure, and that they must have been specially chosen for him by his priests.

James, then, showed mercy to Nell by making financial arrangements to support her, but she was killed by typhus only two years after Charles's death. Charles's more formal connection with the Theatre Royal, Drury Lane continued long after his and Nell's deaths and is still there today with the theatre's royal charter – under whose terms it still technically operates – and its name. Certainly into the late 1930s the Theatre Royal proudly announced its debt to the King's patronage by having plain front covers to the programme for every performance at the theatre: plain covers that displayed only the name of the show with, above it, a facsimile of the Royal Charter, incorporating Charles II's portrait.

There have been four theatres on the site since the first went up in 1663. The current vast building, which seats 2,500 people, was built in the 1810s, and was substantially improved in the 1920s. The portico and the colonnade on the north side date from the 1820s and 1830s respectively.

The theatre has, naturally, had a number of owners, one of the most distinguished of whom was David Garrick. Garrick (1717–1779) was an actor and theatre manager as well as a theatre owner. He revolutionized the playing of Shakespeare and performance in general, expecting his fellow cast members to behave like a united company rather than a collection of prima donnas.

He also expected better behaviour from the audience than had been the case in the past. He is credited, for example, with ending the very seventeenth-century practice of the wealthier (and showier) members of the audience actually sitting on stage, where they would not only watch the performance but greet each other and their friends in the auditorium.

Another improvement that helped focus attention on the performance itself was the dimming of lights in the auditorium, so that the audience were in darkness and only the stage was lit. Garrick lived near the Theatre Royal, in Southampton Street, a few hundred yards across Covent Garden piazza. His residence is marked by an elaborate plaque – which he would enjoy. The house is now owned and occupied by a company that provides offices and office facilities for businessmen, and though Garrick was first and foremost an artist, he was also a businessman, so his ghost would approve of his home's current usage.

Drury Lane has the distinction of being Theatreland's most haunted theatre, which, given its age and size, is unsurprising. The best-known ghost is also the most unusual, in that the Man in Grey, dressed in eighteenth-century costume and a tricorn hat, only appears during the day. If he is seen crossing from one side of the Upper Circle to the other during a dress rehearsal, it is supposed to be great good luck for the show involved. Most of the cast of Ivor Novello's *The Dancing Years*, which opened at Drury Lane in 1939 and went on (elsewhere) to be the greatest British musical hit of the Second World War, saw the Man in Grey.

On the other hand, for those who are sceptical about the supernatural, no one in the cast of *Miss Saigon* saw this benevolent apparition during rehearsals on stage, yet the show went on to be, at the time of writing, the longest-running production (over 4,000 performances) in the Lane's history.

David Garrick was replaced, in the role of theatre owner, by Richard Brinsley Sheridan (1751–1816), an Irish wit and playwright best known now, as in his own time, for *The Rivals* and *The School for Scandal*.

Sheridan's wife, Elizabeth Linley, was not only beautiful but was also an accomplished singer, whose career he insisted on terminating when they married, as it was unseemly for the wife of a gentleman to earn a living.

Admittedly, Sheridan lived in an era that was, by today's standards, absurdly class-conscious, and where the upper classes really did have the upper hand. Although he was a very talented writer and therefore a cut above mere actors, and despite the fact that he was, as a theatre owner, a substantial man of property, Sheridan fretted about his social status, and yearned for a more respectable profession. Ironically, to a modern sensibility, he chose politics. In his day, however, when Members of Parliament were unpaid and therefore drawn from among the wealthy, this was a sensible choice. It also offered the chance of power, as well as a public platform of a different sort, in the House of Commons.

It was while Sheridan was making a speech in 'The House', in February 1809, that disaster struck. The Theatre Royal, which he had rebuilt at great expense

RICHARD BRINSLEY SHERIDAN

Poet and Dramatist

b 1751 ; d 1816

*From an engraving by Hicks after Reynolds
in the collection of Mr. Harry R. Beard*

Richard Brinsley Sheridan, playwright and theatre owner

some years after buying it from David Garrick, caught fire. So quickly did the flames spread, and so brightly did they burn, that the blaze could be seen from the Palace of Westminster.

Sheridan was alerted to the catastrophe but, maintaining the stiff upper lip of the English gentleman that he so wanted to be, he insisted on finishing his speech as if nothing had happened, before making his way, with a group of worried friends, back to the theatre.

Sheridan saw his playhouse on fire and his fortune literally going up in smoke. Catherine Street had a row of the early nineteenth-century establishments equivalent to today's wine bars, pubs and restaurants – some of the buildings whose windows, shut against the heat and cinders, would have reflected the blaze, are still standing.

Maintaining an almost superhuman calm, along with his trademark wit, Sheridan sat outside one such establishment, drinking. When one of his friends, concerned for his mind as well as his safety, said 'Richard, come away!', Sheridan simply smiled, refilled his glass and said 'May a man not take wine at his own fireside?'

Sheridan's *sangfroid* may have been helped by his having been tested on previous occasions. As a young man he had been forced to fight a duel not once but twice to defend his wife's honour from the attentions of an army officer who would today be labelled a stalker. Later, in 1800, Sheridan, as the theatre owner, was with King George III at Drury Lane when a man discharged a pistol at the King. Fortunately, he missed, the King showed himself to a relieved audience, and the national anthem was duly sung.

George had a significant effect on the theatre, though not until after the terrible fire of 1809 and the subsequent rebuilding a couple of years later. The Hanoverian dynasty that ruled from the reign of George I onwards was marked by a regular antipathy between fathers and sons – especially their heirs.

George III's mental instability was, centuries later, to inspire Alan Bennett's superb play *The Madness of George III* (filmed as *The Madness of King George*, in case American audiences thought it the third in a series of Hanoverian psycho-slasher movies). In his own lifetime one of its manifestations was a deep hatred of his eldest son, the Prince of Wales – later Prince Regent during his father's final mental illness, and, on his father's death, King George IV.

George, Prince of Wales, was a maddening figure of whom any father might have despaired, especially one as blunt as George III, who revelled in the nickname of 'Farmer George' and could not have been more different from his wilful, difficult, but artistically knowledgeable and enthusiastic son. Despite this, the King was expected to behave politely to him in public, which is why the incident at Drury Lane was so shocking.

One evening the King was paying a visit to the theatre. The management were being suitably attentive, not to mention self-abasing, when he noticed them looking over his shoulder. Most of us are accustomed to fellow guests at parties looking over our shoulders at someone younger/prettier/richer/more important. The King certainly was not used to this, and swivelled round to see who it could be. It was the Prince of Wales.

George III strode towards his son – and physically assaulted him. Both men's guards and flunkeys felt unable to intervene, so it was a little while before the Prince of Wales managed to extricate himself from his father's flailing fists.

It was decided that this scene must never be allowed to happen again so, when the theatre was rebuilt in its fourth and current incarnation, two separate staircases, each leading from the foyer, were built – the King's and the Prince's – leading to the only auditorium in the world to have two royal boxes – the King's and the Prince's.

These boxes are still there: the King's with George III's royal coat of arms, the Prince's with the Prince of Wales's feathers. They face each other across one of the widest stages in Theatreland, safely far apart, a permanent reminder of a brief but shocking royal family upset.

The vastness of Drury Lane's stage, and its backstage and understage area, made it ideal for great spectacles, a tradition that has continued to the present day with a string of musicals that have included *The Lord of the Rings* – at over £12 million the most expensive musical ever staged in London. Much of the money was spent on the stage itself, an incredibly complicated and effective piece of machinery that created awe-inspiring vistas of Tolkien's Middle Earth.

Victorian theatregoers were particularly fond of spectacle, preferably involving lots of animals, as was recognized by the Italian composer Verdi, in the 'Triumphal March' in his opera *Aida*, which saw processions of camels and elephants wherever possible.

Augustus Harris, who ran Drury Lane from 1879 to 1896 and was nicknamed Druriolanus, was an impresario who was more than happy to match public expectations of spectacle at the Lane. He is less well known than Garrick or Sheridan, but fully deserves the memorial on the wall outside the theatre, on the corner of Catherine Street and Russell Street.

Inside the theatre, in the foyer near the box office, is a seated statue (with trademark cigarette) of Sir Noël Coward, the actor, playwright, composer and wit (and painter and diarist and letter writer and poet . . .) who is discussed more fully in Chapter 10, alongside his friend and rival Ivor Novello.

Coward continued Harris's tradition of huge casts and lavish spectacle with his *Cavalcade*. Opening in 1931, this was more of a historical pageant than a play, and was a rousingly patriotic evening, looking at British society from late Victorian times to the contemporary world of its audience.

Drury Lane earned a great deal from its traditional winter pantomime (an art form seen more often outside London rather than in the heart of Theatreland) but after *Cavalcade* the board of directors found it almost impossible to fill the theatre; especially as the country was going through the Depression. Harry Tennent (of H.M. Tennent, the theatre producers who were to dominate the West End from the 1930s to the 1960s) decided that, having tried Noël Coward, he would now approach Ivor Novello and, in 1934, took him to lunch.

Over a long and lavish meal, he asked Novello whether he couldn't come up with something to save 'the Lane'. The board were desperate, he said. They might well have to close the theatre and sell the site for redevelopment. Novello was appalled. After all, his earliest theatrical memories were of coming to London to see shows at Drury Lane. And since 1913 he had lived almost next door, in a flat above the Strand Theatre (now renamed the Novello).

Harry Tennent stressed that he knew Ivor – could he call him Ivor? Yes, of course – everyone did. Well, he knew that Ivor was a hugely successful playwright, of thrillers, romantic comedies and the occasional drama, and that he was the most popular actor in the West End (starring in his own plays), but Tennent so clearly remembered Ivor's hit song of the First World War, 'Keep The Home Fires Burning'. Not to mention all those witty and tuneful musical comedies that kept soldiers on leave cheerful when they came back from the trenches to the West End.

Well, this was a new crisis, albeit an economic rather than a military one. It needed someone who knew how theatre worked but who could also produce wonderful tunes. Someone who loved not just the theatre in general, but the very stones and staircases of Drury Lane. Someone with the vision to fill that vast stage and, more importantly from the board's point of view, who could fill all those seats with paying customers. Harry was sure that Ivor was that man.

Intoxicated by the concept as much as the claret, Ivor said that yes, he did indeed have something in mind, and came up with an amazingly exotic, glamorous scenario featuring a handsome young hero (to be played by Ivor, of course, despite being 41 at the time), a gorgeous heroine who happened to be an opera singer, a King who was in love with her, a cruise ship that sank on stage and wonderful, soaring tunes.

A thrilled Harry announced that the board would love to see Ivor in a couple of days' time, for a presentation where he could go over the script in more detail, play a selection of the major songs and so on.

Ivor, now far more sober, went home and spent 48 hours, fuelled by cigarettes and black coffee, producing enough material to wow the board. The next spring, in May 1935, *Glamorous Night* opened at Drury Lane and saved the theatre.

Ivor's *The Dancing Years* was playing at Drury Lane in 1939 when war was declared over the radio by the Prime Minister, Neville Chamberlain: 'I have to tell you that no such assurance [to pull back their armies from Poland] has been received and that we are therefore at war with Germany. God save the King!'

The government immediately closed all London theatres, for what would today be called 'health and safety' reasons, before belatedly realizing its mistake and letting them re-open, for the sake of public morale. *The Dancing Years* had already left (it would tour and also play at the Adelphi, at the other end of the Strand, towards Charing Cross) and Drury Lane was given over, for the duration of the war, to the Entertainments National Service Association, or ENSA. This, the official body for producing morale-boosting entertainment for the armed forces across every battle-zone, was rapidly given the unflattering nickname, based on its acronym, of 'Every Night Something Awful'.

In October 1940 something awful nearly happened to Drury Lane. A German bomb, dropped in the course of one of the Luftwaffe raids that made up the Blitz campaign of late 1940 and early 1941, crashed through the roof and ploughed through the rest of the building to bury itself below the floor where, miraculously, it failed to explode. Most of the damage wreaked on London during the Blitz was due to the Luftwaffe using incendiary bombs, and it was these that set London's docks and large swathes of the City on fire, devastating so much of the historic heart of the capital.

The nose cone of the bomb, suitably defused, can still be seen at Drury Lane. After the war it was discretely placed in the corridor that leads to the Royal Retiring Room behind the Royal Box – next to a chair that was taken from the ruins of the Reichstag by Basil Dean, a theatre producer, and presented to the theatre as a trophy of war.

More recently, during the run of *The Lord of the Rings*, the bomb was moved to the inner part of the foyer, just inside the doors where ushers stand to check theatregoers' tickets, and between the two historic staircases designed to stop open warfare within the royal family.

Drury Lane re-opened after the war with *Pacific 1860*, a Noël Coward musical that was a major flop. Ivor Novello was suitably sympathetic in public but must have taken a certain pleasure in Coward failing to take over his theatre. Noël had the last laugh in terms of that rivalry, however, as his statue sits in the foyer, while Ivor is commemorated by a small – though beautifully executed – bust by their mutual friend, the artist and playwright Clemence Dane, in the rotunda further inside the theatre.

Inexplicably, the brass plaque, which records that the bust is of Ivor, lists only some of his Drury Lane shows. It does not, at the time of writing this book, mention *Crest of the Wave* (1937) which was his least successful Drury Lane musical but which certainly deserves recording. Nor does it refer to his *Henry V*. Ivor played his fellow Welshman in Shakespeare's history play at the Lane in 1938. Martial glory was not his strong suit, though he did look lovely in the armour and there were plenty of banners and an astonishing amount of incidental music.

After the war London was in the mood for something fresh and fun, and Londoners turned to America to provide this. Drury Lane hosted many American musicals, one of the most popular and enduring of which has been *My Fair Lady*. It was this musical that provided a favourite Drury Lane anecdote.

Rex Harrison was starring in *My Fair Lady* at the Lane. An elegant and impeccable actor, he was, in private life, known to be a difficult man who got through several wives and far more domestic staff and restaurant managers. As Sheridan Morley once observed of Sir Rex, it takes a certain amount of snobbery for a man to send back a bottle of wine – at his own dinner table!

Harrison was leaving the stage door of the Lane after a performance of *My Fair Lady* that had run longer than expected that night due to some technical hitch. He was tired and bad tempered. It was cold and wet. There were fewer than usual fans waiting for an autograph, thanks to the ghastly weather. Harrison's car had drawn up to the stage door and the great man (still Mr Harrison at this point) couldn't wait to get in and drive off to dinner.

As he ignored theatre protocol and brushed past the small crowd of well-wishers, one old lady approached him, proffering her programme for him to sign: 'Oh, Mr Harrison! It would mean so much to me if you could just sign this for me . . .' Harrison barely looked at her and said 'Don't be ridiculous. It's cold. It's wet. It's late. I haven't the time.'

The old dear was so upset at her hero's less than heroic behaviour that she did something that was probably the closest she had ever come to real violence in her life. She hit Rex Harrison on his beautifully tailored shoulder.

As she did so, Stanley Holloway, who played Eliza's father, the dustman determined to get to the church on time, saw her and instantly summed up the situation. A less sophisticated man than Rex Harrison, he was nonetheless sharp-witted, with a quick sense of humour, as he proved in the exchange that followed, which went along the lines of:

Holloway: Rex! Wait!
Harrison: What is it?
Holloway: Thanks to your bad temper and even worse manners to this lady you've made not just theatre history, but world history!

Harrison: What the hell do you mean?
Holloway: Thanks to your bad behaviour, Rex, for the first time in history the fan has
            hit the shit!

There have been many memorable shows at Drury Lane, including, in the mid-1970s, *Billy*. This was the musical version of Keith Waterhouse's book (filmed with Tom Courtenay and Julie Christie) about a young undertaker's clerk with a rich fantasy life that was far more vivid and indeed real to him than his drab, restricted, everyday life. At the Lane, the title role was played by Michael Crawford, a decade before his later and even bigger West End musical hit with *The Phantom of the Opera* at Her Majesty's Theatre in the Haymarket. One of his character's several girlfriends – the raunchy one – was played by a young actress called Elaine Paige. Miss Paige later went on to become one of the most popular musical theatre stars of the last 40 years, with leading roles in shows as diverse as *Cats, Evita, Piaf* and *Sunset Boulevard*.

Other shows at the Lane have included a lively *The Pirates of Penzance, 42nd Street, Miss Saigon* (whose record has already been mentioned), *Anything Goes* (a transfer from the National Theatre, co-starring Sally Ann Triplett and John Barrowman) and *The Producers*.

Mel Brooks's *The Producers* came over from New York, where it had played at the St James Theatre. Some people who had seen the show there thought that Drury Lane, which is much larger, would be too big for it. There was also a certain doubt as to whether the very New York humour would work as well on this side of the Atlantic. The doubters were proved wrong, as the show was an immediate hit, thanks to Mel Brooks's genius and to the combined acting and comic skills of Nathan Lane and Lee Evans, as well as Conleth Hill, who had first come to Londoners' attention in the Irish two-hander *Stones In His Pockets* and who, in *The Producers*, played a wildly camp – 'Keep it gay!' – theatre producer.

Most recently, *The Lord of the Rings*, which has already been mentioned, played to over half a million theatregoers and achieved the seemingly impossible, to realize Tolkien's extraordinary imagination and bring Middle Earth to the West End. When the producer, Kevin Wallace, installed the multi-million pound set at Drury Lane, the existing stage, which was 'listed' (i.e. protected by law) by English Heritage, had to be dismantled under careful supervision and removed.

One of the attractive features of *The Lord of the Rings* was the backstage atmosphere. Cliques and jealousies are not unknown in West End shows. The bigger the show, the greater the chance for this sort of fragmentation within a cast to take place, but, as numerous cast members made clear in the public after-show question and answer sessions on stage (a very popular part of the matinee performances, and an idea that many other large-scale shows could offer theatregoers), the company of *The Lord of the Rings* was a very happy one. This atmosphere was tangible, in the wings during the show, on stage, and at the curtain call when the cast, lifted upwards by the stage, radiated genuine goodwill to the cheering audiences, rather than the fixed stage smiles that can sometimes be seen at line-ups.

After *The Lord of the Rings* closed in July 2008, the original stage was put back in the theatre, which prepared to welcome Sir Cameron Mackintosh's production of Lionel Bart's *Oliver!* This production makes full use of the depth of Drury Lane's stage and has a full-scale orchestra of over 20 musicians, in comparison with the more usual 10–12 in the orchestra pit.

Drury Lane continues to be one of the most impressive playhouses in Theatreland and a natural choice for a producer wanting to stage a large-scale musical in the best possible environment. The theatre has regular tours in which actors playing historical characters help bring the place to life.

In this they are naturally aided by the building's size, splendour and history but they are not helped by the inexplicable decision to decorate the walls of this extraordinary piece of living theatre history with paintings of rock performers (among others) by Ronnie Wood of The Rolling Stones.

Wood is a great musician, an interesting character and clearly a good painter of his style, but his works seem out of place in the context of London's oldest playhouse. They should be in a more suitable setting: an art gallery or a modern venue where they would be better displayed and appreciated – perhaps O2?

True, there are selections of photos from historic Drury Lane shows on some of the walls, and various other historical artefacts, but the predominant impression is, at the time of writing, of Wood's art work.

Even the Grand Saloon, the large and imposing room, plus bar and restaurant area, which runs along the length of the Catherine Street frontage, has been, for some years, dominated by one of his paintings. Perhaps the Lane will eventually get a Stones musical and the decorative theme will come into its own. Until then, it would seem more appropriate to have some of the Theatre Museum's collection, or the Theatre Royal's own archives, displayed on the walls instead.

The theatre has its own archivist, Mark Fox, who has spent a lifetime in the industry, including theatre management for Lloyd Webber's company and for the previous owners of the Lane, Stoll Moss Theatres. He provided a brief historical video tour of the Lane's historic features as part of *The Lord of the Rings'* state-of-the-art website – and is also a theatre director. His knowledge of Drury Lane's history and architecture has only been matched by one man: George Hoare, who was General Manager of the Lane for decades and who was responsible for creating the archive that Mark Fox has since built on.

The archive mirrors the theatre itself, in that it is formed by the past and informed by its achievements and the interest that people today have in it, but it is a living thing that continues to change and grow as new shows arrive, new personalities make their mark on stage and a fresh generation of performers are able to say that they too have 'played the Lane'.

4

Boys Will Be Girls

The French have traditionally liked to dismiss Englishmen as fundamentally homosexual, and a (female) French government minister made some such disparaging remarks in the 1990s, causing a lot of amusement in the press, along with some pithy letters to newspaper editors. While the slur is clearly untrue, some ammunition has been provided by the traditional English love of boys dressing up as girls and parading around the stage.

Teenage boys playing women's roles on stage dates back to the Tudor and Stuart reigns, as discussed earlier. This practice was considered as bizarre by continental contemporaries as it is by current-day British theatre audiences – though it hasn't prevented a number of all-male Shakespeare productions from scoring hits with the public. Ed Hall's Propeller Theatre Company is a good example of this, and one whose appeal works in the United States as well as in England, though it can be assumed that the style has more of a novelty value than it does in the historic home of boys playing girls on stage.

In a case of clear hypocrisy – or taking coals to Newcastle – Jerry Herman's Broadway musical *La Cage Aux Folles*, based on a French play and set on the French Riviera, transferred from the plucky little Menier Chocolate Factory in Southwark to the Playhouse Theatre on the Embankment in 2008.

The show is about two gay men, Georges and Albin, who live together above the eponymous revue bar where the show is headed by the camper of the two, Albin, who drags up (as does his supporting cast) to entertain the punters. The drama comes when the son of the (relatively) butch Georges, who had a brief heterosexual fling in his youth, announces that he is in love and wants to bring his girlfriend home.

The trouble is the girlfriend's parents are very strait-laced, and the father is a leading right-wing politician. The wildly camp Albin has to disappear for the duration of the visit, so the parents can remain unaware of the true nature of their prospective son-in-law's family background.

In the end Albin drags up as the absentee real mother (she fails to show up, as she has done throughout her son's life) and wows the parents – until 'her' true sex is discovered. All ends happily in this light, jolly tale of the home life of a French drag artist.

The Playhouse production starred Denis Lawson (still remembered for the film *Local Hero*) as Georges and Douglas Hodge as his cross-dressing partner. Stuart Neal, clearly a young actor to watch, played George's son, having already, fresh from drama school, been directed by Michael Grandage in *Evita*, Matthew Warchus in *The Lord of the Rings* and Grandage again in *Piaf*.

La Cage aux Folles may seem a riposte to the idea that it is the English (and their cousins the Americans) who are prone to cross-dressing, but it can always be claimed that it is no wonder that the action takes place on the Riviera. This stretch of coastal Southern France was, after all, 'discovered' by the English, who made it fashionable from Victorian times to its heyday in the 1920s and 1930s, when English luminaries and exiles as varied as playwright and author Somerset Maugham and the Duke and Duchess of Windsor chose to make the Côte d'Azur their summer home, if not their permanent one.

The English who could afford to travel to the South of France tended to be from the moneyed class that sent its children to public schools. It was these institutions that kept the whole boys-as-girls theatre tradition going for centuries, with teenage boys living together in essentially all-male institutions and therefore having to draw on younger boys for female roles in school plays.

Sir Michael Redgrave, as a schoolboy at Clifton College in Bristol, played a girl on stage, as did a distinguished classical actor who was also at Clifton some 50 years later. The many fans of Simon Russell Beale would be surprised to learn that at school he was a remarkably convincing Desdemona.

Another Old Cliftonian was the poet Sir Henry Newbolt, whose poem '*Vitai Lampada*' ('They Pass On The Torch of Life') celebrated the public school ethos and had a chorus whose cry of 'Play up! Play up! And play the game!' has been used, in speeches and in newspaper editorials ever since. The game that Newbolt had in mind was war. This was seen as having been learnt (as the Duke of Wellington said of the connection between Eton and the Battle of Waterloo) on the school playing field, which in Clifton's case was the Close.

The narrative of '*Vitai Lampada*' moves from the cricket pitch: 'a bumping pitch and a blinding light, an hour to play and the last man in . . .' to a savage battle against the Dervishes: 'The sand of the desert was sodden red, red with the wreck of a square that broke, The Gatling's jammed and the Colonel dead, and the regiment blind with dust and smoke . . .'

Whatever the situation – including the third verse in which, like a metaphorical version of one of Lady Butler's war paintings, a host of public schoolboys are charging towards an undefined enemy – the hero of the poem treats everything as a game, in which the prize is not selfish reward or outward signs of glory but the approbation of the other chaps in his boarding house: 'It's not for the sake of a ribboned coat, or the selfish hope of a season's fame, but his captain's hand on his shoulder smote – "Play up! Play Up! And play the game!"'

If wartime was when Newbolt's late-Victorian imperial ethos came into its own, whether in the stoicism of young subalterns on the Western Front or the dashing gallantry of equally young boys, straight out of public school, flying Spitfires and Hurricanes in what Churchill rightly referred to as 'their finest hour', it was also when the public school tradition of acting seemed as validated as playing games. For British prisoners of war passed their time in captivity not just digging tunnels so that generations of families could watch *The Great Escape* every Easter Bank Holiday, but in putting on plays and revues to keep their morale up.

In this they were, as they had been in their tanks or warplanes, simply taking their schoolboy experiences into adult life: from boarding to battlefield, as it were. Theatre was as much a morale booster for their friends and relatives at home as it was for them, but they had to revert to all-male casts unlike the more fortunate theatregoers who braved the Blitz and then the V1s and V2s to get to the theatre.

Theatreland did not stay in the West End, however. Touring parties of actors and singers entertained the troops all over the Empire, and as close to the front line (especially after Allied troops were back in France after the D-Day landings) as was possible. Ivor Novello gave concerts and plays in Normandy against a backdrop of planes roaring overhead towards the Germans.

It was at one such concert that he introduced a new song, one which he would, in 1945, incorporate into his latest musical, *Perchance to Dream*. Just as he had with 'Keep The Home Fires Burning' in the First World War, he summed up the mood of the British public towards the end of the long struggle of the Second.

Troops wanted to get the war over and return home, to simple, everyday pleasures. This made the lyrics of 'We'll Gather Lilacs', with their images of walks in the English countryside and of quiet cuddles at home in front of the fire, all the more poignant. If Newbolt, the impeccable Establishment spokesman of Empire and Navy had captured the militarism of Victorian and Edwardian England before it met the horrors of total war, it was Novello, the apotheosis of

Theatreland, whose entire life was devoted to theatre, to the extent of living above one, who spoke for a nation that was exhausted by two wars and a Depression and just wanted it all to stop.

The end of the war saw the social revolution of a Labour government committed to nationalization and the Welfare State, but theatre and public schools alike took a decade or more to reflect the wider changes of society. It was not until the 1960s that the public school system really began to liberalize, and even then it took another 30 years or so and the fundamental change of co-education to really alter the way of life that had characterized the system for a century.

Until co-education (which now affects the great majority of all leading public schools, with Eton a notable exception), the public school theatrical tradition – not just of plays but of all-male casts – continued: hence Russell Beale's experiences at Clifton in the 1980s.

Public schools continued to give their pupils an advantage over state schoolboys not just in the general level of education but also in their exposure to theatre and experience of acting on stage. This meant that, even though working class backgrounds and accents had become not just acceptable but preferred from the early 1960s onwards, public schoolboys still had an in-built advantage when it came to trying for drama schools, in terms of experience if not of fashion.

In an example of how Theatreland shows a mirror to British society as a whole, the mid-1980s saw a West End play, at the Queen's, Shaftesbury Avenue, that caught one of the defining features of the age – nostalgia for a pre-war upper class public school England. The play was Julian Mitchell's modern masterpiece *Another Country*.

Another Country was inspired by the life of Guy Burgess, an Old Etonian who spied for the Soviet Union, as part of a spy ring that included Kim Philby (who defected to Moscow several years after Burgess had fled there to avoid imminent arrest) and Anthony Blunt, the art historian.

The play shows the rigidly old-fashioned way of a life in a leading English public school of the 1930s, where the apex of the class system within the school (a microcosm of the English class structure of the time) was to be appointed as a superior type of prefect, nicknamed a 'God'. The central character in *Another Country* is Guy Bennet (his initials emphasizing that he was based on the young Burgess). His long-cherished ambition is to become a God, which would give him the same status that belonging to 'Pop' did at Guy Burgess's Eton.

Young Guy Bennett is, however, openly gay and this ultimately ruins his chance to become a God. Socially he may 'play the game' but sexually he is an outcast – as gays were to be, legally, until 1967. Mitchell's play suggests that it is in this environment and through this experience that an attractive young man who seems to have everything going for him might turn into a spy for a foreign power – playing his own game, in a life-long retaliation for his schooldays.

The play opened at the perfect time. The 1981 television series of *Brideshead Revisited* had made short haircuts, stately homes, the upper classes, up-market homosexuality – and teddy bears – fashionable again, and helped pave the way for a profitable run of Merchant Ivory films that also lovingly recreated pre-war, pre-union power, pre-industrial and imperial-decline eras in a world of rose-tinted, linen-suited, behatted, steam-train nostalgia.

This was all given a further boost a year later when Margaret Thatcher's swift victory in the Falklands restored British military prestige and earned her the soubriquet of 'The Iron Lady'. With the Queen in Buckingham Palace and a Boadicea in Downing Street, not to mention an economy finally taking off after a decade in the doldrums, it seemed safe to climb out of recession and into the Rolls.

Another Country not only reflected this sea change, it was also a major contribution to it. Though it seemed to be celebrating an anti-Establishment figure, and a Communist spy at that, it was the environment that appealed to audiences. The unashamed wallowing (theirs rather than the playwright's) in the trappings of 1930s public schools meant that though they liked Guy Bennett – and, as written by Mitchell, who could resist him? – they loved the very things he was rebelling against. Besides which, it was the fact that he was upper class, rather than some stroppy workman, that made him all the more attractive.

The other impact the play had on Theatreland and, ultimately, the wider world, was that it was a showcase that launched several careers, most notably those of four young actors: Kenneth Branagh (Judd) and Rupert Everett, Colin Firth and Daniel Day Lewis (the latter three all playing Bennett).

It is very rare for one show to spawn such a range of talent. More usually it is a genre rather than a particular example of it. During the war and in the National Service years (which ended in 1960) that followed it, one such genre was service revues, where national servicemen entertained their fellow squaddies – which brings us back to boys as girls, for a feature of such entertainments was that the casts were all male.

Leading British entertainers who cut their theatrical teeth in this way included Kenneth Williams and Stanley Baxter, both of them brilliant comic performers.

Williams also had a strong early start in theatre, being a convincing Dauphin in George Bernard Shaw's *Saint Joan*, before he slipped off the stage and onto the radio and, later, into films.

The playwright Peter Nichols, who himself served in one such touring concert party, wrote a play, *Privates on Parade*, that not only captured this world – the campness and the camaraderie – but also the violence and racism that were the backdrop to the wars and insurgencies that British troops were engaged in dealing with.

Privates on Parade which opened in 1982, was revived in 2001 at the Donmar Warehouse with Roger Allam playing the camp captain Terri Dennis, who heads the troupe; a part first played (and subsequently filmed with) Denis Quilley. The part of the well-meaning but Blimpish commanding officer of the unlikely soldiers was played by Malcolm Sinclair, an actor whose consistently first-rate performances have included a number of military men, including that of 'Uncle' in David Grindley's production of R. C. Sherriff's *Journey's End*.

In the cast at the Donmar was James McAvoy, who is now one of the country's most bankable – and watchable – film stars, but who was then a young unknown who even in that small role showed considerable promise. He also showed his all, standing naked by his bunk bed in one scene, something that would today have fans queuing round the block. But then Donmar productions often do have queues right up Earlham Street in any case.

Privates on Parade is set in the Far East, where British troops were (success-fully) combating the Malaysian insurgency. By this time, though all-male concert parties were still acceptable in the jungle, all-male entertainments had fallen out of the brief fashion they had enjoyed back home in England.

For in the aftermath of the Second World War, and as a direct result of the all-male shows and revues brought about by it, there was a short period when young men in drag were a popular touring entertainment, in shows like *Soldiers in Skirts* and *Forces Showboat*. This was, in a way, a means for the public to poke fun at the militarism that had been necessary to save the country from the Nazis, but of which everyone was tired. The military were still respected, of course, and most families had men who had been or still were in uniform, but the shows were a way of seeing (and in a curious way celebrating) men in the armed services in a fun, and certainly unthreatening way. This was militarism not as in a Nazi propaganda film, but as in a saucy seaside postcard.

One career that started with service revues and continued into the post-war world was that of Danny La Rue. Said to have remarked, when someone gushed that he was one of the last true stars, 'I'm not a star, darling . . . I'm a ****ing legend!' La Rue's career really is an extraordinary one, giving a unique take on the boys in frocks stage tradition.

La Rue was born Danny Carroll, in Ireland; his mother brought him over to London as a child. He served in the navy during the war and was due to take part in the allied assault on Japan, but fortunately by the time he reached Singapore the conflict was over and he could develop his taste for acting. The combination of stunning good looks and the contemporary taste for drag shows meant that he easily secured a part in one, before being hired for the cabaret circuit by one of its leading figures, Ted Gatty, who also gave him his stage name of La Rue.

He has always dismissed the phrase 'drag artist', preferring the term 'female impersonator'. A distinctive feature of his stage show was that his final number would be out of frock and wig, dressed like a man: 'I'm a performer, not a transvestite.' He also enjoyed addressing audiences, when appearing on stage looking like an impossibly glamorous diva, with 'Wotcha mates!', delivered in a deep guttural voice that was more miner than Marlene.

His preference for being described as a female impersonator may seem a semantic distinction but it marks a difference in ambition if not in genre. La Rue enjoyed the growing reputation and income that came with being a star in the cabarets and revues of 1950s London, in the rival nightclubs Winston's and Churchill's. Among the young talent he worked with was Barbara Windsor, whom he once defended from the attentions of an over-eager customer by telling the man 'Don't be fooled by the wig, mate' before landing a well-placed punch. It was, perhaps, incidents like these that made him want to move on.

He took an important step in making the transition from performer to owner when he set up his own club, called simply Danny La Rue's, in Hanover Square, where his late-night shows attracted a highly theatrical audience of actors and dancers who came on to La Rue's for dinner and cabaret. Princess Margaret and Lord Snowdon were regulars, as was Rudolf Nureyev. Patrons were always very generous tippers and La Rue was not the only person to rake in money from his club: 'The woman who ran the ladies' loo had bought herself three houses by the time we closed.'

La Rue's success was part of the wider trend for dinner and entertainment in relatively sophisticated surroundings, which had been cashed in on by Bernard (Lord) Delfont, who had turned the Hippodrome Theatre off Leicester Square into The Talk of The Town.

La Rue offered more than cross-dressing glamour and some songs – of which 'On Mother Kelly's Doorstep' became his party piece. He also offered satire. This was very different satire from that provided by Peter Cook and the young alternative comedians in his circle, at Cook's Establishment Club in Greek Street.

It was satire nonetheless and La Rue, as with generations of female impersonators before and since, was able to make some punchy political points under the cover of wig, frock and sexual innuendo. This gave his act and his club the edge that made them a must-see part of the theatre scene throughout the 1960s. He took pride in the sharpness of that edge, compared with today's much more explicit sexual humour, saying in one interview: 'They used to call me

Danny La Rude. Goodness knows what they'd make of today's lot.'

Not content with 'just' revue, he went on to star in a West End theatre, the Whitehall (now converted into the Trafalgar Studios) in *Come Spy With Me*, in 1966.

Given his humour and outrageous stage persona, La Rue was, unsurprisingly, in great demand for pantomime, but here too he set his sights higher than most and appeared not just in the provinces or the outskirts of London but also deep into Theatreland – at the Saville Theatre, in *Queen Passionella and the Sleeping Beauty*, in 1968.

Building on this experience, in 1971 he played the Palace Theatre, along with Roy Hudd, a large number of dishy backing dancers and an outrageously large clothes budget. To fill the Palace as a female impersonator was a remarkable achievement. Not only was it a tribute to his star power and sense of complete confidence and control on stage, but also it showed the influence on theatregoing audiences of television publicity.

The programme that beamed him into millions of living rooms was *The Good Old Days*, a long-running series, hosted by Leonard Sachs, in which an evening of Victorian music hall, with audiences dressed in period costumes, was televised and broadcast to a nation whose older members still remembered the dying days of the genre in the 1920s, and so had a personal connection with the type of entertainment on offer.

La Rue's appearances – singing music hall numbers while dressed as an Edwardian woman or a pantomime Principal Boy, but in any case making sure, where possible, to show his long and shapely legs to good effect – were invariably the top of the bill, and helped make him a household name.

The other factor that contributed to this was that he was at that time unique, a cross-dressing performer who worked in the theatre rather than in just pubs or working men's clubs. His popularity in England, given the historic attraction for audiences of boys in frocks, is not surprising. What is more impressive is that he went on to have a very prosperous career in Australia.

At the time, some 30 years ago, Australia and drag were not two words one would normally speak in the same sentence. That has now changed, thanks largely to the impact made by the film *Priscilla, Queen of the Desert*, about a group of drag artists (one of whom is a transsexual) touring their act in the Outback. The movie has now been turned into a stage musical, which will be opening at La Rue's old theatre, the Palace, in London in 2009.

As if La Rue's career were not singular enough, he made theatrical history in 1984 when he starred, in the title role – a part immortalized by Carol Channing in the United States – in *Hello Dolly!* at the Prince of Wales. Never before had a man played a female role, simply as a female rather than as part of some plot device where a male character impersonates a female one, on the London stage.

The nearest anyone came to this was as an understudy; an emergency measure rather than a planned performance. This was when the actor-manager Seymour Hicks, one of the leading figures of early twentieth-century Theatreland, covered for his sick wife, Ellaline Terriss, for several performances in the run of *The Darling Little Duke*, which had opened at the Queen's Theatre in 1909.

La Rue is now in his 80s and his days as a lithe beauty are behind him, but he has continued to perform as a female impersonator, retaining a certain grandeur along with the wigs and eyelashes. His skill these days lies, as it did back in the 1960s and 1970s on *The Good Old Days*, in performing classic music hall numbers.

At a performance of his one-man show at the Pleasance Theatre in North London, about ten years ago, he was entertaining when discussing his showbiz career, and how in the late 1960s there were never empty seats at his shows until the night when two seats had been reserved for his old friend Judy Garland. She had been due to see him the night she collapsed and died at her home in Chelsea.

This was a sad story, and there was, at the Pleasance, a gently wistful feel behind the brass and the bonhomie, a sense of a man who had had an extraordinary career, but who had now aged beyond the natural appeal of his prime, when sexual energy was a crucial part of his act. Yet when he asked if anyone had any requests, and a young member of the audience surprisingly asked for a music hall standard 'Only A Glass Of Champagne', La Rue suddenly seemed stronger. Not exactly rejuvenated, but somehow more authoritative.

He gave a brief history of the song, mentioned Evelyn Laye (nicknamed 'Boo', and from whom the 1970s pop singer Patti Boulaye took the second part of her stage name) as a great interpreter of the piece, and then sang the song himself. As the song's name implies, it is about drink – the perils of a young woman accepting a glass of champagne from a dashing older man, determined to have his wicked way with her. As he stood on stage, resplendent in his frock and wig, La Rue seemed to personify the nostalgic appeal, the comedy and the pathos of music hall.

He has performed at the Brick Lane Music Hall, which used to be in the East End but subsequently moved further out of the area with which it had historic ties. At these shows he was again in his element and afterwards queues of fans lined up to buy merchandise. He may be old-fashioned, but so is making money: Ivor Novello used to write the nightly box-office takings on his dressing-room mirror – in lipstick.

Yet it was at the Pleasance, in a less likely setting, and without the trappings of stardom, that La Rue seemed most a star. *La Cage Aux Folles* shows the sadness as well as the glitter of a drag artist's life, notably in the song 'I Am What I Am', which closes the first half of the show. La Rue has recorded 'I Am What I Am' on CD but it is his signature tune, which was on the same album, 'On Mother Kelly's Doorstep', with its memories of Irish immigrants and the warmth – and poverty – of street life before the war, which best sums up his career and his appeal.

It should be La Rue who has the last word on this section on boys as girls, and a line from his triumphant return visit to an Irish theatre, decades after he had emigrated as a boy to London, sums up the uniqueness of the English love of drag, and the entertainer's sense of humour: 'Look what the English did to me! I left Ireland in short trousers and I've come back to you in a frock!'

5

Royalty at the Theatre

Theatreland has always embraced royalty. Not literally, of course, given the restrictions of royal protocol, but as the supplier of royal charters to companies and buildings and drama schools, as inspiration for characters in plays, as VIP visitors and as a useful marketing tool. Boxes with hospitality suites are far more sellable for corporate functions if they can, legitimately, be linked with the royal family – even if no member of it has actually sat there, formally, for decades. Really Useful Theatres, owned by Andrew Lloyd Webber, has a hospitality division called Royal Box, which arranges canapés and champagne for visitors to the group's theatres.

Royal boxes may have a social cachet, but they are rarely used by royalty. It is the sight-lines from these boxes to the stage, rather than the boxes themselves, that are responsible for the modern-day absence of tiaras and furs. Even more than other boxes, royal ones are designed to show off their occupants to the rest of the auditorium, rather than give the guests themselves a decent view of the stage.

Royals' entire lives are a form of theatre, conducted in flashlight, so you would think trips to the playhouse would have a certain appeal, that it might evoke a fellow-feeling for those on stage. In fact, with a few notable exceptions, the opposite seems to be the case, as if the royals find their being looked at in an environment where the public have, for once, come to see someone else being paid to perform, is an intrusion too far.

It could also be that there is a sort of folk memory among them, about the risks posed to heads of state by appearing in the relatively vulnerable situation of a theatre auditorium where, with the lights off, it would be relatively easy for an assassin to pull a gun without being noticed – until it was too late.

President Lincoln's fate immediately springs to most people's minds, but given the English royal family's extraordinary ability to see the world through the prism of their extended family rather than anyone else's experience, they may be more conscious of the attempt on George III's life at Drury Lane, in 1800, when a would-be assassin fired off two shots from a pistol at the King.

George had more than his fair share of assassination attempts, as did his great-niece Queen Victoria, but, as did Victoria, he survived them all unscathed. In the royal box with the King at Drury Lane was Richard Brinsley Sheridan, the dramatist and theatre owner, who called out to the shocked audience that the King was alive and asked them to sing the national anthem.

This expression of patriotism and relief was particularly appropriate as it was at the Theatre Royal that the tune had one of its first recorded public performances in London. Sung in defence of the Hanoverian dynasty against the attempted retaking of the crown by the glamorous but doomed Stuarts, the national anthem is (contrary to the tired complaints of those who would prefer something flashier) as stirring as any other when played with suitable verve, brass and a decent drum roll.

Another case of assassination connected with royalty occurred a century or so later, and in another country. Tsar Nicholas II was present in the Opera House in Kiev, when his Prime Minister, the highly effective and suitably conservative (though reforming) Peter Stolypin, was assassinated by a double agent who was supposedly working for the police but was actually a revolutionary.

It was during an interval, and Stolypin had come to the front of the auditorium, by the rail of the orchestra pit. Wearing full evening dress he was talking with colleagues when the gunman walked up to him and opened fire.

The Tsar, hearing the shots, immediately walked back into the royal box – something no modern-day police protection officer would have allowed. Rising to the sense of occasion, despite what were to prove fatal wounds, Stolypin turned to the royal box and made the sign of the cross in a blessing on the Tsar, before collapsing and being rushed to hospital.

This may seem a far way from today's West End, but the events of the Bolshevik Revolution were deeply traumatic and lasting for the British royal family, who were very close to their relatives in St Petersburg. As Prince Philip was to say of the Bolsheviks, in his characteristically forthright way, 'The bastards shot half my family!'

Indeed, another royal sailor, King George V, the current Queen's grandfather, looked less like a cousin of Nicholas II than an identical twin. A group of Russian émigrés, presented to the King after the Revolution, reportedly fell to their knees in astonishment, believing themselves to be in the presence of a miraculously saved Tsar.

George may have looked amazingly like his doomed relative, but he was far more down to earth and definitely less theatrical. Whereas Nicholas loved the ballet and the opera – preferably Russian in both cases – George had to be dragged to the theatre by his wife, the stately Queen Mary.

The King was famously asked 'And what, Sir, is your favourite opera?' '*La Boheme*', he replied. 'And may I ask why, Sir?' queried the courtier. 'Because it's the shortest!' He also, in response to a question about his favourite tune, said, entirely seriously, 'God Save the King!'

George's favourite habits were sticking in stamps and slaughtering huge numbers of game birds on his Norfolk estate at Sandringham. Theatre was something he only attended out of duty. He was persuaded to attend Ivor Novello's musical spectacular, *Glamorous Night*, at the Theatre Royal, Drury Lane, in 1935.

This was George's Silver Jubilee Year, a celebration of 25 years on the throne. Towards the beginning of his reign he had, in the royal retiring room behind the royal box, knighted Frank Benson, a leading actor-manager who was starring in *Julius Caesar*.

There was, however, no question of King George repeating this romantic gesture and knighting Ivor Novello in the same room in the interval of *Glamorous Night*. Novello was obviously (to those who chose to recognize it and most of his female fans preferred not to) gay. George's view of homosexual men was typically reactionary – and blunt: 'I thought men like that shot themselves!'

Despite this he was persuaded to invite Novello to a Garden Party at Buckingham Palace, where the matinee idol was presented to the King who, for once, showed a surprisingly human side when talking about his consort. 'Next time, Mr Novello, I hope you will write a story with a happy ending. I don't like to see the Queen cry!'

Mary had plenty of reason to cry the following year when George died in January and in December their eldest son, Edward VIII, abdicated in order to marry a twice-divorced American, Wallis Simpson. This constitutional crisis was the inspiration for Royce Royton's play, *Crown Matrimonial*, in which Peter Barkworth played Edward VIII to Wendy Hiller's Queen Mary at the Theatre Royal, Haymarket, in 1972. It also inspired a musical, *Always*, at the Victoria Palace Theatre (2003) and several fringe plays.

As Prince of Wales, Edward had been much more into nightclubs than theatres, even though the newly built Prince Edward Theatre in Old Compton Street, Soho, had been named after him in 1930. There was also the Prince of Wales Theatre, named after his grandfather and opened, on the edge of Leicester Square, in 1884. It had a reputation for staging revues, which were more Edward's idea of a night at the theatre than a play was. The Prince of Wales is today one of the seven theatres owned by the Delfont Mackintosh theatre chain, and there is a memorial plaque to the late Lord Delfont (1909–1994) at the side of the theatre, in Oxenden Street.

The Duke of York's Theatre, in St Martin's Lane, was named after Edward's father when the latter was still Duke of York. It would have been far more appropriate if the Prince Edward had been named the Duke of Kent because of all Edward's siblings only the second youngest, George, Duke of Kent, showed any theatrical inclinations: too many, in fact, when he embarked on an affair with Noël Coward.

During the abdication crisis it was suggested that the next in line, the Duke of York, should be passed over, due to his unsuitability to the role. The Duke was a painfully shy man who struggled with a nervous stammer: there are newsreels of him making a public speech where, 75 years later, you can almost touch the frozen embarrassment of the bystanders as the Duke struggles for breath and the strength to move forward with his prepared text.

The next brother, the Duke of Gloucester, was well-meaning and dutiful, but considered to be something of a joke, so there was support in some quarters for the Duke of Kent to take over – not least because he was the only sibling who came anywhere close to Edward in terms of looks and charisma. As one of Coward's friends quipped, once the dust had settled: 'My dear! To think you could have been Queen of England!'

The woman who did become Queen Consort was Elizabeth, Duchess of York. Though she enjoyed the usual country sports and especially horses, a passion she passed on to her eldest daughter, Elizabeth II, she also had a relatively rare royal interest in the theatre.

This expressed itself in the form of a long-lasting friendship with Noël Coward, and in regular visits, once she was widowed in 1952, to either the theatre or the ballet on her birthday. Coward enjoyed this friendship, though he confided to his diary that he was irritated by the fact that royal protocol demanded that he refrain from making any sexually charged jokes. Not that he particularly wanted to; it was the mere fact of the social restriction that grated.

Another friend of the Queen Mother was Dorothy Dickson, the American actress and dancer who had been the star of two Novello musicals at Drury Lane – *Careless Rapture* (1936) and *Crest of the Wave* (1937). Dickson was a great beauty. With a very 1930s face, her big eyes, superb cheekbones and dramatically plucked eyebrows, she looked a little like the young Marlene Dietrich.

Dickson's daughter, Dorothy Hyson, was as great a beauty as her mother, and was also in the theatre. She went on to marry Anthony (later Sir Anthony) Quayle.

He is remembered primarily as a film actor, thanks to classics like *Ice Cold in Alex*, in which he co-starred with John Mills, who was also knighted later in life.

Mills started his acting life on stage – where his career was helped by Noël Coward, who 'discovered' him in Singapore – but went on to specialize in film, whereas Quayle, despite being a stalwart of the British film industry, returned to the stage and proved to be a reliable leading man, especially in Shakespeare.

Dorothy Hyson was not only as attractive as her mother, but also looked strikingly like her. There is a double portrait of her in the National Portrait Gallery's collection. The photograph is by Dorothy Wilding (1893–1976), one of the few women photographers who made a professional name for herself. In her portrait of the actresses, the Dorothies look like sisters rather than mother and daughter.

Dorothy Dickson was a regular luncheon guest of the Queen Mother and was the filter through which appropriate members of the stage could be invited to meet Her Majesty. Her love of the performing arts was reciprocated by the theatre profession, a mutual admiration society whose apotheosis was reached in the 1990s when the Queen Mother paid a birthday visit to the Comedy Theatre in Panton Street. This small jewel of a playhouse, with its lamp-bearing female statue and suitably regal lions' heads on the façade, was occupied, at the time, by a collection of Alan Bennett's *Talking Heads* – monologues delivered by different characters, about their lives.

With the Queen Mother in her box, Bennett, playing a repressed gay character speaking about his mother, said of her, when she had been compared to the Virgin Mary by an over-enthusiastic visiting vicar, that if she couldn't be compared to the Queen Mother, then the Virgin Mary was the next best thing. The line, which always got a good response, naturally brought the house down, as all eyes turned from the stage to the Queen Mother's box, where she beamed happily at the author.

Queen Elizabeth II and Princess Margaret used to accompany their mother on many of these excursions, and the Princess proved to be a great supporter of the arts in her own right. At the Royal Opera House, on the landing between the old Crush Bar and the stairs leading to the stunning Floral Hall, there is a plaque to the Princess's memory, recording her long association with, and patronage of, the Royal Ballet. The Princess these days seems to be discussed only in terms of her marriage and various affairs, but she promoted the performing arts throughout her public life.

Royals tended to visit the Coliseum in the 1970s and 1980s because the director of English National Opera was Lord Harewood. He grew up as a minor royal – the son of Princess Mary, George V's only daughter, and of the 6th Earl of Harewood, a wealthy and much older aristocrat to whom the young princess was married off.

The younger (7th Earl) Harewood bucked the usual royal preference for stable rather than stage by being fascinated by opera, and took what was then Sadler's Wells Opera into the London Coliseum in 1968, giving it a new home and a new name – English National Opera (ENO).

Given that he was their relative – albeit one temporarily disgraced when he divorced his first wife and married a musician without consulting the Queen – various royals, including Princess Alexandra and Princess Michael of Kent, used to be fairly frequent visitors. In recognition of the fact that ENO was a national company with a royal patron, under Lord Harewood ENO's new season each autumn began with a spirited rendition of the National Anthem before the audience settled down to the overture to whichever opera had been programmed. This enjoyable tradition ended when Lord Harewood resigned as Director. The feeble argument given to explain this change of policy (the company shamelessly hung on to its other royal connections, which were useful to it in fundraising) was that the National Anthem was somehow distracting for audiences who had, after all, come to hear an opera. The company showed no such hyper-sensitivity to their patrons when it came to making announcements from the stage, before the overture, begging for cash to support ENO's work.

Harewood was a genial presence at the Coliseum but was also an imposing one. This was a combination of several factors: his height, the quality of his clothes, and his magnificent head of hair. In an industry where hair (like costume and make-up) is an important part of presentation, Harewood clearly paid regular attention to his, visiting Trumper's, a leading barber's in Jermyn Street which has a distinguished clientele (that used to include Margaret Thatcher's husband, Denis) and which looks like every tourist's vision of Edwardian England.

Most impressive, however, were his very Hanoverian looks: a solid and strong personal presence and the slightly bulging eyes that can be seen in contemporary portraits of George III and his relatives. Harewood naturally spoke to visiting members of his extended family in familiar terms – he used to call the Queen Mother 'Auntie' when escorting her to the royal box.

On one such occasion, the royal party were ascending the main staircase from the foyer to the dress circle level, which is the public route to the royal box. The ornate wood and glass doors near the foot of the staircase were shut, for the Queen Mother's comfort and security. Fascinated opera-goers were crammed behind them, watching her pass. As she walked up the stairs, giving the traditional royal wave, a slight circling motion of the hand, with the forearm held rigid at the elbow, she was heard to say to Lord Harewood, while maintaining her smile to the masses and in effect talking like a ventriloquist: 'Really, George! It's like being at a zoo!'

The Queen Mother and Princess Margaret were both known to enjoy a drink when visiting Lord Harewood's opera house. One theatre manager, who tended them in the royal retiring room, remembered asking Queen Elizabeth (as she was officially referred to) whether she would like a gin and tonic: a question to which he already knew the answer. The only real issue was how much gin should be poured into the glass before the tonic was added.

The manager showed Her Majesty a generously sized glass. 'How much shall I pour, M'am?' he asked. 'I shall say "When",' replied Queen Elizabeth. He started, reached a double measure and, with her unwavering gaze fixed on the rapidly rising level of gin, carried on pouring. Eventually, and with a characteristic twinkle in her eye, she exclaimed 'When!', sharing the joke with him as he added a tiny amount of tonic.

Princess Margaret preferred whisky (Famous Grouse) to gin, and she still managed to get through a surprising amount, especially if there were more than one interval in the show. As she refused to sit in a box and chose a dress circle seat because of the better view, this meant that several seats had to be set aside by the management, to accommodate her lady in waiting, other guests and police bodyguards. It also meant that, as she walked back to her seat from the royal retiring room, Her Royal Highness had, at the end of the second interval, to focus very carefully indeed on reaching it without mishap.

Princess Margaret was known for her occasional haughtiness – usually expressed just after someone had begun to feel comfortable with her. This tendency was reined in for a while after Princess Diana's death in a car crash in Paris in August 1997. There was a wave of public hostility to the older members of the royal family and their rigid adherence to Court protocol. Princess Margaret made an effort to be more amiable on visits to the theatre after this, to try to repair some of the tarnished public image that senior members of the family had (unfairly) earned in the immediate aftermath of Diana's death.

Ironically, the one royal who escaped this was the Queen Mother, who had actually been one of Diana's most formidable enemies at Court: partly because of her determinedly pre-war approach to the formality required in everyday royal life; and partly because she was devoted to Prince Charles, whom she had virtually brought up during his mother's many absences on official duties.

The Queen Mother even escaped lightly in Stephen Frears's 2006 film, *The Queen*, in which a catty comment made by the Queen Mother was attributed not to her but to the more predictably haughty Princess Margaret. On hearing of the turmoil caused by the aftermath of the crash, Her Majesty had drawled:

'Who would have thought that girl could be even more tiresome in death than when she was alive?'

That the public assumed that was the sort of thing Margaret would say was due to a lifetime of making just such comments. Of the various overheard remarks she made at the theatre, one of the most typically dismissive and abrupt was a riposte she made to someone who, on being presented to her in the foyer, had the temerity to comment on the magnificent jewels she was wearing.

Though well-meant, this was a major faux pas in terms of royal protocol. One is never supposed to mention anything a royal is wearing. Comment, however fawning, is considered impertinent. The Queen was quite prepared to deliver a withering put-down to Mrs Thatcher when, as Prime Minister, she had the audacity to suggest to Buckingham Palace that the two women should compare notes so that they wouldn't both be wearing the same colour when they appeared together at State functions. 'The Queen', Thatcher was frostily informed, 'never notices what other people are wearing.'

Her sister's reply to the well-wisher's remarks about her jewels was sharper: 'Yes!, she snapped, 'Big, aren't they?'

Elizabeth II was played by Helen Mirren in *The Queen*, and played so well that she has become indelibly associated with the real-life sovereign. Following the release of the film, when, at the State Opening of Parliament, the House of Commons is summoned by the royal official with the unfortunate title of Black Rod to 'attend Her Majesty' in the House of Lords, Dennis Skinner, the Labour MP with a penchant for witticisms, quipped that he hoped Helen Mirren was available as a stand-in for the Queen.

Dame Helen's portrayal of the monarch has eclipsed an equally convincing stage version of Her Majesty, when Prunella Scales played her in Alan Bennett's play *A Question of Attribution*, part of a double bill at the National in 1988 titled *Single Spies*, in which Bennett himself played the spy and Surveyor of the Queen's Pictures, Anthony Blunt.

Scales caught the Queen's voice, walk and mannerisms perfectly. Similar in height to the real thing, she was eerily convincing – so much so that the Queen was reportedly persuaded to visit the theatre incognito to see herself on stage.

Charles and Diana have also been portrayed in the theatre, as since the ending of the Lord Chamberlain's censorship of the stage in 1968 and the throwing open of palace doors to film crews in the highly influential documentary film *Royal Family* in 1969, the current royal generation have been seen as fair game. Theatre has presented them in a far more affectionate light than television, though even the satirical TV series *Spitting Image* seemed to laugh with the Queen and her mother rather than at them.

Shakespeare suggested that 'divinity doth hedge a king', and that remains as true for twenty-first-century audiences as it was for sixteenth-century ones. We are used to seeing kings and queens on stage, largely thanks to Shakespeare, and though we may see their flaws, they are nonetheless presented as majestic and awe-inspiring individuals who possess that divinity, even if on occasion, as in *Richard II*, it is ripped from them. The very act of doing so was so shocking to contemporaries that it continues to resonate in Shakespeare's other history plays, where Henry IV is seen as guilty of Richard's death and permanently tainted by it. Crucially, it is the King's deposition (and therefore the weakness of Henry's own right to expect the loyalty of others) that is as much a crime against nature as his murder.

The divinity that Shakespeare celebrated hedges foreign royals, too. The most haunting case of this – involving another deposition followed by a murder – is that of Atahualpa, the King of the Incas, who was treacherously captured by the Spanish conquistador Ferdinand Pizarro when the two men met following Pizarro's invasion of the Inca kingdom of Peru. These events were dramatized by Sir Peter Shaffer in his play *The Royal Hunt of the Sun*, which opened at the National in 1964 starring Robert Stephens as Atahualpa and Colin Blakely as Pizarro.

The historic incident – involving Atahualpa's seizure by the Spaniards who slaughter his bodyguards and then Pizarro's offer to ransom his captive if he could fill a room with gold – was staged with a brutal reality, as was the Pizarro's going back on his word and having the king executed. Shaffer's genius was not only to show that a modern playwright could, like Shakespeare's Richard II, 'tell sad stories of the death of kings', but also to make theatre magic out of seemingly unpromising material.

Robert Stephens's Atahualpa was an exotic but entirely regal figure, but what gave the play such impact (it was later filmed with Christopher Plummer as the Inca and Robert Shaw as Pizarro) was the way that Shaffer's script made a poetic leap that took the idea of kings as somehow ordained by God and decided to treat it literally.

In *The Royal Hunt of the Sun*, Pizarro, through his one-on-one encounters with Atahualpa, comes to believe that the Inca king might indeed be divine, as Inca culture insisted he was, and that if he were to be killed and his body left intact, when the sun rose with the following dawn it would bring him back to life.

Determined to see if this would happen, Pizarro insists that the king is spared from being burned at the stake (a death the attendant Catholic priests are keen to inflict on him, supposedly to cleanse his soul) and that he is garrotted instead, with his body left on his throne so the rays of the sun cover it when dawn arrives.

The play touches so many themes, but the religious one is among the most powerful. Years before cultural relativism and political correctness led to any belief system being taken as equally valid as the great historical world religions, Shaffer's Pizarro argues that if the Christian God can rise again after death why should not this Inca one? Prince Charles, who is rumoured to want to adopt the title 'Defender of Faith' rather than the historic 'Defender of the Faith', would presumably approve.

Elizabeth II's Christianity does not allow for her to have any Inca-style delusions of divinity, but she is nevertheless the Supreme Governor of the Church of England, was anointed by Holy Oil at her coronation in Westminster Abbey in 1953, enjoys singing hymns to herself, and believes she is ordained (literally so, at the coronation) by God to fulfil the role she was born into.

While this doesn't make her godlike, it does mean that she carries an aura of self-belief which, as plays from Shakespeare to Shaffer have shown, helps create the sense of power and otherness that radiates from a crowned head – however uneasily that head may sleep.

Alan Bennett, with his professional interest in the Queen (he also wrote a successful short novel about her, *The Uncommon Reader* in which she makes a late-in-life discovery of the joy of books) should be allowed the final comment about her, and the divinity that hedges her. In his *A Question of Attribution*, Prunella Scales's Elizabeth discusses Heaven with Bennett's Anthony Blunt, and wistfully remarks that for everyone else it will be delightful to be treated alike before God – but that for her it would feel like something of a demotion.

6

Dynasties

Theatre has its own royalty: actors and actresses whose thespian genes are pooled by marriage and passed on to other generations.

In the mid-twentieth century, there were three actors generally regarded as at the top of their profession: Sir Ralph Richardson, Sir John Gielgud and Sir (later Lord) Laurence Olivier. Bringing up the rear, as it were, was Sir Michael Redgrave. Sir Alec Guinness is generally regarded as being as accomplished as the other four, but was essentially a film actor, while the others, despite some memorable performances on screen at various stages of their careers, were seen as belonging, at heart, to the theatre.

The irony is that is was the fourth, Michael Redgrave, who went on to head a theatre dynasty that can now claim to be the royal family of the English stage. It was, equally ironically, specifically thanks to Redgrave being married – unlike the bachelor John Gielgud who had blotted his copybook by being arrested for importuning in a public lavatory – that he received his knighthood. That incident not only nearly put paid to Gielgud's career, it led the Establishment to decide that the next actor to be knighted must be a happily married man. The man they chose was the bisexual Redgrave. This amused Gielgud, as did Redgrave's penchant for bondage, so when he bumped into him in the street soon after Redgrave had received his honour, Sir John greeted the mortified actor with the exclamation: 'Ah! *Sir* Michael Redgrave, I'll be bound!'

Ralph Richardson, by contrast, was happily but quietly married to his wife, Meriel. Laurence Olivier's first wife, Jill Esmond, was an actress and they had a son, Tarquin, who looks much like his father did in his prime.

Olivier's second wife, Vivien Leigh, was of course as big a star as her husband, and Olivier was reportedly almost sick with jealousy when she won the Best Actress Oscar in 1940 for her role as Scarlett O'Hara in *Gone with the Wind*, the epic movie released in 1939.

The Oliviers were the theatre royalty of the 1940s and 1950s, appearing in the West End and on tour, where (particularly when abroad) they travelled like visiting heads of state rather than 'vagabonds and players'. It helped that both were very good looking, with Vivien Leigh frequently recalled in the memories of those who met her as being the most beautiful woman they had ever seen.

The Oliviers combined beauty with talent, as both were superb actors who, though noted for their Shakespearean roles, were as at home in modern classics. Vivien Leigh appeared at the Aldwych in *A Streetcar Named Desire*, the Tennessee Williams classic about a faded beauty, Blanche DuBois, who is losing her mind but has kept her libido – with devastating results. The role has been immortalized in the film version, where she played opposite a young Marlon Brando.

One of the reasons that Vivien Leigh still exerts such a fascination, over 40 years after her death, is that her troubled private life (she suffered from manic depression that often manifested itself in over-sexed and 'hyper' behaviour) mirrored those of the tragic figures she played on stage. She later said that playing Blanche night after night tipped her into madness.

Laurence Olivier is commemorated by a rather effete statue of him playing Hamlet, with a sword upraised, just in front of the National Theatre. Vivien Leigh has her own commemorative plaque at the back of the actors' church, St Paul's, Covent Garden, with a quote from Antony and Cleopatra: 'Now boast thee, death, in thy possession lies a lass unparalleled'.

Rosemary Geddes, who worked for Miss Leigh for several years as a very young personal secretary, has nothing but praise for her as a person and an employer. An elegant woman herself, Geddes says that many of the stories of Vivien Leigh's 'madness' have been exaggerated and though of course there were periods of instability in the actress's life, when she knew her she lived a fairly quiet and restrained London life at her flat in Eaton Square.

She died in that flat in the summer of 1967, from tuberculosis, a rather old-fashioned disease, but then, with her convent school private education, tours of Europe with her wealthy father, and a finishing school in Switzerland, Leigh was in many ways an old-fashioned figure.

There was a touching twist to Rosemary Geddes' tribute to her sometime employer at the Theatre Museum in 2003. Here she told, with the help of an interviewer, the story of her work for Miss Leigh and looked back on the actress's stage and screen career. The talk naturally attracted a large audience, at the back of which, discretely, sat the man she had gone on to work for after Leigh's death – the actor Alan Bates.

Alan Bates had twin sons, one of whom, Tristan, died aged 19 while in Japan.

Bates' wife, Victoria, died not long after – of grief. A small theatre, part of the Actors' Centre in Tower Street, Covent Garden, is named after Tarquin. His surviving twin, Ben, is also an actor and appeared on stage with his father in England and in America.

Bates, who had been given a knighthood earlier in 2003, was suffering from the cancer that would kill him just after Christmas that year, and had lost his trademark mass of black hair, but he was determined to attend Rosemary Geddes' event. She worshipped him as much as she had Vivien Leigh and it was moving to see that, despite his illness, he clearly felt a similar loyalty to her.

At the time of Miss Leigh's death, Laurence Olivier was married to Joan Plowright, a rising young actress decades younger than the great actor. Plowright is now a Dame of the British Empire in her own right, thanks to her long and distinguished acting career, but though she provided Olivier with a longed-for new family, their children, despite well-reviewed acting and directing on stage, have not gone on to have as remarkable a career as either of their parents – though Richard Olivier has been very successful with seminars and speeches about leadership and motivation, using Shakespearean characters and performances as illustrations of these qualities.

Michael Redgrave's three children by his wife, the actress Rachael Kempson, have all had leading stage careers, taking the Redgrave name forward and indeed achieving greater fame than their father – a key hallmark of a successful dynasty.

Vanessa Redgrave has been a star since the 1960s, helped by being one of the great beauties of her generation. She also earned notoriety as well as fame through her left-wing political views, which were not shared by her sister, Lynn, but definitely were by their brother, Corin.

Lynn has spent much of her career in America, where a few years ago she toured with a one-woman show called *Shakespeare For My Father*, in which she explored Shakespeare's work and her own relationship with Sir Michael. The show crossed the Atlantic to London, where she performed it at the Theatre Royal, Haymarket – one of the most attractive playhouses in Theatreland.

Corin, unlike his sisters, matured later as an actor, but in middle age he seemed suddenly to push himself centre stage with a series of riveting performances, including, at the National Theatre, that of a prison governor in a minor but very powerful Tennessee Williams play, *Not About Nightingales*.

It was even later in his career that Corin was united on stage for the very first time with his sister, Vanessa, in the Noël Coward play *Song At Twilight*, at the Gielgud Theatre. A severe stroke cruelly brought a temporary halt to Corin Redgrave's upwards trajectory, but he has lately returned to the stage, reading Oscar Wilde's *De Profundis* at the National.

The next generation, including Vanessa's daughters Natasha and Joely Richardson, have continued to demonstrate that acting is in the family's blood, and have given their grandfather some posthumous fame in the process.

Another Theatreland dynasty is the Williams family. Simon Williams, a tall, handsome and debonair actor who was himself the son of actor Hugh Williams, has had a long career on stage, punctuated by appearances on television, especially the very popular 1970s series *Upstairs, Downstairs*, where he played James Bellamy, the son of the owners of the house where the series was set.

Simon Williams combines an acting career with various charitable good works on behalf of the theatre world, and has been one of the trustees of Ivor Novello's estate for many years, deciding whether producers can stage revivals of his plays or musicals. Williams's son Tam is also an actor, and has starred in the West End, in the play *Birdy* at the Comedy Theatre (opposite Adam Garcia, star of the stage version of *Saturday Night Fever* at the Dominion Theatre), and has appeared in several Shakespearean plays for Edward ('Ed') Hall's Propeller Company.

Propeller bring a physical-theatre sensibility to Shakespearean plays, and also play them, as Shakespeare would have expected, with all male casts. Tam being as good looking (if in a less classical way) as his father, has often been cast in female roles. The company director, Ed Hall, is the son of Sir Peter Hall, one of the most distinguished English stage directors of the twentieth century, who established the Royal Shakespeare Company in the 1960s and is still directing plays well into the current century. Ed Hall has married Issy Van Randwyck, an actress and cabaret performer who was part of the very successful cabaret group Fascinating Aida, so a further generation of theatrical Halls may well be on their way.

Timothy West and his wife Prunella Scales are both hugely popular actors, whose son Samuel West is a leading actor and director in his own right. His Hamlet for the Royal Shakespeare Company was a critical success and he recently had another hit with T. S. Eliot's *The Family Reunion* at the Donmar.

An even younger generation of sons on stage is represented by Rory Kinnear, whose father was the much-loved (mainly cinema) star Roy Kinnear. Rory was a superb Laertes to Ben Wishaw's *Hamlet* at the Old Vic, and has concentrated on a stage career where he is increasingly seen as a classic actor, especially since his astonishing central performance in Thomas Middleton's *The Revenger's Tragedy* at the National Theatre in 2008.

There are numerous other examples of sons or daughters following their parents onto the stage, sometimes when a parent has had a theatrical career but not an acting one – like Ed Stoppard, son of playwright Sir Tom – and it is in the nature of the theatre that those exposed to it at a young age because of their parents' careers will often want, despite their parents' warnings about the irregularity and unreliability of work, to see if they can earn the standing ovation and rave reviews in the next day's newspapers that their parents – or uncles, or aunts – have themselves enjoyed.

Potential future dynasties include husband and wife thespians James McAvoy and Anne-Marie Duff. McAvoy has largely (despite a run in Richard Greenberg's *Three Days of Rain* at the Apollo, Shaftesbury Avenue) concentrated on a film career, but Duff is still very much a regular part of the Theatreland scene and gave an award-winning performance in the title role in George Bernard Shaw's *Saint Joan* at the National Theatre. She is photographed in armour, in her dressing room, in Simon Annand's *The Half*, discussed in Chapter 1.

7

Americans in London

British politicians like to bang on about the 'special relationship' between the UK and the United States, largely because they seem to enjoy the attention they get from Washington and the apparent endorsement by the American establishment when they visit the White House.

Whatever the degree of fantasy involved at the Downing Street end of the transatlantic hotline, it remains true that America has fought on the side of the British Empire in two world wars, and troops from both nations have fought together against a common foe in both of the wars against Iraq, and also in Afghanistan. There is, undoubtedly, a connection and a belief in a common interest.

There is also, crucially, the common language which, despite various quotes about mutual misunderstanding, is a vital part of the sense of cousinship between the two countries. This shared language is why so many Americans have immediate access to British literary culture, and why so many of them make a visit to Theatreland a central part of their vacation (or business trip) to London. According to the latest Society of London Theatre audience survey, there has been a substantial increase in the number of overseas visitors since the last such survey – they made up 28 per cent of the West End theatre public, up from 18 per cent in 1997. Over half of these (17 per cent of total theatre audiences) came from North America.

Given the joint language – and that New York is the other great theatre city of the world – it isn't surprising that there should be such strong American connections with Theatreland. These connections go far beyond mere visiting: Americans and American culture have been an important part of the London theatre scene for much of the last 100 years.

American actors have long been a part of the English theatrical scene, just as the Brits have enjoyed a very long relationship with Broadway, transferring plays and musicals (especially those written by Andrew Lloyd Webber and those produced by Cameron Mackintosh) to New York after successful runs in the West End.

These links can take the strangest forms. One of the most curious is that of Sir Charles Wyndham, the actor and theatre owner. Wyndham built the theatre named after him, on the Charing Cross Road, near Leicester Square tube station, in 1899. He also bought a building plot at the back, where he took his time in building a second theatre. Following endless enquiries as to when he was going to build his new theatre, he simply called it 'The New' when it opened in 1903: the year after he had been knighted for services to theatre.

His theatre empire also included the Criterion, on Piccadilly circus, which is why his monogram can be seen decorating the walls of the stalls in that small jewel of a playhouse – where Patrick Barlow's adaptation of *The 39 Steps* (discussed in more detail in Chapter 25) has followed another long-runner, *The Complete Works of Shakespeare (Abridged)*.

Wyndham trained as a doctor, but his real love was the stage. Despite an early success with Ellen Terry, his career failed to take off as quickly as he had hoped, so he crossed over to America to work as surgeon on the Union side in the American Civil War. In the course of this he attended the injured at several battles, including that of Gettysburg, which was immortalized in Abraham Lincoln's address, a speech considered one of the great political orations of all time.

Returning from this conflict, in which over a million people were to lose their lives, he turned his back on medicine forever and managed to find more acting work. He went on to be one of the most popular performers in late Victorian London, and made enough money to fund a career as a producer and theatre owner as well.

At the age of nearly 80 he married his long-time leading lady, Mary Moore, who was the widow of playwright James Albery. Her son, Bronson Albery was to be a theatre producer and owner in turn, as was his son, Donald, and then his son Ian, whose career has included running Sadler's Wells Theatre in Islington.

Mary Moore, who is also referred to in Chapter 12, was a fascinating character. Born into a well-off family that suffered a complete reversal of fortune and was plunged into poverty when she was 12 years old, she left school at 16 to become an actress (following the example of her older sister) to help the family finances.

Moore's career was just taking off at the Gaiety, which specialized in musical theatre, when she met James Albery, married him and had three sons by him. The family struggled financially and so, for a second time in her life, she was forced to go onto the stage. Charles Wyndham hired her in 1885, quickly realized he had a star on his hands, and made her his regular leading lady thereafter.

Wyndham also had the wit to realize that, offstage, she had a good business brain: so much so that he took her on as his business partner in 1896. It was thanks to her that Wyndham's and the New were built, and she was their co-owner. Wyndham retired in 1913 after finding he had trouble (he was then 76) remembering his lines.

When his wife died in early 1916 he proposed to Mary Moore, herself a widow since 1889, and she became Lady Wyndham. He died three years later, while she survived into a prosperous old age, dying in April 1931. The report into her death in The *Daily Herald* recognized her business acumen, with the headline 'Death of Lady Wyndham, Wealthiest Theatre Manager'.

The alleyways that run along each side of Wyndham's Theatre are both very old-world in feel, especially at the corner where Wyndham's stage door backs onto that of the Noël Coward. This rather Dickensian feel is typically English, which is part of its charm, but such alleyways, which criss-cross Covent Garden and St James's can also have American connections.

One of the most picturesque examples of this is in St James's, a short stroll from the site of the St James's Theatre, which for many years was run by the American impresario Gilbert Miller.

Situated towards the bottom of St James's Street, on the east side of the road and few yards from the clock tower of St James's Palace, is the narrow entrance to a little passage way that runs along the side of Berry Brothers & Rudd, London's oldest wine merchants, who have been on these premises since the 1690s.

This alleyway, which leads to a small courtyard overlooked by Georgian houses and the side of a smart restaurant, L'Oranger, is Pickering Place. Given its size – a couple of boxing rings – and hidden location, away from prying eyes, the courtyard was one of the last places in London to be used for fighting duels. A look-out could be stationed at the St James's Street end of the passage way to alert the duellists and their supporters if there was any sign of a policeman.

At that corner of the wine merchant's, the street and the alley is a reminder of another long-vanished period of history. This is a gold-coloured plaque commemorating the presence of the Texas Legation, from 1845 to 1846. At the time Texas was not yet a part of the United States, and the British were keen to keep it that way. As a separate state, in every sense of the word, it would be a counterpoint to the expansion and growing power of the youthful nation – in effect, a southern version of Canada.

In the end, Texas did become part of the Union, but for those few months it was represented in an office a few yards away from the clock tower of St James's Palace. This was then, and still is (despite the fact that her London home is

Buckingham Palace), the official residence of the monarch and the place to which all embassies are accredited – all ambassadors are technically ambassadors from their country to the Court of St James's.

A much more visible American presence in London is the sight of their movie stars staring down from publicity posters and hoardings on West End theatres. These visiting stars bring a touch of Hollywood to Theatreland, and are generally welcomed by London audiences, keen to see the stars in the flesh.

Jake Gyllenhaal, whose best-known film is probably *Brokeback Mountain* (2005), in which he played a gay cowboy opposite Heath Ledger, appeared at the Garrick Theatre on Charing Cross Road in *This is Our Youth* in 2002, though in his case this was a young film actor making an appearance before he became an international star: the appeal was his youth and acting ability rather than his fame.

An earlier star who had enjoyed a massive teen following when at his youngest and prettiest is Christian Slater, who has something of a love affair with the London stage – a passion fully reciprocated by audiences who flocked to see him in the stage version of *One Flew Over the Cuckoo's Nest* in 2004 and then again in *Swimming With Sharks* in 2007. He enjoyed being in London so much he decided to move here, and seems to be a regular fixture on the social scene between acting engagements.

Another teen idol, Rob Lowe, also came to London to appear in a stage play, *A Few Good Men*, at the Theatre Royal, Haymarket in 2005.

Representing an older Hollywood generation, Dustin Hoffman made a moving Shylock in *The Merchant of Venice* at the Phoenix Theatre in 1989. More recently, movie star Kathleen Turner has played Mrs Robinson in *The Graduate* (the stage version of the film that effectively launched Hoffman's career) on Shaftesbury Avenue; Kim Cattrall starred in *Whose Life Is It Anyway?* at the Comedy Theatre; Brendan (*The Mummy*) Fraser made a convincing Brick in a London production of Tennessee Williams's American classic, *Cat on a Hot Tin Roof*, while ex child star Macaulay Culkin proved that he is as good an actor as an adult as he was as a precocious pre-teen in the *Home Alone* franchise, with his winning performance in *Madame Melville* at the Vaudeville Theatre where he played a teenage American who is seduced by his tutor, played by Irene Jacob.

Many visiting Americans seem to like to stay at the Covent Garden hotel, a five-star boutique hotel on the site of an old French hospital near Seven Dials. Even if they don't stay at the hotel they seem to enjoy giving interviews there – a library on the first floor is well-suited to these.

In the flesh Culkin may be surprisingly small (like many Hollywood stars) but his body is normally proportioned – he just looks like a shorter version of an adult man. His role in *Madame Melville* may have been similarly surprising in that many people almost automatically rule out the possibility of ex-child stars developing into serious adult performers, yet, as mentioned above, Culkin earned excellent reviews from London's unsentimental theatre critics, who took to his engaging performance. It would be good to see him back on a London stage.

It is not just American actors and actresses who are popular in London: British theatre directors and audiences can't get enough of American playwrights. The three classic writers whose plays seem the most popular are Arthur Miller (who in later life seemed to prefer the West End to Broadway), Tennessee Williams, whose over-the-top and quasi-operatic plays appeal to the English sensibility for the romantic underdog, and Edward Albee, whose brilliantly witty dramas produce devastating one-liners against a backdrop of sour and stormy dysfunctional relationships.

Dame Maggie Smith headed a cast that included Frances de la Tour and Samantha Bond in Albee's *Three Tall Women* at Wyndham's Theatre in 1994. In the course of the play the audience comes to realize that the women are all playing the same character, but at different stages of her life.

Albee's best-known play is *Who's Afraid of Virginia Wolf?*, a long, emotionally exhausting but rewarding play about the failed marriage of a provincial university professor and his embittered wife who welcome a distraction in the form of a visit by a well-built young male lecturer, new to the campus, and his rather mousy little wife.

Although Arthur Miller's work is highly respected, and his play *The Crucible*, technically about seventeenth-century American witch hunts, but actually about the McCarthyite campaign against communists in 1950s America, remains a favourite with London audiences, the playwright whom Theatreland has taken most to its heart is Tennessee Williams.

This is partly because he was so good at writing roles for older women, something English actresses have always been deeply grateful for. One of the best interpreters of his roles was the late Sheila Gish, who took to his damaged heroines like a swan to water. Her early death from cancer has robbed Theatreland of one its most accomplished actresses.

Americans have also had an impact on Theatreland as administrators Gilbert Miller and the St James's Theatre have already been mentioned. This century has seen the appointment of Hollywood star Kevin Spacey as the artistic director of the Old Vic.

Spacey's tenure got off to a slightly shaky start, with a production of a modern European play called *Cloaca* (Latin for sewer) but later productions have been more assured, and Spacey (who appeared in *Cloaca*) has always pushed up the box office when he is on stage, thanks to his continuing high profile in Hollywood, where he starred in *American Beauty*, directed by Sam Mendes, who had been in his time another leading example of Theatreland's select group of artistic directors, in his case at the Donmar Warehouse.

Spacey has proved to have an adept touch at the Old Vic, and his commitment to the theatre, despite his film-making, has been impressive as well as lengthy. This is a long-term passion for the London stage rather than a temporary infatuation with it.

A far longer commitment (mixed with infatuation) was that of Dan Crawford at the little fringe theatre, the King's Head, Islington. Crawford was a one-off, but in his own way he was typical of a breed of foreigner who falls in love with another country and dedicates himself to working for it. This tends to be especially true where an appreciation of foreign culture (in this case the English Theatre) is concerned.

The English have a long tradition of falling for other people and places themselves. Lord Byron wrote a poem (Adieu My Native Shore) saying farewell to his homeland before heading to the Continent and falling in love first with Venice and then with the idea of Greek independence from the Ottoman (Turkish) Empire.

Venice in particular seems to do something for the English (maybe, as an island race, it's all that water), and characters as disparate as the art historian and writer John Ruskin and Viscount Norwich (son of Lady Diana Cooper, the society beauty and actress who starred in Max Reinhardt's theatre production *The Miracle* in the 1920s) have headed the Venice in Peril campaign to save the stunningly beautiful city from sinking irretrievably into the lagoon.

Crawford chose the less picturesque Upper Street in Islington as his life's project. He began his lasting impact on London theatre by buying an old pub, the King's Head, and while keeping the pub running at the front of the building, turned a backroom area, which had been used for billiards and boxing contests, among other activities, into a theatre space.

The King's Head is not in Theatreland, but it has an unrivalled track record for transferring shows from Upper Street to the West End, and Dan is certainly relevant to an article or chapter discussing Americans in Theatreland, given the influence that his work had.

For his was the theatre where actors including Alan Rickman and Hugh Grant both played roles early in their career, and it was also at the King's Head that the overdue revival in Sir Terence Rattigan's career began. The string of Rattigan revivals that graced Shaftesbury Avenue in the 1990s owed a lot to Dan's determination to give the dying playwright (who did at least make it to *The Browning Version* at the King's Head) his due.

As well as straight plays, the King's Head staged musicals, and both genres transferred to the West End after their Islington launch. Dan's example was to inspire many other prospective impresarios and theatre owners to set up their own theatre spaces in pub rooms. As this book has discussed already, there is nothing new in theatre being performed in converted spaces, but the King's Head showed that it could be done in pubs, that it could be done to a very high standard, despite the restrictions on budget and space, and that shows could potentially transfer to the West End.

Dan Crawford's portrait now hangs happily on the King's Head wall with those of so many of the actors and actresses who performed at the theatre. The photographs look benevolently down on customers in the pub, many of whom seem quite content just to treat it as a rather theatrical local and would not dream of going past the end of the bar – where the box office is a lady sitting in an armchair with a batch of tickets and a tin for the money.

As a pub, the King's Head has charm, not least because it looks at least 70 years out of date. Dan's anglophilia extended to the old currency of pound shillings and pence, and he used to insist that his bar staff gave prices in the term that would have been used before decimalization.

The eccentricity with which he ran a pub was matched by the way he managed the theatre. A loather of bureaucracy, he was unwilling to fill in reams of forms and follow standard procedures, which is why the King's Head, despite its longevity and its remarkable artistic record, was gradually starved of funds by official bodies who would not tolerate Dan's sense of independence.

The result was what came to be a King's Head ritual. Before the play started, he would appear in front of the small but surprisingly versatile stage, bucket in hand, to ask patrons for some cash to help the roof fund, which was set up to plug assorted leaks.

Dan's heroic refusal to bend to bureaucracy, however inconvenient the result, ultimately showed up how sterile and unnecessary so much of officialdom really is. It may seem a long way from Upper Street to St Martin's Lane, and further out to the Cut at Waterloo, but Dan Crawford was in a way the inheritor of the mantle once worn by Lilian Baylis.

The programme credits at the Coliseum, home of the opera company that Miss Baylis was responsible for founding, show dozens of administrative staff, under a variety of different sections or areas of responsibility. This may be to be expected, given the range of activity needed to maintain a leading opera company, but Miss Baylis managed to run The Old Vic, and then Sadler's Wells too, with little more than herself and a handful of old dears.

Throughout the arts world today, by contrast, (museums and galleries are just as bad as theatre companies) it seems to take a remarkable number of administrators, outreach workers and so on to keep the show on the road. Miss Baylis (on a wing and, given her Christian convictions, a prayer) and Dan on the stage of the King's Head with his charming smile, soft voice, battered jacket and a bucket, both managed to produce a major and much-appreciated contribution to Theatreland without the grinding apparatus of subsidy, endless forms and 'mission statements'.

Since Dan Crawford's death in 2005 his widow, Stephanie, herself American, has kept the place running. It now has much-improved seating and a more secure roof, but still lives on its wits and the box-office receipts from the shows. These continue to be very varied in style, and to attract new acting talent, such as James Jagger, who appeared there in 2007 in a double bill, *Lone Star* and *Private Wars*. Dan may have gone, but the King's Head retains the love and support of a great many patrons of this little outpost of Theatreland who seem as determined as its founder was to keep his creation going.

8

St Martin's Lane

St Martin's Lane stretches from south of Seven Dials to just south of the London Coliseum and a little north of Trafalgar Square, in St Martin's Place. At its start, where it meets Monmouth Street (a long and attractive road that is divided in two by the Seven Dials monument) it is technically a different street, called Upper St Martin's Lane.

Upper St Martin's Lane is the least interesting part of the road but on the plus side it contains the headquarters of Equity, the actors' union. One of the current senior officers (Vice President in 2008) of Equity is Malcolm Sinclair.

He sees the changes brought in by Margaret Thatcher's government in the early 1980s as detrimental to Equity. In union terms, theatre used to be a closed shop, but that practice was outlawed. Actors and others working in the theatre could be members of unions if they so chose, but it was no longer compulsory.

This fundamental change may have meant that Theatreland was part of the 1980s Thatcher revolution, but it wasn't exactly like the miners being charged by police horses – something that theatre director Stephen Daldry put into his film, *Billy Elliot*. Daldry's stage musical version of that story, playing at the Victoria Palace, retains the anti-Thatcher sentiments of the film – while throwing in some jibes against Michael Heseltine as well.

Sinclair is less preachy about Thatcher but clearly feels her administration has something to answer for, as the lack of a closed shop has by definition made Equity's bargaining position weaker in any given situation. The situation with which he and his colleagues were involved at the end of 2008 was the wide-ranging discussion, with the Society of London Theatre, over rates of pay in Theatreland.

Sinclair argues that although some other costs that producers have to meet may have gone up, actors' wages have in effect gone down over the last 20 years.

When speaking about the union he is clearly passionate about the work it carries out on behalf of its members:

> Equity was founded by actors for the benefit of their fellow professionals. It was designed so that there would in effect be a pooling of resources between actors, at whatever stage of their careers they were at. It was very much the theatre community in action.

There is an equity representative, or deputy, in each theatre, from among the company – they are part of the company and acting on their behalf, not some sort of outside appointee from the union. Deputies have, among other things, the historic duty of collecting dues, though these tend to be collected by direct debit these days. The representatives are conduits for problems that need dealing with on the actors' behalf.

One major change in Equity over the last 20 or so years has been (despite the lingering dislike for some of the changes Mrs Thatcher initiated) the way that the union is now seen as very much less political – in the general sense of the word. Under the terms of its own rules Equity cannot be party political. As Sinclair points out, the union is not allowed to get involved in political issues like the Iraq war: it restricts itself to its members' commercial interests, negotiating deals on their behalf.

There is some pressure for Equity to save money by moving from its central London offices to outer London: the Musicians' Union is in Stockwell, south of the river, while the National Union of Journalists is in King's Cross. Sinclair believes, understandably, that it is psychologically important for the actors' union to be located in Theatreland and therefore within walking distance for most of Theatreland's actors.

As an actor himself, Sinclair is maintaining the tradition, stretching back to Dame May Whitty and other equity pioneers, of working on behalf of his professional colleagues. Leaving that to one side and talking instead about an actor's experience of Theatreland, he talks of life in the theatre rather than the union while sitting in a café by the stage door of Wyndham's Theatre.

Sinclair sees a fundamental difference between New York's theatre and London's, which is that most actors tend to live in Manhattan, whereas in London it is increasingly the case, especially among younger actors, that they cannot afford to live centrally and have to commute home after the show.

This has an inevitable effect on the sort of after-show 'family' relationship within a company of actors in a play, as rather than unwinding over a glass or wine or a coffee after the show they are rushing for a train or a last bus before the much slower night bus services begin.

Another noticeable change is the demise of the purely theatre star. In New

York there is Patti LuPone, and in London there is Simon Russell Beale, but by and large, Sinclair argues, theatre actors who are national or international names are so not because they have spent an entire career in the theatre but because, however distinguished their stage experience, they have become known through film and, to a degree, television work.

Sinclair gives as an example the actor he was appearing with in the *Ivanov* company at Wyndham's in 2008 – Kenneth Branagh. Branagh is a major stage actor but his public profile rests also on his film work, including film adaptations of Shakespeare plays, among which is his full-text *Hamlet*.

The same could be said of the stars of the other three plays in the Donmar's West End season at Wyndham's in 2008 and 2009. Sir Derek Jacobi has spent most of his career on stage but came to wider public attention through the television series *I, Claudius* and he subsequently starred in another TV hit, *Cadfael*.

Dame Judi Dench has also had a long stage career punctuated with hits like her Lady Macbeth (opposite Ian McKellen), but is best-known for television work and for a series of films, including her Oscar-winning role as Elizabeth I in *Shakespeare in Love*. She has also become known to a younger non-theatrical audience through her role as 'M', the spy chief in the James Bond films.

Jude Law, says Sinclair, is a further case of an actor who has proved himself on many occasions in the theatre – his forthcoming stage Hamlet has aroused a huge amount of advance interest – but whose fame rests on eye-catching film roles rather than his achievements on stage.

Sinclair clearly loves today's Theatreland and speaks of working in *Ivanov* with real pleasure: 'It was great fun and had a wonderful company feel'. However, he misses aspects of an earlier theatre industry: the stars who came up almost exclusively through theatre work; the glamour that theatre undoubtedly had; and also the sense of history that younger actors used to be inducted into. These days, he feels, many actors all too often have no idea of the great names of even the recent past – citing a case of a reference made about Peggy Ashcroft being greeted with complete incomprehension.

'It is not as if there are no stars left – Ken Branagh has real star appeal, as does Ian McKellen,' notes Sinclair – 'It's just that younger actors seem to have little interest in the stars who preceeded them.' He says that he doesn't want to come across as a nostalgist, but in person that's the last thing that he appears. He has an energy and an enjoyment for his profession that is very engaging.

One problem Sinclair identifies in terms of a sense of community is the lack of a range of theatre magazines, like the old *Plays and Players*, that catered for theatre lovers. The modern equivalent is *Whatsonstage*, a free monthly magazine available at theatres, which he feels carries on the *Plays and Players* tradition.

There are also numerous theatrical websites and blogs, but there is nothing like being able to sit in a dressing room or on the bus or train home, reading a magazine devoted to what's happening in London's theatre.

On the other hand, Sinclair felt the importance of sharing theatre history with the younger actors with whom he was working in *The History Boys*, and the company of David Grindley's production of *Journey's End* were fascinated by the military history of the First World War and very moved by a visit to the Cenotaph.

Their interest in the Cenotaph as a memorial to the dead of that conflict is understandable given the emotional power that Grindley brought to his production of R. C. Sherriff's 1929 drama set in a dug-out in a front-line trench on the Western Front, just before the final major German assault in 1918. Grindley's version had a curtain call where the actors stood in a silent line at the front of the stage, with a backcloth of row after row of the names of the dead.

Moving south from the Equity headquarters, past Stringfellow's nightclub, where Peter Stringfellow has been providing erotically charged conviviality for over 20 years, you come to a crossroads. From here you can turn immediately right into Long Acre, or take a gentler right down Garrick Street, where the Garrick Club is located.

The Garrick is a Victorian clubhouse whose purpose was to enable actors and gentlemen (the two initially being considered clearly separate) to meet in civilized surroundings. It is one of the more fashionable of the gentlemen's clubs of London, a collection of mansions and palaces that are centred in St James's, their historic homeland, but are also to be found in Covent Garden (the Garrick) and Mayfair (the Savile).

Unlike any other club, all of which tend to count unobtrusiveness as a cardinal virtue (outside the clubhouse at least: inside the places can be astonishingly imposing), the members of the Garrick have their own dual-toned tie. Salmon pink alternated with cucumber green, it is a distinctive badge of belonging.

Membership is still drawn from the senior ranks of the stage. The veteran Sir Donald Sinden, who acted as a young man with an ex-member of Sir Henry Irving's company, provides a much appreciated sense of continuity with the twentieth-century stage. Today more members tend to be drawn from the professions, especially the law, which has, like the church, always had an element of theatre about it.

The clubhouse has a superb collection of theatrical memorabilia and paintings, including one of the actress Dame Gladys Cooper, whose grandson, the theatre critic Sheridan Morley, is discussed in Chapter 15.

The Garrick was one of the last of the major London clubs to have a make-over, with its stone exterior being fully cleaned and restored to its creamy original, and all traces of a century and a half of London soot (which had rendered it a deep and grimy black) being happily removed in the process.

For the acting profession, membership is something that only a handful will want or afford, and those usually well into middle age, but just as gardening becomes more attractive as one ages, so presumably does membership of a club where well-dressed old boys (women have been resisted here far longer than they were even by the Church of England) lunch at length and then snooze through the afternoon in leather chairs before waking for an aperitif before dinner. Younger actors have other places in their sights, and these will be looked at elsewhere in this book.

The Garrick can be seen from the junction between Upper St Martin's Lane and St Martin's Lane itself. Continuing down St Martin's Lane brings you to two historic theatres and two small alleyways (one barely passable at its St Martin's Lane opening). On the left hand side, Goodwin's Court lies between St Martin's Lane and Bedfordbury, the street that runs past the back of the Coliseum and it stage door. The entrance at either end of the court is narrow, especially on St Martin's Lane, where it is easy to miss if you don't know where to look, or whether to look at all in the first place.

Goodwin's Court is a row of late seventeenth-century houses on the south side, while the north consists of offices and the backs of the various shops and restaurants of the south side of New Row, one of the most attractive little streets in Covent Garden. New Row, which forms part of the route from Covent Garden to Leicester Square, is usually very busy, from early in the morning when office workers pop into Farmer Brown's for one of its trademark bacon sandwiches, to late at night when the theatres close and audiences pour out onto the street.

In contrast, Goodwin's Court is a quiet backwater, a secret pathway through the heart of one of the busiest parts of central London. The court was condemned to be demolished in the 1930s, on the grounds that the picturesque, bow-fronted little houses were unfit for human habitation; a dangerous row of slums that should be replaced by something modern.

Fortunately, a Mr Sympson bought the court and set about refurbishing it. The family still own most of it today, and the little houses that were once overflowing with people are now smart offices for advertising companies and other commercial enterprises. Leslie Sympson, of the children of the saviour of Goodwin's Court, used to live at the Bedfordbury end, and would, every week, hold Sunday lunches that saw a mixture of elderly women of a theatrical background and presentable young actors and dancers brought together for a traditional Sunday roast, preceded by Leslie's home-made soup. The soup that was not drunk that day tended to be saved and added to by fresh soup the following week, which led to a local legend that some of any given serving of soup had probably been first made 30 years earlier.

Leslie's brother, Tony, was himself an actor. He was the sort of performer who never really made it in terms of major roles, let alone fame, but who was good at his job, reliable and always in work. There is a plaque to him at St Paul's, Covent Garden. Among the tributes to the major stars, the glamorous dancers and the smartest playwrights it simply says: 'Tony Sympson. An inspired player of small parts'.

Among the doors on the north side of Goodwin's Court is number 14a. This used to be the office of Peggy Ramsay, a towering figure in Theatreland from the 1960s to the 1990s. A literary agent, her speciality was in playwrights, and she helped steer the careers of many of the major names of the 1960s and beyond. She is vividly recalled in Simon Callow's memoir, *Love Is Where It Falls*, in which he discusses his friendship with her.

Among the many talented playwrights on her list – which included David Hare and Alan Ayckbourn – her most notorious client was Joe Orton, the author of the black comedies *Loot*, *What the Butler Saw*, and *Entertaining Mr Sloane*, which brought an anarchic sexuality and irrepressible sense of anti-Establishment fun into the West End.

Orton was a promiscuous gay who spent years living in a tiny bedsit in Islington with his partner, Kenneth Halliwell. Halliwell was the older and better educated of the two when they met at RADA, London's most prestigious drama school. Halliwell lived off a family inheritance and, when that ran out, the pair managed on social security. They were happy to sacrifice prosperity for their art, which was originally writing fiction rather than plays.

Orton sent a manuscript – *The Boy Hairdresser* – to Charles Monteith, the publisher (at Faber & Faber) who had discovered William Golding. Golding's *The Lord of the Flies* had been turned down by about a dozen publishers and was already on Faber's 'Reject' pile, awaiting a polite letter to be sent turning the book down, when Monteith happened to pick it up.

A large man who had, like the central character, Piggy, been a fat and bespectacled boy at school, Monteith immediately identified with Piggy and was drawn into the story, which his editorial skill later ensured had various major improvements to it. The result was a bestseller that made Golding's name and fortune, and did Monteith's career no harm either. Among his other discoveries were the crime writer P. D. James and the poets Philip Larkin and Seamus Heaney. He also published Samuel Beckett's plays.

Having heard of Monteith's reputation as a publisher with an eye for a promising manuscript, Orton, who was then still known by his real first name, John, sent his manuscript to him at Faber's. Hoping to use his personal charm – he was very attractive in a boyish-faced, well-built way – as well as his writing skill, he invited Monteith and a friend of his, another publisher, Richard Brain, to dinner at his flat. Dinner in that financially-challenged household consisted of rice pudding as main course and rice pudding with syrup as dessert.

Monteith returned the hospitality, in rather grander style at his flat in Maida Vale, where he invited Orton – and the inevitable Halliwell – to a drinks party so that John could meet other literary figures, in the hope they might be helpful, in terms of contacts or advice. Orton and Halliwell spent most of the evening sitting on Monteith's enormous sofa, talking to each other rather than socializing with the other guests. The publisher, who co-incidentally turned down the novel, assumed they had not enjoyed themselves, but it was a case of their being nervous and rather intimidated by the more socially adept fellow guests rather than a lack of interest, and the Publisher was amused to see pen portraits of some of those present at the drinks party in later (equally unsuccessful) manuscripts that they wrote.

Orton changed direction as well as his name when he tried writing plays rather than novels, and found that the results – an *Evening Standard* Best Play award, for example – were very different too. His brief but starry career as Theatreland's favourite naughty boy came to an abrupt end when Halliwell, jealous of his sometime protégé's success, and fearful that Orton was tired of their claustrophobic living arrangements and living quarters, beat him to death with a hammer, before taking an overdose of pills.

This grisly end was somehow in tune with a career that celebrated the macabre and the unusual, and a life that saw Orton indulge in frequent and potentially dangerous sex with strangers. John Lahr's biography of Orton, *Prick Up Your Ears*, was followed by Alan Bennett's screenplay, in the film of which Orton was played by Gary Oldman and Halliwell by Alfred Molina. At the time of writing there have been suggestions that Matt Lucas, of *Little Britain* fame, might play Halliwell in a stage drama that sees the tortured and ultimately fatal relationship between the two men from Halliwell's point of view.

In the film, Peggy Ramsay was played by Vanessa Redgrave, who played her as stylish and mordantly witty, as she was in real life. Ramsay had been very fond of Orton, and was horrified at his death, but her stable of playwrights was an extensive one and she continued to work out of her offices at Goodwin's Court until her death in 1991.

Looking at the door to 14a today, it is strange to think that this quiet little alleyway was such a powerhouse of theatrical writing talent, for so long. Tom

Erhardt, an American who worked for Peggy for decades, still represents, at the age of 80, those clients of hers – and new ones of his own – who moved to the amalgamated company of Casarotto Ramsay & Associates that was formed after Peggy's death.

That firm has its headquarters behind Oxford Street, not New Row, and in large modern offices rather than Peggy's little warren in Goodwin's Court, but Erhardt, still a handsome, tall and powerfully built man, remains a fixture of theatrical first nights and after-show parties, looking after the interests of Casarotto Ramsay's clients who continue to include many of the biggest names in Theatreland. Peggy would approve.

Almost opposite the St Martin's Lane entrance to Goodwin's Court is the Salisbury. This gives a real feel for what a Victorian pub would have been like, decorated with glass, brass and wood, with plush velvet seats. Unfortunately the log fire that used to burn in the grate has been permanently put out – presumably for the ubiquitous health and safety reasons, which lessens the atmosphere.

The pub sign shows the imposingly bearded figure of the 3rd Marquess of Salisbury, a dedicated Tory who in the course of his career was not just a hawkish Foreign Secretary but three-time Prime Minister. It was Salisbury who laid down the doctrine that the Royal Navy should at all times be bigger than the next two navies in the world combined, to ensure that Britannia still ruled the waves. Speaking of which, Thomas Arne, the composer of 'Rule Britannia', lived a couple of minutes' walk away from the pub, in King Street, Covent Garden. Both Salisbury – whose family own the land on which the pub and neighbouring theatres stand – and Arne would have been appalled at the pathetic level to which the Royal Navy has been shrunk, not just by Labour but by Conservative governments too.

Carrying down St Martin's Lane, on the same side as the Salisbury, is Cecil Court, an alleyway of antiquarian bookshops, which includes another Theatreland institution: David Drummond's shop, The Pleasure of Past Times.

This is a nostalgist's idea of heaven, packed as it is with old posters, books about and by actors, postcards with pictures of long-dead performers, various manuscripts and a range of other memorabilia. His frequently changing window display draws the passer-by not so much into the shop as back in time, with its posters advertising long-dead trapeze artists, its copies of programmes from early Harold Pinter plays, or its copies of books packed with photographs of long-vanished music halls.

Drummond's own theatrical experience includes clowning, and he is as effortlessly knowledgeable about this as he is about the most arcane theatre lore. There is something, both about the shop and about Drummond himself, with his old-world manners and aura of calm, that suggests the shop should be in a Harry Potter film – where perhaps the wizard or one of his friends pops in to retrieve a seemingly innocuous wand, once owned by a master magician like Eric Mason (known as 'The Great Masoni'), and which really does have magic powers . . .

Past Cecil Court and further down St Martin's Lane is the Duke of York's Theatre. This modestly sized building tends, due to its size, to stage plays rather than musicals. Its moment of glory (every theatre has one) came on 27 December 1904, when it was the venue for the world premiere of James Barrie's *Peter Pan*.

The play was an immediate success and gave birth to subsequent books – and films – about Barrie's boy who would never grow up. Hollywood filmed a version of the story in *Hook*, co-starring Robin Williams as Peter and Dustin Hoffman as the villain, Captain Hook.

Hook was played at the premiere by Gerald Du Maurier, son of George Du Maurier who wrote the best-selling Victorian novel *Trilby*, whose lead character (despite being a woman) gave the world the name for the Trilby hat. The casting of Gerald Du Maurier as the pirate chief was a case of keeping things in the family, as Du Maurier's sister, Sylvia, had married a young barrister, Arthur Llewellyn-Davies. They were the parents of the group of boys who jointly inspired Barrie to invent the character of Peter Pan.

The opening night of *Peter Pan* was recreated for the screen in the film *Finding Neverland*, starring Johnny Depp. In the film, the Duke of York's is represented by the sweeping frontage of the Palace Theatre, in Cambridge Circus. Opened in 1891 as the Royal English Opera House, the Palace looks far more imposingly Victorian than the slender and elegant little frontage of the Duke of York's, with its charming little balcony where customers can enjoy their drinks on the rare London summer evenings that are actually warm.

The Palace was also used, for similar reasons, as a stand-in for the St James's Theatre in *Wilde*, the film about Oscar Wilde's doomed relationship with Lord Alfred Douglas, in which Wilde was played by Stephen Fry and Lord Alfred by Jude Law.

In 2008 the theatre saw a revival of Harold Pinter's *No Man's Land*. This had, in the original 1970s production, co-starred Ralph Richardson and John Gielgud. The revival had in their place David Bradley and Sir Michael Gambon, with a supporting cast of David Walliams (of *Little Britain* and cross-channel-swim fame) and Nick Dunning. The latter's presence as a butch homosexual was rather unnerving: partly because he acted the part so well, but partly, too because audiences has spent the last few months seeing him on their televisions every night as the father of Natalie Dormer's Anne Boleyn in *The Tudors*.

Pinter's plays are characterized by a sense of violence, which was strongly suggested in this production, but his work also has a strong streak of humour, albeit of a very dark kind. He also has the rather Elizabethan combination of playwriting and poetry and is an accomplished poet – as the programme notes to this *No Man's Land* make clear.

Across the road from the Duke of York's is the London Coliseum. This, like its counterpart in Bow Street, is an opera house, though when Londoners or visitors alike say 'opera house' they invariably mean the Royal Opera House rather than Frank Matcham's vast edifice.

The Coliseum was renovated to mark its centenary in 2004, and the major change by architects RHWL's arts team was to make all areas accessible via the main foyer on St Martin's Lane, rather than having to send those with seats in the Balcony to the Siberia of May's Court, round the side of the building, to then walk up a long flight of stairs to reach their seats where, as in the Royal Opera House, they were segregated from the rest of the audience, who appeared rather like dots far beneath the steep balcony tiers.

When opened, this was a variety house rather than an opera one. Despite this the rigid segregation of classes was insisted on by the owner, Oswald Stoll, and the Coliseum took the usual snobbery one step further when a compartment, resembling a railway carriage, was constructed, The idea was that when the King and Queen (Edward VII and Queen Alexandra) arrived at the front of the theatre, the doors would open and the royal couple would walk into the carriage, which would take them through the foyer on a little track, on which it would effortlessly glide, taking its precious cargo, insulated from the other theatergoers, to a royal box at the rear of the stalls. Parked outside the box, the compartment would provide a handy reception room.

Unfortunately the contraption broke as soon as the King (a massive man; his weight may have had something to do with it) entered. The King found this hilarious, but an appalled Stoll had the thing removed the next day.

The refurbishment of the Coliseum shows (as does that of the Royal Opera House) that there is huge scope, providing buildings are large enough, to give old theatres radical makeovers, ensuring they fit the requirements of early twenty-first-century audiences and actors.

This is just as well, given that new mainstream theatres are not likely ever to be built in central London again. According to Rosemary Squire (a past President of the Society of London Theatre, and a leading theatre owner and producer), the economics of the property and income ratio in the West End mean that theatres will always lose out to shops or offices.

Given this situation, Theatreland has to make the most of the building stock that it has, and the Coliseum's architects have done so here. The upper circle has been given a modern version of its Edwardian glass roof, and another use of glass (apart from allowing far more natural light into the public spaces) has been to create a small conservatory-style area from which some of Trafalgar Square can be seen – a miniature version of the windows in the National Portrait Gallery's restaurant, with their Mary Poppins-style view over the Square's rooftops.

The stalls area has been opened up as well, with a staircase now leading down to an area where the old staff changing rooms have been swept away to create new open space and plenty of lavatories.

The bar areas have also been improved, both in terms of size and style, while the auditorium, which had been styled in a greenish-blue colour scheme, has now reverted to the imperial red and purple that was always intended. Lifts take patrons to all levels, and the whole effect is one of prosperity and comfort, much as it must have seemed when the theatre was first opened in 1904.

Not every change in recent years has been for the best. There used to be more of a community feel within English National Opera, and the front-of-house staff tended to be drawn more from the ranks of full-time music students than they appear to be now. As a result a number of today's leading singers and conductors appearing at the Coliseum began their association with the building 20 or more years ago, wearing the battered green velvet jackets that used to be the ushers' uniform. Among those checking customers' tickets in the 1980s were the conductor Mark Wigglesworth and singers John Hudson and Jason Howard.

One of the perks of the poorly paid job was to be able see as much opera as you could bear, while there was (in that pre-accountant-led age) another perk of regular access to complimentary tickets for families and friends. This second perk was all the more generous given that so many of English National Opera's performances sold very strongly. Thanks to Lord Harewood's artistic policy the Coliseum was once referred to in the press as the home of the best musical theatre productions in Theatreland.

The sense of community was continued in after-show parties and events. Once these had finished and the corporate clients had been seen off, the staff who attended them would be fed from the same menu as the City bankers at long trestle tables in the upper circle restaurant area.

When the staff left the building they passed, at the side of the Coliseum, London's narrowest little alleyway: Brydges Place. It has been made marginally less dingy and threatening by some extra lighting and by painting the walls, up to head height, in white paint. Despite this, no tourist in their right mind would venture up this dark and often urine-soaked passageway on a wet winter evening unescorted by a local. The urine may be from tramps or it may be a sort of folk memory etched in the pavement, as there used to be a public urinal in the alley.

Brydges Place gets wider as it moves away from St Martin's Lane and towards Bedfordbury. On the left are a set of doors with attractively etched glass. These lead directly to the back of the Royal Retiring Room, behind the Royal Box. When opened, royals or other VIPS can leave the theatre discretely and safely, avoiding the crowds in the foyer and at the front of the building.

Opposite these doors, on the other side of the passageway, are a set of wooden doors. When open, they reveal an empty arch with a similar set of other doors which, when opened, would take a party of VIPs straight into a limousine and off (to a palace or a hotel) without having been caught in the traffic snarl at the bottom of St Martin's Lane.

For those without the advantages of bodyguards and outriders, but with more leisure time, there is, a few feet further towards Bedfordbury, the pleasure of a drink or a meal at 2 Brydges Place. This is the name as well as the address of a private members' bar and restaurant run for over 20 years by Rod Lane. A good-looking man with a penchant for chunky sweaters in winter, he presides over Brydges Place with a genial charm. This, along with the club's discreet entrance flanked by two miniature trees, its real fire, panelled walls and theatrical atmosphere (many of the members are in the industry) make it a perfect place to retreat to after a hard night on stage.

St Martin's Lane also contains the Coliseum's CD and DVD shop, specializing in opera but with a certain amount of ballet, too. It is well stocked and the staff tend to be knowledgeable about what they're selling, which is not always true of London record shops. On one such visit to another central London store, a girl – on the information desk, no less – was asked where you find CDs by Noël Coward. 'Who are they?' she asked, blankly. When assured 'they' were not an obscure pop group but a composer from the 1920s and 1930s, she dismissed the whole conversation with 'Well, I wouldn't have heard of him then, innit?'

9

Shaftesbury Avenue

Shaftesbury Avenue, known in the trade simply as The Avenue, is for many people the most obvious part of Theatreland – a row of high-profile theatres at the centre of London. For Shaftesbury Avenue starts at Piccadilly Circus, the roundabout that (despite Charing Cross being technically the centre of London) has been traditionally seen, since its creation, as the hub of the West End.

Shaftesbury Avenue was created in the early 1880s by sweeping away slums to form a new highway that would bring prosperity to the area, arcing away from Piccadilly Circus in a lower-scale mirror version of the majestic sweep of Regent Street.

It used to be said that if you stood at Piccadilly Circus for long enough you would see everyone you knew pass by. What you would certainly see, until the late 1980s, was a collection of rent boys, either at the 'meat rack' under the arches on the north-western side of the Circus, or walking around lower Regent Street and the alleys off it.

The advent first of the mobile phone and latterly of the internet has meant that rent boys can now advertise on the web and operate from the comfort and safety (or at least warmth) of their own homes, rather than pacing the pavement, whatever the weather, in hope of catching a customer's eye.

The presence of rent boys in this area was curiously appropriate. The statue by Sir Alfred Gilbert that is the centrepiece of Piccadilly Circus and an instantly recognizable symbol of central London (it is used by the capital's main evening paper, the *Evening Standard*), is of a winged youth, naked except for a billowing and strategically-placed scarf, firing an arrow from a bow.

The statue is usually referred to as Eros, the Greek god of love, though it has also been taken as representing the spirit of Christian compassion, as Lord Shaftesbury, after whom the Avenue is named, was a philanthropic Christian much concerned with trying to improve the living conditions of London's poor.

The statue is, officially, not of Eros, but of Anteros, Eros' twin. Anteros represents fulfilled desire, as in lust that follows through and is reciprocated and rewarded with physical passion, unlike Eros who can pierce your heart with his arrow but does not guarantee that that love will be requited. The exact meaning of each name can best be left to scholars of ancient Greek and that culture's mythology. For passers-by in Piccadilly, the name Eros, and the association with love/lust will do.

The direction of the arrow is away from the great line of theatres in Shaftesbury Avenue but it would still hit a theatre: the tiny gem named after the road in which it is located – Jermyn Street. This little space, once used as a changing room for the neighbouring Italian Restaurant, is run by Penny Horner, a one-woman whirlwind of energy who not only put the theatre on the map but managed to get it a royal patron: Princess Michael of Kent.

Princess Michael has often had a less than flattering press, and has been given the nickname 'Princess Pushy' but she is a strikingly attractive woman who looks superb in evening dress and tiara. Whether in the Royal Box at the Coliseum in the 1980s or the more modest surroundings of Jermyn Street Theatre in the 1990s, she has brought some continental glamour to Royal duties, for which she should be congratulated rather than mocked.

Jermyn Street Theatre's heyday was in the late 1990s and early 2000s. It has, arguably, lost some of its well-deserved cachet since then, but it continues to stage a variety of plays and musical theatre, along with one-night specials, and Penny Horner continues her labour of love in keeping the venue going: a little touch of theatre amid the shirt shops, barbers and restaurants of this historic street.

In the other direction from that pointed at by Gilbert's statue is the start of Shaftesbury Avenue. To the right of the opening from Piccadilly Circus is what remains of the London Pavilion, which opened in 1885. By the 1920s it specialized in revues, including those of the legendary impresario C. B. Cochran. Cochran's glamorous life came to a grisly end. A sufferer from arthritis, he decided, when staying at a hotel with his wife, to ease the pain with a hot bath.

Having for some reason locked the door of the bathroom, he sat in the vast tub and started to run the hot water. Going to reach for the cold tap, his joints froze, and he was unable to move as the increasingly hot water gushed out of the tap and onto his terribly scalded skin. He screamed for his wife who had to get the hotel manager up to their room to break the bathroom door down, by which time Cochran was fatally injured.

In 1934 the London Pavilion was converted into a cinema. This was later more or less demolished (apart from the façade) and replaced with the large shopping mall that now stands on the site, called the London Trocadero. Fortunately its nearest neighbours are still playhouses.

The building of these theatres in Shaftesbury Avenue reflected their profitability as commercial ventures in an age when live theatre was the main entertainment for a capital city that appeared to be bursting with people and money. If Piccadilly was the hub of London, then London was the hub of the largest and most prosperous empire in history – one reason so many theatres were called after it.

Shaftesbury Avenue's theatres are, in ascending order from Piccadilly Circus, the Lyric, the Apollo, the Gielgud, the Queen's and, at the unfashionable and rather isolated very top end of the road, the Shaftesbury.

The Lyric, a not very attractive building, has its stage door in Great Windmill Street, named after the Windmill Theatre that staged nude tableaux and famously never closed during the Second World War, despite the bombing raids. Martin Sherman, an American playwright living in London, wrote the screenplay for *Mrs Henderson Presents*, a film about the woman who owned the theatre and made a fortune from the Windmill's sexually charged presentations.

The Lyric stands on the site of a house that showed off flesh in a very different way. A London County Council plaque on the eighteenth-century wall that is incorporated into the building reminds passers-by that 'This was the house and museum of Dr William Hunter, Anatomist 1718–1783'.

The Lyric opened in 1888 with a comic opera called *Dorothy* – which should be noted by those who think that the dominance of musicals is something new. The building has an elegant glass awning to protect anyone queuing outside the box office or waiting to get in. Both eventualities needed to be catered for with the opening of two other musicals, *Blood Brothers* in 1983 and *Five Guys Named Moe* in 1990.

One of the best straight plays that the Lyric has hosted in recent years was a revival of the comedy *Hobson's Choice* in 1995, with Leo McKern as a domineering Edwardian shopkeeper and Nichola McAuliffe as the long-suffering spinster daughter who finally turns the tables on her tyrannical parent.

McAuliffe is an accomplished comic actor who has also shown real talent as the writer of a novel with the eye-catching title of *A Fanny Full of Soap*. This is set in a West End show where everything is going wrong, a fortunately rare eventuality but one that offers a lot of comic potential.

The neighbouring Apollo is a much prettier theatre, with a pleasanter atmosphere than the Lyric, whose modern front-of-house area has a drab and unloved feel to it. The Apollo's drawback is that the foyer is shallow and small, so on first nights and indeed any night of a popular play, it's a struggle to get past the box office window and the ushers and into the theatre.

The Apollo opened 20 years after the Lyric, with a short run of an American musical called *The Belle of Bohemia*, in 1901. Further musicals and revues formed a staple diet until the 1920s, when plays included Edgar Wallace's 1928 thriller *The Squeaker*. Revue returned in the 1950s, which saw Kenneth Williams and Fenella Fielding star in *Pieces of Eight* (1959).

The 1950s and 1960s were Fenella Fielding's heyday but she still appears on stage from time to time and her name remains a draw, as the indefinable star presence about her has never faded. A devastating sex symbol in her day, she still carries herself with the straight-backed poise that only stars from the 1950s seem able to manage – Joan Collins is another example.

Miss Fielding's sultry voice, which has enthralled susceptible male theatregoers for decades was recorded for posterity when she appeared opposite her theatre colleague Kenneth Williams in a Carry On film. In *Carry On Screaming*, where she plays a vampire, she asks 'Do you mind if I smoke?' and then emits wafts of the stuff from her body.

Comedy has been a mainstay of the Apollo, with prime examples being Alan Bennett's *Forty Years On* (1968), which is a series of sketches set in a boys' public school. The headmaster was played by John Gielgud, who was as good in comedic roles as he was in the tragic ones for which he was best known – including David Story's *Home*, which was also staged at the Apollo, and which co-starred Ralph Richardson. Among the schoolboys in *Forty Years On* was a young Anthony Andrews (Lord Sebastian Flyte in the television version of Evelyn Waugh's *Brideshead Revisited*), who decades later made an excellent Henry Higgins in *My Fair Lady* at Drury Lane.

Another comedy at the Apollo was *Jeffrey Bernard is Unwell*, in which the stage was transformed into the interior of a Soho landmark, the Coach and Horses. The Coach and Horses, in Greek Street, just round the corner from the Palace Theatre, was the favourite 'local' for legendary journalist Jeffrey Bernard. Bernard achieved his fame through chronicling his drink- and cigarette-fuelled life, his lovers and his betting losses, in the pages of the *Spectator*, where he wrote the 'Low Life' weekly column, a counterpoint to the 'High Life' recorded by the yacht-owning Greek playboy (and karate champion) Taki.

Bernard's life revolved around drink, women and horses, and he was one of the last of the great twentieth-century Soho characters. He knew the artist Francis Bacon, who used to take him to dinner when as a young man he had run out of money and needed a decent meal. He was on first-name terms with most of the Bohemian group that propped up the bar at the Colony, one of Soho's best-known drinking clubs. It was a lifestyle that many envied, but it took a toll of Bernard's film-star good looks, and though despite his doctors' fears he sailed past the age of 40; his early death was directly attributable to his years of vast alcohol intake.

The Coach and Horses was his favourite place to drink, and though as a pub it looks very ordinary it was its situation – and the acerbic wit of its veteran landlord, Norman Balon – that attracted him: the Soho streets, the sex shops and the stage doors provided a perfect backdrop to a drinking session.

Bernard's career was bookended by the theatre. As a young man he had swept stages and broken several actresses' hearts as a stage hand, while in later life he was portrayed on stage in *Jeffrey Bernard is Unwell*. From stage hand, then, to stage personality.

The title came from the laconic line that replaced his column in the *Spectator* when he was too drunk to write it in time for the weekly deadline. Keith Waterhouse wrote a very sharp, darkly comic piece whose central premise was that Bernard had been accidentally locked in overnight at the Coach and Horses, where he had collapsed in a drunken stupor.

Several actors played Bernard in the course of several productions, but the best was the man who originated the role – Peter O'Toole. This was a perfect piece of casting, given O'Toole's charisma on stage and the added frisson that everyone in the audience knew of his own hell-raising past. The play was directed by Ned Sherrin, and made Bernard internationally famous.

Bernard used to visit the Apollo while the play was running, though he was more interesting in soaking up the atmosphere in the stalls bar during the show rather than sit inside the auditorium watching it. On one occasion a member of staff tried to remove him, as the bars are only meant to be used before the show and in the interval. Having a disreputable-looking old man (Bernard looked old enough to be his own father) in the bar was an annoyance. He was asked to leave. He protested that he had every right to be there, as he was Jeffrey Bernard. 'You're not fooling me,' the man replied. 'Jeffrey Bernard is in there – on stage!'

The next theatre up the Avenue is the Gielgud. This used to be called the Globe but was renamed in honour of Sir John Gielgud, the actor who made his name as Hamlet and spent the next 50-plus years on stage and even longer on screen. The name change was initiated because the opening of Shakespeare's Globe would lead to confusion between the two Globe theatres. Janet Holmes à Court, who at the time ran Stoll Moss, the theatre company that owned the Globe, came up with the ideal solution: another name for the Globe, beginning with the same letter, and which would honour England's greatest living actor in the year (1994) of his 90th birthday.

Gielgud, whose bust adorns the downstairs bar, came from a theatrical background. His mother was a Terry, a stage family whose most famous member was Ellen, Sir Henry Irving's favourite actress at the Lyceum.

He and Laurence Olivier were rivals for the position of best classical actor, a rivalry that had an early and unusual start when they both appeared in *Romeo and Juliet*, in 1935. They alternated in the roles of Romeo and Mercutio. Olivier was the better-looking, more masculine (though he always had a feminine quality about him, too), while Gielgud was the more poetic.

Gielgud had an extraordinary voice, whose quality entranced generations of theatregoers and which has been recorded for posterity in numerous films, including the 1953 film of *Julius Caesar*, which co-starred Marlon Brando as Mark Antony.

In one of the best scenes of the play, Cassius (Gielgud) is talking to Brutus (James Mason) and speaks the lines which inspired James Barrie to write his play *Dear Brutus*, which has as its theme the human longing for a second chance and the fondly held belief that if we could start over again we would avoid the mistakes which can blight our lives.

The lines that Gielgud spoke are 'The fault, dear Brutus, is not in our stars, but in ourselves, that we are underlings.' The scene is especially worth watching in that it shows the actors with the two most gorgeous voices of the twentieth century. Gielgud, essentially a stage actor, despite being best-known to many Americans as Dudley Moore's butler in *Arthur*, had a voice often described as being like silver. Mason, a film actor, had a voice like velvet, or an alcohol-enhanced cream.

Gielgud earned the right of having a theatre named after him not just for his longevity (born in 1904, he died in 2000) but because of his dedication to theatre as an art form, however much films rather than plays paid his bills. An unworldly man, he was taken advantage of for many years by Hugh 'Binkie' Beaumont, the producer whose company, H.M. Tennent, dominated Theatreland for decades. Beaumont not only paid Gielgud far less than the actor could have demanded, he also stole his boyfriend, John Perry, from him. Gielgud had no choice but to put a brave face on this, however bitter he may have been in private, for the sake of his career.

That career nearly came to a catastrophic end in 1953, when he was arrested for importuning for sex in a public lavatory. Charged and fined, he had claimed in court that he was drunk at the time. The magistrate, who clearly held an old-fashioned view of the nature of human sexuality, advised him, after issuing a fine rather than the possible prison sentence that really would have wrecked the newly knighted actor's professional life, 'Go and see your doctor at once!'

The theatrical profession rallied round Gielgud, as did the general public, though Laurence Olivier was less than fulsome in his support, and Binkie Beaumont had in effect to be blackmailed by Gielgud's brother. Beaumont was worried about the effect of the scandal on the box office for the play, *A Day By The Sea*, that Gielgud was shortly to appear in, and seriously considered firing him until Val Gielgud, who was head of Drama at the BBC, phoned Beaumont and said that unless he kept Sir John in work he, Val, would consider letting the authorities know about Beaumont's own sexual history.

When Sir John walked into the rehearsal room he was greeted by his co-star Sybil Thorndike (who had been in a spot of bother with the law herself when as a suffragette she had hurled a brick through a window) and the immortal words: 'Well, Johnny, you have been a silly bugger!' The tension was broken by laughter, and when Gielgud appeared on stage he was received by equally reassuring applause.

As a result, Gielgud's career continued for another half a century on stage, his final appearance being as Sir Sydney Cockerell in *The Best of Friends* at the Apollo in 1988. A consistent theme in his life, along with rave reviews, was his habit of dropping 'bricks' – saying things that he shouldn't, at the worse possible time.

There are many examples of this, including an ill-fated attempt to retrieve the situation immediately after one such 'faux pas'. When lunching with the curiously named writer Edward Knoblock (who adapted J. B. Priestley's *The Good Companions* for the stage), he said, of another customer arriving in the restaurant, 'Oh! Look at that man over there! He's the most tremendous bore. Worse even than Eddie Knoblock . . . Oh! Oh! I mean the *other* Eddie Knoblock, of course!'

Sir John Gielgud when taken to lunch at the House of Commons to celebrate his 90th birthday by Gyles Brandreth, who had written a very readable biography of him and had befriended him, Sir John turned to Brandreth and said 'It's so nice of you to invite me. I don't know what I should have done, otherwise. You see all my *real* friends are dead!'

He also managed to upset Richard Burton, whom he directed in *Hamlet*. Appearing in Burton's dressing room when the actor was getting out of costume, Gielgud, who never fully took to Burton's portrayal – he thought he wasn't princely enough – let his subconscious thought break into arrangements for a post-show dinner. Seeing that Burton wasn't yet ready to leave he said 'Oh, dear! I'll come back when you're better!'

Another theatrical knight associated with Shaftesbury Avenue was Sir Terence Rattigan (1911–1977). Rattigan was a playwright rather than an actor, and a very old-fashioned writer at that. Educated at Harrow and the son of a diplomat, he made his name with a pre-war comedy, *French Without Tears*. During the war,

Rattigan served with the RAF and this experience inspired *Flare Path*, set on a wartime RAF station.

After the war Rattigan enjoyed a six-year run of successes, with *The Winslow Boy* (1946), *The Browning Version* (1948), *The Deep Blue Sea* (1952) and *Separate Tables* (1954) – all dramas featuring the English middle classes.

Rattigan dressed like a prosperous stockbroker rather than a thespian, but the stage was his life and his greatest skill as a writer was in generating emotion without hysterics. His characters may have kept stiff upper lips on stage, but their efforts in doing so saw the lips of the audience quivering in sympathy as they watched. Both characters and audience felt emotion just as deeply as other, far more histrionic nationalities – or classes. As Noël Coward once said, when accused of writing 'irrelevant' plays about the upper classes rather than the working man, 'Duchesses have feelings, too!'

Rattigan's women suffer agonies beneath a façade of well-bred self-restraint, though even they sometimes crack – like Hester Collyer, the central character of *The Deep Blue Sea*. The play is about an upper-class woman who has left her husband (a judge) for a much younger ex-RAF fighter pilot, with whom she has fallen passionately in love. Her sexual hunger, which was unsatisfied in her marriage and only fully awakened by her affair, now embarrasses the younger man.

At the start of the play her frustration leads her to despair and a suicide attempt – by gassing herself. *The Deep Blue Sea* was based on the suicide of a (male) lover of Rattigan's, and was written at a time when a serious play about homosexual love was out of the question. This doesn't mean that Hester (or any of his other female characters) are second-rate creations. The playwright may have used his own experience, or that of others, as inspiration for the stage, but his female characters are well-drawn and ring true, which is why revivals of his plays have touched audiences more cynical than those for whom the play was written.

Rattigan's connection with his public seemed unbreakable, but his reputation was fatally wounded with the opening, in 1956, of John Osborne's *Look Back in Anger* at the Royal Court. This play introduced 'kitchen sink' drama, and when the kitchen sink came on stage the French windows and well-cut suits that Rattigan represented went straight out the stage door.

For a man who was the embodiment of the smart commercial theatre of 1940s and early 1950s Shaftesbury Avenue, this was a devastating blow, from which he never really recovered. His move to Bermuda was prompted as much by a sense of dissociation from the realities of modern English life and theatre as by the need to avoid tax on his highly lucrative work writing screenplays, most notably for *The V.I.P.s* and *The Yellow Rolls-Royce*.

In the latter, Rex Harrison played one of the owners of the car, and the actor – who was perfectly suited to such a vehicle – was presented with it at the end of the filming. When someone told Harrison it was an outrageously lavish reward for a short period of filming he replied that the car was not a recognition of a few days' work but a lifetime's.

Rattigan saw – just – his own damaged reputation rethought within his own lifetime. The revival in his standing among theatre critics came in the unlikely form of Dan Crawford's King's Head in Islington, which staged a revival of *The Browning Version* in 1976. Rattigan, by then a seriously ill man, went to the opening, but when he realized that he was dying, it was Shaftesbury Avenue that he wanted to see again, and he was driven up and down the Avenue to see the lights of its theatres for one last time.

In subsequent years the Avenue has seen revivals of both *Separate Tables* and *The Deep Blue Sea*, the latter starring Penelope Wilton as Hester Collyer. Wilton, who has recently earned rave reviews for her performance in T. S. Eliot's *The Family Reunion* at the Donmar Warehouse, and an *Evening Standard* award (jointly, with Margaret Tyzack) for *The Chalk Garden* (at the same theatre), has proved herself to be one of Theatreland's leading actresses in revivals of twentieth-century classics, and it can't be long before she receives a damehood.

In her youth she was a great beauty, her good looks recorded in a studio portrait by Cornel Lucas, the British photographer who was a favourite with British and Hollywood stars alike. There are a number of Lucas's photographs in the National Portrait Gallery, including an iconic one of Marlene Dietrich sitting on a pile of expensive-looking luggage as if she has just disembarked from the Queen Mary.

Dietrich was a friend of both Noël Coward and Ivor Novello. The two men, friends and rivals, worked together only once, in 1927, in a play called *Sirocco* (after the Mediterranean wind) which was a resounding flop. By co-incidence, Sirocco is the name of a popular bar situated on the west side of Shaftesbury Avenue, between the Gielgud and the Queen's. This is a happy co-incidence which reminds the passing theatre historian or tour guide that Theatreland is a story of failures as well as first-night standing ovations.

Sirocco has an absurd plot about a young English tourist and a sexually violent young Italian waiter. Coward offered the play to Novello, whose own dark good looks were sufficiently Italian-looking to have landed him his first starring role in a silent movie in 1919, eight years earlier.

Novello had a few misses as well as hits in his acting and playwriting career but was, fundamentally, a shrewd judge of what would or would not work on stage. He realized that *Sirocco* would not work, and declined. Furious, Coward said that in that case he would play the male lead himself. Appalled at the idea of Coward as a passionate Italian waiter, Novello relented and agreed to perform the part, even though he knew he couldn't bring the required machismo to the part.

True, he had a stage (and then film) success with his own play, *The Rat*, three years earlier, when he had played a supposedly rough young thug in a louche Paris nightclub, but even here he had brought his trademark delicacy and beauty to the role – so much so that one fan, waiting for his autograph at the stage door, had gushed 'Oh, Mr Novello! You looked so *lovely* when you spat!'

Novello's fears for *Sirocco* were well-founded. The audience – or at least those in the cheaper seats – were restive almost from the start. They made loud and comic kissing noises in the love scenes, and as the evening wore on began to heckle, too. By the time of the curtain call the theatre was in uproar, one which was added to by Coward's insistence, despite everything, on taking an author's bow – something that infuriated the critics in the balcony even more.

Basil Dean, the director, had spent the first night in a Soho restaurant, trying to forget what was going on, yards away, on stage. When he returned in time to supervise the curtain call, he thought (he had very poor hearing) that the noise must be one of cheers. Thinking he had a surprise hit on his hands, he kept ordering the stage manager to raise the curtain, to the despair of the actors.

Coward reacted to this unnecessarily extended ordeal by gallantly and defiantly taking the leading lady, Frances Doble, by the hand and ushering her forward – to a shout of 'Hide behind a woman, would yer?!' and a follow-up cry of 'Coward!' Miss Doble, trapped on stage and punished further by the author of her misfortune by being pushed closer to the lion's den of enraged theatregoers, had a fit of hysterics. With tears pouring down her face as programmes and other objects rained down on her from the auditorium, she stuttered out her pre-prepared curtain call speech. 'Ladies and gentlemen!' she sobbed, as a beaming Basil Dean looked on from the stalls, 'Tonight is the happiest night of my life!'

Sirocco entered the theatrical lexicon as a by-word for a dreadful first night, and the presence of its title in the middle of Shaftesbury Avenue stands as a ghostly warning to all those who believe, in the words of a Novello song, that 'It's Bound to Be Right on the Night'.

The Queen's Theatre used to have a façade very like that of the Gielgud, but it was ripped apart by a German bomb in 1940, during the run of a dramatization of Daphne Du Maurier's *Rebecca*. This was a novel that lent itself to the stage, and a twenty-first-century (touring) version starring Nigel Havers as Maxim de Winter broke national box-office records. This was partly thanks to Havers's now weathered upper-class charm (seen in more youthful form in the film *Chariots of Fire*), but was also proof of the enduring emotional impact of a play about a young woman coping with the influence of another (albeit dead) lover on her husband.

John Gielgud appeared often at the Queen's, from the West End transfer of his Old Vic sensation as Hamlet in 1930 to his one-man show of excerpts from Shakespeare, *The Ages of Man* in 1959. Ten years later Joe Orton's final play, *What The Butler Saw*, was posthumously performed at the Queen's, in a disastrous production with Ralph Richardson and Coral Browne. A much stronger revival at Wyndham's in 1991 was followed in 1995 by another production at the National Theatre, starring Richard Wilson and John Alderton.

The end of the play still seems rather feeble but Orton, like most playwrights, continued to adapt his work, especially in rehearsals, where you can see far more clearly what does or does not work on stage. Had he not had his skull staved in by his desperately insecure and jealous lover, he would inevitably have improved on the script that casts work with today.

After the Queen's, Shaftesbury Avenue winds up to Cambridge Circus, where the vast Palace Theatre stands. Its stage door has a stone above it that says 'The world's greatest artists have passed and will pass through these doors'. This is all very inspiring until you walk round the corner to the stage door of the Prince Edward. The theatre fronts Old Compton Street while the stage door is in Frith Street. Above the stage door (in addition to a plaque recording the young Mozart's stay in a house on that site) is a stone which boasts that 'The world's greatest artists have passed and will pass through these doors'. Plagiarism or economy?

For most people, this is where Shaftesbury Avenue ends, but it actually carries on past Cambridge Circus, towards Holborn. Angels, the theatrical costumier which hires out costumes to thespians and party-goers alike, is on the west side of this part of the street. The Avenue ends a little before the theatre that bears its name, the Shaftesbury.

The Shaftesbury has had a mixed run of shows, and for a while had a reputation, despite the occasional hit, as an 'unlucky' theatre. This spell is now comprehensively broken, with the continuing runaway success of *Hairspray*, the stage musical inspired by the original John Waters film starring the late American drag star Divine.

Playing Divine's role is Michael Ball. Ball made his name in the West End through singing the song 'Love Changes Everything' in Andrew Lloyd Webber's *Aspects of Love*, at the Prince of Wales Theatre. Roger Moore, who was scheduled to appear in the musical before he had a change of heart and pulled out, said, in a typically debonair press conference that he thought Ball would soon become a star, which he duly did.

Ball's career has included playing a matador who inspires a stalker-like devotion from a strange woman, in Stephen Sondheim's musical *Passion* at the Queen's. He certainly inspires passion in perfectly normal women, as was shown by the crowd outside the stage door at the Theatre Royal, Haymarket, where he appeared in a one-man show as part of a cabaret season there. Given the size of the crowd, all of whom presumably hoped for an autograph or at least a word, it must have taken him hours to get home each night.

One of Ball's co-stars is Ben James-Ellis, a contestant on *Any Dream Will Do*, who has proved that title right. He may not have become Joseph but he made it into Theatreland and his image beams down from the Shaftesbury's wall. Another lead actor in this production is Ian Talbot. For several years Talbot was the artistic director of the Open Air Theatre, Regent's Park. He combined business skill, artistic flair and an engaging good humour, which made Regent's Park an important part of London theatre's summer season.

Naturally *A Midsummer Night's Dream* was regularly performed, but whatever the show Talbot chose, the experience itself was as magical as the goings-on in Shakespeare's fantasy about fairies, forests and actors. Sitting in one of the tiers of seats on a balmy English summer's evening (they do occasionally happen), watching a well-performed play while the sky gradually darkens and the wind gently rustles the leaves of the trees that tower behind the playing area is one of the great pleasures of London life.

This was particularly the case with the last two musicals that Talbot brought into the Park: *High Society* (a stage version of the Bing Crosby/Frank Sinatra/Grace Kelly film) and, best of all, Sandy Wilson's *The Boyfriend*. First a hit in 1954, when it opened at the Player's Theatre in Charing Cross before transferring to Wyndham's, this is a delightful musical pastiche of 1920s plays.

Most pastiches are just clever approximations of whatever material it is they are making affectionate fun of, but *The Boyfriend* rises above mere parody to be a wonderful example, in its own right, of the style of show that it represents. At Regent's Park Talbot played an old roué who sings of the charms of love late in life. At the first night curtain call he welcomed Sandy Wilson onto the stage and into the line-up, where the composer received a well-deserved standing ovation, half a century after *The Boyfriend* first opened.

Also appearing in *The Boyfriend* was Summer Strallen, a stunningly attractive actress and singer who followed Connie Fisher into the role of Maria von Trapp in *The Sound of Music* at the Palladium, one of Theatreland's largest and most historic theatres, which (like Drury Lane) offers tours of the building to the general public. Strallen is following in the footsteps of a great many young stars who went on to become household names, even if many of them came from the world of variety rather than straight theatre. The photos of many of them line the walls of the corridor that leads from the Palladium's entrance lobby through to the box office where *The Sound of Music* has been ensuring the tills are alive since it opened in 2006.

Although the Shaftesbury is safe in the hands of *Hairspray*, the same cannot be said of the Saville Theatre, which has been turned into a several-screen cinema. This was the home of the last of Ivor Novello's musicals. *Gay's the Word* opened in February 1951, starring Cicely Courtneidge as a retired showgirl, Gay Daventry (hence the show's title), who runs a drama school. The musical had one major hit number, 'Vitality', in which Novello celebrated the musical theatre stars of his youth, comparing them favourably with the crooners (by inference Bing Crosby and Frank Sinatra) who were then at the height of fashion.

The show, which opened to the usual rave reviews, was to be the last Novello musical. Given commercial imperatives, it seems unlikely the Saville will be returned to its original use as a theatre, but the potential remains. It may not make economic sense to build a new theatre in the West End anymore, but for an enterprising producer or theatre owner the Saville, thinly disguised as a cinema, stands waiting in the wings for its return to the spotlight.

10

Drama Queens: Ivor Novello and Noël Coward

Ivor Novello made it to the first night of *Gay's the Word* at the Saville, but died not long after, in the early hours of 6 March 1951, aged 58.

He died in the flat he had lived in since he moved there with his mother, the formidable Clara Novello Davies, in 1913. That flat is now a suite of offices, owned by Sir Cameron Mackintosh, whose director of operations, William Differ, has his office in what was Ivor's bedroom.

The theatre below was called the Strand – a misleading name as well as a bland one, for the theatre is not in the Strand at all, but in the Aldwych: the semi-circular road that sweeps round the BBC's Bush House (home of its World Service) before rejoining the final, eastern section of the Strand that leads up to Fleet Street.

Immediately opposite the Strand is a new hotel – still being constructed as this book went to press. The hotel is on the site of one of the great Victorian West End theatres, the Gaiety. The Gaiety specialized in musical theatre, and the leggy chorus, the Gaiety Girls, were much sought after by the young and wealthy stage door Johnnies who were interested in a different sort of performance to that found on stage. The girls were often willing to oblige – but sometimes for a very high price: several of them married into the aristocracy.

The young Ivor Novello, a classically trained musician who had been a choral scholar at Oxford until his voice broke, was stage-struck. His mother, Clara, known to all as 'Mam', disapproved, wanting her prodigy to become a distinguished classical composer. Given this, it seems odd that she should arrange for her and her 20-year-old son to move to a flat above one theatre, opposite another, and a stone's throw from half a dozen more.

Ivor (as he was generally known in the profession, though stagehands at Drury Lane always called him the 'Guv'nor') took full advantage of his new home's location, which fuelled his desire for a life on stage. He was to achieve this ambition via the silent movie screen, but theatre was always his great love, as it was of another talented actor whose career included stage and screen, his friend and rival, Noël Coward (1899–1973).

Both men now deservedly have theatres named after them, in belated recognition of their major place in twentieth-century British theatre. The Strand was renamed the Novello in 2005; the Albery (formerly the New) became the Noël Coward in 2007. Both are owned by Delfont Mackintosh, the chain run by Sir Cameron but co-named after Bernard, Lord Delfont, a major twentieth-century theatre owner and West End figure, whom generations of television viewers saw greeting the Queen or Queen Mother at Royal Variety Performances at the London Palladium.

Of the two men, Noël Coward's reputation has been the most enduring. When the renaming took place, people recognized Coward's name and understood the reason for honouring him. Ivor Novello, however, is a name that these days only has a resonance with the very elderly or fans of pre-war British musical theatre. Yet Novello was, in his day, even more famous – and popular in the theatre industry – than Coward.

Coward, who lived longer and was around for the eventual revival in his theatrical reputation (after a 15-year dip), also lasted into the age of the documentary and the television interview, both vital for publicity and public recognition. In addition, some of Coward's best plays (including *Private Lives* and *Blithe Spirit*) have small casts, which makes them affordable to perform as well as entertaining to watch. In 2008 there were, worldwide, 59 productions of *Blithe Spirit* alone.

Novello was also a prolific playwright, and like Coward often starred in his own shows. However, the plays do not stand up nearly as well to scrutiny, let alone revival, as Coward's do. The honourable exceptions are *I Lived With You* – in which an exiled Russian Prince is found in the Hampton Court maze by a young lower-middle class girl and taken home to Clapham, with devastating consequences for the morality and happiness of her family – and *Proscenium*, in which an older actress fears she will lose her younger husband to the vixenish wiles of an even younger actress.

Novello was not as good a playwright as Coward, and his humour, based on warmth rather than Noël's trademark waspishness was certainly less sharp. Despite this, what really rankled with Coward, and comes as a surprise to us today, was that in his lifetime Novello was easily the more successful of the two when it came to writing musicals.

Ivor was not just a superb composer with an ability to write astonishingly effective melodies; he was also ideally placed to play the romantic lead in his own shows. The reason for this was his extraordinary good looks. Noël was to quip, in a typical mix of wit and bitterness, that 'There are two perfect things in this world: my mind and Ivor's profile.'

That profile, with the dark, Italianate hair, the ivory skin, the soulful yet smouldering eyes and the full, sensual lips, was Ivor's passport to a career in film and then on stage. His first professional success had come in 1914, when he wrote one of the great hits of the First World War: 'Keep The Home Fires Burning'. Aged 21, he was, like Lord Byron, famous overnight. Unlike Byron he was not a poet – that role was to be filled by his lyricist, Christopher Hassall, from the mid 1930s onwards – but he was, thanks to this hit, financially independent.

Beautiful, talented and clearly gay, the young Ivor Novello had no shortage of admirers. His principal patron, mentor and friend was Sir Edward Marsh, a highly educated man who was to become Winston Churchill's Private Secretary, but who was in any case independently wealthy – not least from a family legacy, a

Noël Coward's *Private Lives* at the Phoenix Theatre, 1930

fortune granted by Parliament to the family of England's only assassinated Prime Minister, Spencer Perceval, who was shot in the lobby of the House of Commons in 1812. Marsh was descended from him and, as a high-spending man of the world, he found the 'blood money' very useful.

It was when attending the opera with Marsh that Ivor met the young actor Robert ('Bobby') Andrews who was to be his life partner, and with whom he would often act on stage. The acting career didn't really take off until after the war, and then only through the prism of a camera lens. Thanks entirely to his good looks (he had zero professional acting experience at this point, unlike Noël, who was a boy actor on stage and screen), Ivor was cast in the male lead in a French film, *L'Appel du Sang* (*The Call of the Blood*).

This melodrama was followed by several others. The good looks quickly earned him a following, and by ensuring, after a tip-off that the legendary film director D. W. Griffith would be dining at the Savoy, that his profile was displayed to best advantage at a strategically placed table, Ivor was duly signed up to appear in Griffith's *The White Rose*.

Ivor's numerous silent and very few talking films are largely forgotten today, but at the time they made him an international star and, with that public recognition attached to his name, enabled him to appear in West End plays – in the lead role. No long apprenticeship for him, unlike Noël Coward, who would not have been human had he not resented Ivor's seemingly effortless rise, propelled by his beauty rather than his brains or experience.

The only film of Ivor's that is known today is the 1926 film *The Lodger*, directed by a young Alfred Hitchcock. A thriller about a serial killer of young blondes, it has several Hitchcock hallmarks and was to preview several aspects of *Psycho* – including the dark old house and a beautiful blonde in danger in a bathroom, though in *The Lodger* she is taking a bath rather than a shower.

Not content with having used his film stardom to break into acting on stage, Ivor went on to write a string of plays, many of which were subsequently filmed with him in the lead on screen, as in the theatre. Some of these were dramas; many were comedies. As noted above, Ivor's humour was warmer and less acid that Noël Coward's. It worked well when spoken by the performers to whose characters Ivor had moulded it, but doesn't read that well on the printed page – unlike Noël's lines, which certainly display a far higher level of wit than anything Ivor ever produced. On the other hand, he inspired some good one-liners from his friends.

One such example was when Dame Lilian Braithwaite attended a Novello first night. On hearing the orchestra strike up the overture, her companion, who thought she recognized one of the melodies, turned to her and said 'Oh! Naughty

Ivor! That's an old Welsh hymn!' To which Dame Lilian replied 'Which is more than one can say of the composer!'

It was as a composer of lavish musicals (sometimes with a cast of over 80) that Ivor was to earn his greatest fame: a further career that would eclipse his previous ones as actor and author of straight plays and of films. The first of these stage musicals, *Glamorous Night* (1935) was to save the Theatre Royal, Drury Lane, from threatened closure. *Careless Rapture* (1936), *Crest of the Wave* (1937) and *The Dancing Years* (1939) followed at Drury Lane, though the latter transferred to the Adelphi as the Theatre Royal was taken over by ENSA, the armed forces entertainments organization, when the Second World War broke out.

In the last weeks of the war Novello's *Perchance to Dream* (1945) opened, and toured not just the provinces, like his other shows, but South Africa too. George VI also toured South Africa to get some post-war sunshine, though he was wracked with guilt at leaving his subjects to freeze in what has been called 'Austerity Britain' (1945–1951). Ivor, as theatre royalty, had no such qualms.

Ivor's love of the sun led him to buy a holiday home in Jamaica – as did Noël Coward. Even in the location of their holidays the two seemed determined to maintain their Theatreland rivalry. Each thought the other's Jamaican home to be in bad taste, with Noël taking pleasure in noting Ivor's villa's lack of a view compared to his own, which had such a fabulous view of the sea that he eventually chose to be buried there.

The last classic Novello show, with a huge cast, a coronation scene and with Ivor playing the male lead, was *King's Rhapsody* (1949), while his final creation, as discussed earlier, was *Gay's the Word* in 1951.

Gay was not a word associated with homosexuality in 1951, though in some circles it was beginning to have that connotation – though as a code word rather than a call-sign or banner. Ivor enjoyed giving his shows camp nicknames. *The Dancing Years*, the Second World War's biggest musical hit, was called *The Advancing Years* in tribute to its longevity, and, when the company was a safely camp one, *The Prancing Queers*. *Perchance to Dream* had a similar make-over as *Perchance to Scream*. *Gay's The Word* speaks for itself.

The cloud in the otherwise unbroken sunshine of Novello's life came when he was sent to prison in 1944, for a month, for petrol-rationing offences. This crime was usually punished merely by a £50 fine. The presiding magistrate, who was known for disliking the theatre in general and homosexuals in particular, told Novello that a financial penalty of £50 would mean nothing to a wealthy man such as him, so sentenced him instead to two months prison.

Despite Sir Edward Marsh's personal intervention with Churchill, the Prime Minister was not able to interfere with the law and, though the sentence was reduced to a month on appeal, Ivor had to go to prison: to Wormwood Scrubs. He survived his time, and a near nervous breakdown, and returned straight to the stage, in *The Dancing Years* at the Adelphi.

A very popular man in any case, the public reacted strongly to what was generally seen as a clearly vindictive punishment. Far from shunning the shows of a jailbird, as the magistrate had clearly hoped, the public flocked to the theatre in support, and when Ivor made his first post-prison appearance, he was given a prolonged standing ovation.

The prison sentence put paid to any chance of an honour, which would in any case probably have been considerably delayed (as was Noël Coward's) owing to the Establishment's distaste for homosexuality. Laurence Olivier and Ralph Richardson both earned their knighthoods in the 1940s, at which point neither had as prominent a career as either Novello or Coward.

The duo had (separately) done their bit for the war effort: Noël with the morale-boosting film *In Which We Serve*; with his poignant yet defiant song, 'London Pride', and with his tours of his plays round England's theatres.

Both Ivor and Noël entertained the troops with plays and concerts behind the battlefields. Ivor's 'We'll Gather Lilacs', a very popular song at the end of the Second World War, with its poignant melody and lyrics (for once by Ivor rather than Christopher Hassall) about the simple pleasures of peace, was, ironically, first heard by troops in Normandy, only a few miles behind the front line.

Whether on stage or off, whether performing for battle-hardened troops or matrons at West End matinees, both men were careful to be seen with glamorous women on their arms. Even late in life, Coward told his first biographer, Sheridan Morley, that he did not want his homosexuality to be mentioned while he was alive. This wasn't moral cowardice, he explained, but commercial sense. He was a writer and actor and relied on audiences to provide his income.

Despite common sense and all evidence to the contrary, Coward insisted, there were plenty of old dears who came to see him in the theatre in the belief that he was straight. He didn't want to disabuse them or to unnecessarily upset the larger group of fans who knew deep down that he was gay, but with whom he had an unspoken but very firm covenant that neither side would ever acknowledge this fact.

Both men liked women, though Coward had more of a taste for social climbing; the pinnacle of which was reached when he became friends with the Queen Mother – a friendship cemented by their mutual loathing of the Duke and Duchess of Windsor. The Queen Mother thought the Duchess an upstart and resented the abdication that gave her husband the throne – and drastically cut short his life.

Coward had a different but equally personal distaste for the Duke who, as Prince of Wales, had on at least one occasion ruthlessly 'cut' Coward, in a humiliating reminder that though he might be all very amusing as a country house guest who entertained people at the piano, he was not even remotely socially acceptable to His Royal Highness in any other context.

Coward had a justified resentment at being not quite the same as other guests in those country house weekends: he was there not just to relax but to entertain. He literally had to sing for the supper the other guests simply enjoyed as of right.

Although Noël was to create a gay character in his first West End success, *The Vortex* (1924), this role, that of Nicky Lancaster (which Noël played himself) was not allowed to be specifically homosexual – it was just hinted at. Homosexuality was not allowed to be portrayed on stage by order of the Lord Chamberlain, the royal official who censored plays until 1968.

It was not until Coward's old age, and the abolition of the Lord Chamberlain's stranglehold on the theatre, that the author (again starring in his own play) felt able to play a gay character, that of the novelist Hugo Latymer in *A Song at Twilight* (1966). It was Noël's own twilight, but one in which he made an impassioned plea for tolerance of sexuality, while simultaneously expressing his belief that it would take more than changes in the law for the British public to show any real acceptance of homosexuality as just another aspect of everyday life.

The change in the law that he referred to was the 1967 Act of Parliament, steered through by the then Home Secretary, Roy Jenkins and which legalized same-sex relations between consenting male adults. This finally put sex back into the bedroom and out of the courts, though it was to take some 30 years more before the age of consent was lowered (at the insistence of the European Union) to parity with that of heterosexuals.

Throughout their careers, Noël and Ivor had to live up (or down) to the title of Noël's best-known play, *Private Lives*. This didn't stop either of them having – and living with – long-term lovers, or having a succession of flings. But the title, and the shadow of the Lord Chamberlain in the wings of every theatre, lurked in the background of everything they did or wrote.

Despite or perhaps because of this restriction, they channelled their talent into creating plays and musicals that appealed to mainstream audiences, and in that sense it could be argued that they benefited from the restrictions they operated under. Ivor in particular had a genius for writing for women, whether in words or music. The only decent male parts in most of his shows were those he played himself, which is one reason, apart from the changing public taste, his genre of musical theatre disappeared almost immediately after his death.

For Novello shows were just that: though some touring versions coped without him, they, like the London runs, relied on his reputation and the charisma that he brought to the stage. Even hard-bitten critics were won over by the sheer enthusiasm and conviction that he brought to his playing. More importantly, he had an authority on stage that belied his notably camp demeanour outside the theatre. He didn't mask his voice (a strong Welsh accent, whatever the role he was playing) or pretend to be more butch than he was. He just grew in stature. He had a stage presence that held the audience in even the largest theatres, and which inspired an unrivalled affection as well as admiration.

Given the presence of his London home above a playhouse (his English country house, Red Roofs, near Maidenhead, is now a thriving drama school), it is entirely fitting that Ivor should have the belated but very welcome recognition, over 50 years after his death, of a West End theatre named after him.

On the wall at the side of the entrance steps, before you reach the foyer itself, is Angus McBean's composite photo of Ivor, showing his dark good looks, the books (literally) of some of his plays and musicals, his hands playing the piano, and another shot of them writing music – and smoking. McBean's name appears in the photo, on manuscript paper, in mirror writing.

Cigarettes were an essential prop to any major star between the wars and beyond. Just as Ivor's photo shows him smoking, so does Noël's statue in the foyer of the Theatre Royal, Drury Lane. Ivor also has a plaque in St Paul's, Covent Garden, the actors' church – as does Noël. Noël is represented at Westminster Abbey. Ivor, in recognition of his role as a wartime composer in both World Wars, had a plaque to him unveiled in St Paul's Cathedral – by RAF fighter pilot Sir Douglas Bader.

So both men have been given their due, as well as their own theatre. Both were unique: one-offs whose works and personal lives represent the glamour and style of the pre-war world, as well as the darker side. It is the undercurrent, the secrecy, the code, that provided some of the steel beneath the satin, but above all it was their genius to be able to represent, on stage and in song, the needs, fears and hopes of their generation.

They provided the escapism that was desperately needed in the years after the horrors of the First World War and in the Depression that was the hangover of the party decade of the 1920s and which blighted so many people's lives in the run-up to the fresh ordeal of the next global conflict. Though the Second World War ravaged the cityscape that Novello and Coward knew, their world, that of the theatre, was responsible for keeping up morale while the men were away at war, and for providing light relief when they returned to their families on leave.

Coward's *Blithe Spirit* was a way of making light of death, at a time when its sudden appearance was a part of everyday life. Novello's *The Dancing Years*, with its Nazis on stage in prologue and with a story of pre-First World War Vienna as its main plot, gave wartime audiences the chance to feel they were defying the Nazis while simultaneously escaping from the horror they unleashed, back into a gentler, romantic Austria – a case of exchanging Leni Riefensthal for Franz Lehar.

Ivor Novello's ashes are buried – under a lilac tree – in North London's Golders Green crematorium. Noël Coward is buried where he died, in Jamaica, under a lawn looking out over the cliffs to the sea. This may seem a strange and rather lonely resting place for a man so identified in the public's eye with England, and with Theatreland in particular, but one of Coward's song titles, 'I Travel Alone', summed up an aspect of his character.

Yet the loneliness in the title referred to his sexuality rather than his personal habits – he liked to live and travel with a small entourage of lovers and friends, as did Ivor – but he felt very much an exile, in terms not just of tax but of lifestyle. The England he had grown up in and which his works in so many ways personify was not the England that he saw in his final years.

That England is still missed by many people and attracts many more who never experienced it. Nostalgia remains a strong part of the appeal of both Novello and Coward, though the latter's wit is also a major factor in Coward's continuing commercial success.

This had dipped in his lifetime, when he was, as the old theatre joke has it, no longer a *tour de force*, so was forced to tour. He went further afield that the usual provincial run – all the way to Las Vegas where he reinvented himself as a cabaret performer. He traded on his very English image, with one album cover showing him standing in the desert wearing a dinner jacket and holding a cup of tea. The result was a revival in his financial fortune, if not his critical one, which had to wait for a 1964 National Theatre revival of *Hay Fever*.

Novello's musicals still await a director of the National (or of English National Opera) to give him a suitably lavish and professional revival. With all due respect to amateur theatre companies, the fact that they are the only ones to have staged Ivor's musicals means that his reputation has suffered accordingly. Imagine if, in future years, the only time anyone was to see a Lloyd Webber musical was when they were performed by the local amateurs, with the bank manager's wife playing Norma Desmond or Eva Peron. Everyone would wonder what all the fuss had been about.

Ivor's bust, by his and Noël's friend, Clemence Dane, stares rather wistfully at dress circle patrons enjoying an interval drink in the Rotunda at Drury Lane. Noël's statue downstairs looks smugly happy, as well it might given the strength of his reputation today and the tribute that literally falls in his lap on the Saturday nearest his birthday (16 December) when members of the Noël Coward Society lay flowers there in celebration of The Master.

Coward is welcome to this, and to the theatre where his first West End play, *I'll Leave It To You* was staged in 1920, being named after him but though it is he who has the largest memorial at Drury Lane (the theatrical equivalent of tanks on the lawn), the Theatre Royal belongs, if to any one composer and actor, to Ivor Novello, and the most fitting tribute that Theatreland could pay him would be for the Theatre Royal to stage a revival of one of his musicals.

11

The Donmar: The West End's Favourite Warehouse

The Donmar Warehouse, in Earlham Street, Covent Garden, is arguably London's smartest small theatre, with an enviable artistic reputation. Its 250 seats regularly sell well, leading to a daily queue of determined-looking theatregoers, hoping to buy one of the day seats that are reserved for personal callers to the box office and sold there every morning.

The Donmar was originally a banana warehouse, in the days when Covent Garden was the central fruit and vegetable market for London. It was bought and converted for theatrical use in the 1960s by impresario Donald Albery (1914–1988) and ballerina Margot Fonteyn (1919–1991), and named after them. The original purpose of the conversion was to make it available for ballet rehearsals, in which capacity it was used by the London Festival Ballet. From 1977 to 1981 it was used by the Royal Shakespeare Company. From 1981 to 1989 the Donmar, managed by Nica Burns and Ian Albery, was a West End showcase for touring theatre companies. In 1989 the theatre was acquired with a view to redevelopment, and it only came into its current form when in 1990 Sam Mendes, who had noticed the building and approached its owners, was given the remit of producing in-house work.

Mendes' arrangement with the then owners, Maybox, was to run the theatre as Artistic Director, with the intention that any West End transfers from the Donmar would transfer to larger theatres that were part of the same group. Maybox bought a 25-year lease on the Donmar at the start of the 1990s. It subsequently sold this to ATG in 2001 and when it expires in 2016 it will revert to the company that programmes the venue: Donmar Warehouse Projects Ltd. Mendes oversaw a refurbishment of the building, creating the public areas and facilities that it enjoys today.

The Donmar receives modest Arts Council funding but needs to raise a large proportion of its revenue from private sponsorship. As a result, the Donmar, despite its small size, raises three times as much from its box office as it receives from the Arts Council, and raises a further three to four times as much as its grant from private sponsorship, which is why there is such an impressive list of supporters in its small foyer area.

The Donmar appeals to audiences on several levels. Primarily there is the quality of its productions. These have been as consistent under Michael Grandage as they were under Sam Mendes. When Mendes (who is now married to the film star Kate Winslet) left the Donmar in 2002 to pursue other projects, director Michael Grandage, who was then running the Crucible Theatre in Sheffield, took over the Donmar. He was an exciting choice, but had a lot to live up to.

Charismatic leaders are always a hard act to follow, not least in the theatre, but Grandage has proved himself to be Mendes' equal at the Donmar. His artistic programming has naturally been different, and has included a number of fascinating European dramas, as when Michael Sheen played the title role of the deranged Roman Emperor in French novelist and playwright Albert Camus' *Caligula*.

Caligula was designed by Christopher Oram. He is a minimalist whose stages are uncluttered because he believes in clearing the space to tell the story, but he can, with a simple floor design and a wall of beaten copper, create the perfect playing space for a drama, and his designs have been as consistently praised as Grandage's direction.

Grandage's role as Artistic Director means that as well as choosing the plays and who will direct them, he has to be part of the constant fund-raising effort that keeps the Donmar going. This includes maintaining contacts with people and companies who make up the theatre's extensive list of supporters, arranged in several layers of membership, the highest of which (at a subscription of some £12,000) gives a unique access to the inner workings of the Donmar.

This access is another part of the Donmar's success. It is standard practice for the great opera and ballet companies like the Royal Opera and Ballet, and English National Opera and Ballet, to have Friends groups whose members are, through backstage and rehearsal access, able to feel an extended part of the company. This also applies to other subsidised theatres like the The Royal Shakespeare Company and the National. It is very rare among commercial theatre companies.

The Donmar is a charity but that charity's purpose is to put on six plays a year (both new and established) with the highest possible production values, to paying audiences. To have achieved such a rapport with its members and the general public, under two Artistic Directors, is a remarkable achievement.

The theatre's size, layout and location all play a part in this. Covent Garden

The auditorium of the Donmar Warehouse, Covent Garden

has gone from an early 1980s, post-market wasteland whose tube station was shut on a Sunday because no one wanted to go there, to being one of London's main tourist attractions. With its range of shops, restaurants and bars, Covent Garden's problem now is the opposite one – overcrowding.

In summer the street performers (from jugglers and musicians to living statues) can be barely seen, such is the crush of people streaming down James Street towards the Piazza, and so many are the visitors that the station sometimes has to be shut to reduce the overcrowding. The congestion is partly caused by the need for most people to take the lifts from the very deep platforms rather than the seemingly endless stairs, which would defeat all but the fittest.

That Covent Garden is now one of the most attractive and vibrant parts of central London is clearly a bonus for the Donmar. Its own part of Covent Garden is among the quirkiest, with the organic health and natural remedy shops of Neal's Yards close by, and the chic little hub of Seven Dials with the boutique shops of Monmouth Street a minute or two's walk away. In Dickens's time the Seven Dials area was one of the most notorious slums in London, where the police never patrolled unless in a group of at least two or three. Today it is full of tourists and those working in the nearby theatres (including the Cambridge, to which *Chicago* transferred from the Adelphi), as well as Londoners heading for the flower stall which is a local landmark.

The Donmar benefits from its surroundings, being an easy place to travel to and an attractive one to arrive at. The smallness of the foyer ads to a sense of cosiness and camaraderie, even though it can be frustrating getting to the box office to pick up tickets on the night. On the other hand, the ushers who stand at the foot of the staircase that leads from the foyer up to the stalls and dress circle are adept at directing the human traffic up to the bars, lavatories and theatre seats.

Small bar areas are not generally a good thing but because of the equally small number of seats in the theatre, the Donmar's two bars also seem to suggest an unusually cheerful togetherness, something that is further enhanced by the frequent presence of well-known faces, for the Donmar is very much an actor's theatre that attracts other members of the profession to its shows.

It is the combination of the above factors that has made the Donmar one of London's favourite theatres. Its recent foray into the West End, with four plays (*Ivanov*, *Twelfth Night*, *Madame de Sade* and *Hamlet*) at Wyndham's was designed to allow greater access to a series of high-profile Donmar productions. Wyndham's, which was given a substantial renovation treatment by its owner, Cameron Mackintosh, has the required extra space to do this, but it also has an intimate feel to it that in some way replicates the experience of seeing a play at the Donmar. Donald Albery and Margot Fonteyn must be very happy.

12

West End Women

Theatreland has always provided a platform for strong and independent-minded women. Although, as Rosemary Squire, chief executive of theatre owners and producers ATG points out, women are as underrepresented in the theatre industry as any other, they have also, historically, played a greater part in the running of theatres (as opposed to 'just' acting in them) than the public may suppose.

Squire cites the case of Mary Moore, the actress who cemented a 30-year stage partnership with actor-manager Sir Charles Wyndham by marrying him. Although Sir Charles seemed to be the dominant partner, it was Mary who had the business head of the two, arranging contracts and dealing with the company finances, while Wyndham concentrated on acting.

Gladys Cooper (1888–1971) was another leading woman manager. Not content with a career as model and actress, she went into theatre management, running the Playhouse Theatre on the Embankment jointly with Frank Curzon from 1917 to 1927 and then solely until 1933.

Her management skills upset rather than pleased her first husband, Herbert Buckmaster, who returned from the First World War to find that his actress wife was now also a businesswoman. Buckmaster's name lives on in the drink that he created, Buck's Fizz, in which champagne is mixed with orange juice.

Cooper had two children by Buckmaster. Their daughter, Joan, was to marry the actor Robert Morley. Cooper had an almost physical revulsion for those who were less than beautiful, a prejudice that she was punished for in having such a large, round and less than handsome son-in-law.

Her son, John Buckmaster, suffered from mental illness. In a case of birds of a feather, he had a passionate affair with Vivien Leigh, who once had to be rescued from his naked clutches – he was trying to persuade her they could both fly from

Mary Moore, a formidable actress and theatre manager

the roof – by a posse of films stars including David Niven. This troublesome connection would have been enough for any woman, but Leigh had a second bite at one of Cooper's relatives when she became the lover of Cooper's stepson, another John, by Gladys's third husband, Philip Merivale. John Merivale was Leigh's last lover and was living with her in Eaton Square when she died.

Cooper's other daughter, Sally, by her second husband, Sir Neville Pearson, was married for over 20 years to the actor Robert Hardy.

Gladys Cooper's sister Doris appeared with her on stage in the 1920s, and was deeply upset when her first appearance on stage was greeted by what seemed to be a wave of hissing from an inexplicably hostile audience. The sobbing Doris was comforted in the wings, as soon as she was able to leave the stage, by a colleague who assured her that the sibilant noise was made by old ladies in the audience whispering to each other 'She's Gladys Cooper's sister!'

In her mid-40s Cooper discovered California and its sunshine, so happily moved there and appeared in a number of films, including *Rebecca*. One of her best roles was as Bette Davis's over-bearing old mother in *Now Voyager*, the classic weepie starring, alongside Miss Davis, Paul Henreid and Claude Rains. Cooper aged up for the part, and when subsequently interviewed for roles by Hollywood executives they were astonished to find not a well-preserved 70-year old but a very glamorous 50-something woman still radiating a cool sex appeal.

The years of sunbathing took their toll, and as an old woman Gladys Cooper (by now Dame Gladys) had a face almost as lined as the poet W. H. Auden's. She appeared in the film version of *My Fair Lady* as the mother of Henry Higgins (played by Rex Harrison). It is as an actress that she will be remembered, but her contribution to Theatreland had been far more versatile than that, and she proved that there was no reason why a woman couldn't run a commercial theatre along with the men.

There could hardly have been a greater physical contrast to the elegant and lovely Gladys Cooper than the dumpy, bespectacled figure of Lilian Baylis (1874–1937). Miss Baylis ran the Old Vic in Waterloo, which she inherited from another strong woman, her aunt, Emma Cons.

The young Lilian had been trained as a violinist but it was the theatre that was her great love and she built on her aunt's work in what had once been a temperance hall to create a powerhouse of London Theatre. Given its location, the Old Vic was not geographically a part of Theatreland but was an outpost, like her later acquisition, Sadler's Wells Theatre in Islington, North London.

However, despite Baylis seeing the Old Vic as an opportunity to bring Shakespeare to the working classes of South London, her ability as a spotter of talent meant that the Old Vic's productions became a magnet for theatregoers for whom the furthest south they were comfortable with was the Playhouse on the Embankment.

Baylis was responsible not just for theatre but also for the development of ballet and opera in England, through her other companies, but it was as a theatrical manager and artistic director that she excelled and for which she will always be remembered.

An eccentric, she carried out her job in a highly individual style. Not least, she was a devout Christian who believed herself to be in regular touch with the Almighty, to whom she frequently prayed in her office. On one occasion she was overheard to pray out loud 'Oh, Dear Lord, please send me some wonderful actors. But make them cheap!'

The salaries she felt she could afford to pay were indeed very low but actors were prepared to accept them in order to have the cachet – and experience – of working in an Old Vic production, just as they do today at the National Theatre, where leading actors accept far lower wages than they could normally command in commercial playhouses. There was a fitting continuity that Laurence Olivier's National Theatre Company based itself (before its own theatre on the South Bank was built) at the Old Vic.

Baylis died relatively young, in her early 60s, worn out by her constant work. The pressure was partly self-inflicted, in that she managed to combine a great many areas of responsibility that would today be parcelled out among several executives. This is admirable in itself, but all the more so given that she was doing so as a woman in what was still overwhelmingly a man's world. The hours that she put in meant that she virtually lived in the theatre, where she was known to cook her dinner on a small stove in the wings, with the actors distracted by the sound of sizzling sausages, and both cast and audience tantalized by the delicious smells wafting onto the stage and into the stalls.

Dame Monica Mason of the Royal Ballet may be the only female head of a major theatre organization in England today, but there are many women working in Theatreland as directors, designers, producers and theatre owners. They all owe a generalized debt to Baylis's pioneering work but have made their careers on their own terms and by their own talents.

The previous and the current presidents of the Society of London Theatre are both women. Rosemary Squire began her love affair with the theatre at the Nottingham Playhouse, where she was inspired by the work of director Richard Eyre, who was later to run the National Theatre. Nica Burns, the current president, co-owns Nimax, a company that owns several West End theatres. An experienced producer, her range of interests and activities make her the most influential woman in Theatreland.

Sonia Friedman, sister of actress and singer Maria Friedman, is a high-profile producer whose company, Sonia Friedman Productions, is part of the ATG theatre empire. Among the shows she has produced was, at the Palace Theatre, Andrew Lloyd Webber's *The Woman in White*, a musical version of Wilkie Collins's Victorian thriller, with state-of-the-art video designs replacing conventional stage sets.

Before she sold Stoll Moss, Janet Holmes à Court (the widow of tycoon Robert Holmes à Court) was another major player, owning the largest selection of West End theatres, including the flagship Theatre Royal, Drury Lane. Holmes à Court sold the theatres to concentrate on other commercial interests back in Australia, but during her time at the helm of Stoll Moss she proved every inch as capable a manager as her late husband.

Women directors may be less numerous than males but they have as strong a chance as men do. Tamara Harvey is the leading example of her generation, with plays like Tennessee Williams's rarely-performed *Something Cloudy, Something Clear* to her credit. Maria Aitken was primarily an actress, who gave a definitive performance in the 1980s revival of Noël Coward's *The Vortex*, playing Florence Lancaster opposite Rupert Everett as her dissolute son, Nicky. More recently she has taught in New York, but her latest Theatreland venture has been directing Patrick Barlow's adaptation of *The 39 Steps*. This production is discussed in greater detail in Chapter 25, but the point is that this quirky surprise hit, which has transferred from London to Broadway, was directed by a woman.

For the majority, however, women in the theatre means one thing: actresses. Some of these have been influential offstage, like Nell Gwynne, the lover of King Charles II, or in politics, more overtly, like Vanessa Redgrave. Most have been happy to confine their energy to the stage.

Although, as Rosemary Squire points out, there are still far more roles for men than for women (especially older women), Theatreland has always been the one area of public life where women have been major players in their own right rather than as someone's wife, and where they have been free to earn an independent living. They have also been able to earn very large sums of money, and have no 'glass ceiling' keeping them below a certain level.

While there may be more great roles for men than for women, that largely reflects not the domination of male playwrights (though despite the work of Caryl Churchill, Sarah Kane and Timberlake Wertenbaker men continue to dominate this area of creativity), but the historic truth that most decisions have been taken by men, and that therefore there are far more male role models, leaders and other figures on which to build a play than female ones.

Despite this, there are a great many roles for actresses, from Shakespeare via Shaw (whose Saint Joan was played in an award-winning performance by Anne-Marie Duff at the National) to David Hare. Hare wrote a play, *Amy's View*, that transferred from the National Theatre to the Aldwych. The Amy of the title is a young woman (Samantha Bond in the original production) whose mother, Esme (Judi Dench) is an actress. The play contrasts the old-school, theatre-based world of Esme and the modern, television-based career of Amy's boyfriend and later husband.

Hare's drama is one of the greatest plays ever written about the power of the theatre, and it has at its heart a superb female role in which Judi Dench, despite a lifetime of other great performances, was at her finest. Towards the end of the three-act play there is a scene between Esme and her son-in-law, Dominic (Eoin McCarthy) in which Esme delivers some devastating ripostes to a man who still – despite Esme being in a fringe show that has clearly touched a nerve with the general public, who are flocking to see it – simply can't understand the power of theatre.

Having championed the redeeming strength of the stage, Hare ends *Amy's View* with the opening few moments of the play that Esme is now starring in. This takes the audience further into the actor's world, and you leave the theatre feeling elated to have been part of such a celebration of what theatre can achieve. There used to be a saying that went 'One goes to the theatre to be *changed*'. This may seem rather dramatic, but *Amy's View* shows how theatre can be grand without being grandiloquent.

There are other roles for theatre than to change, however – to entertain, for example. The 1953 Hollywood film *The Bandwagon*, starring Fred Astaire, Cyd Charisse and Theatreland's own Jack Buchanan summed this up in the show-stopping number 'That's Entertainment'. Just as the Greek representation of drama was two masks, one comic, one tragic, so the English stage has always valued humour as much as tears.

One of the greatest comic actresses of her generation is Dame Maggie Smith. Dame Maggie's dry wit, delivered with a quavering drawl, made her a favourite with theatregoers, who also admired her for spending most of her career on the stage, despite the occasional high-profile foray into film (including *The Prime of Miss Jean Brodie*, *A Room with a View* and *Private Function*).

Her many triumphs include Peter Shaffer's 1987 comedy *Lettice and Lovage*, where, co-starring with Margaret Tyzack, she played a romantically histrionic tour guide who regularly got carried away with her own eloquence, and who fought valiantly against the drab realities of the real, modern, world.

Smith also made a memorable Lady Bracknell in *The Importance of Being Earnest* and played a charismatic tramp in Alan Bennett's *The Lady in the Van*

– the stage version of Alan Bennett's account of inviting a woman tramp to live in a caravan parked in the drive of his North London home.

Dame Maggie's appearance in Edward Albee's *Three Tall Women* was mentioned in Chapter 7. In this play, in which she acted the eldest incarnation of a formidable American matriarch, one of her co-stars was Frances de la Tour. De La Tour, whose brother Andy has been a stalwart of the National Theatre, still labours under the burden of having played the role of Miss Jones in the long-running 1970s television sitcom *Rising Damp*. Her co-star, Leonard Rossiter, was appearing at the Lyric Theatre, Shaftesbury Avenue in 1984 in a revival of Joe Orton's comedy *Loot*, when he died. His role taken over by Dinsdale Landen, Rossiter was sadly missed by his many fans, for whom he will always be the seedy *Rising Damp* landlord, Rigsby.

Although de la Tour has had an extra quarter of a century to throw off that role, she too is still seen through that prism by the general public, but Theatreland audiences know her as a versatile stage actress. Though she can play serious drama, as in *Duet for One*, written by her then husband Tom Kempinski, her forte is still comedy, and she was a natural choice by director Nick Hytner for the role of the female teacher in Alan Bennett's play *The History Boys*.

This was perhaps the most successful single production in the National Theatre's history, opening in 2004 then going on to tour not just Britain but the world, including a sell-out run in New York as well as more than one cast in the West End transfer to Wyndham's. The play was also filmed, with the original cast, so de La Tour's wry, dry delivery has been captured for posterity.

Her stage career is worth mentioning not just because she is one of the country's most gifted comic actresses, but because it shows how women actresses can, with the support of a director, buck the trend for stereotyping. There is a general assumption, for example, that only very beautiful actresses can play the great romantic leads, and also that between the ages of 40 and 60 actresses have a hard time. Though as with most generalizations there is a kernel of truth, Tennessee Williams provides several great roles for middle-aged rather than very young (Juliet in *Romeo and Juliet*) or very old (Volumnia in *Coriolanus*) actresses.

I hope it is not too ungallant to say that de la Tour, though sexy back in *Rising Damp*, has never been regarded as a beauty. Yet when she played the middle-aged version of Maggie Smith's old woman in *Three Tall Women* she was, well-coiffed and very well-dressed, a revelation. Here was an actress who could, despite her public image, play glamorous and powerful.

It was perhaps with that role in mind that she was cast by director Steven Pimlott as the Egyptian queen in the Royal Shakespeare's *Antony and Cleopatra*, to

Alan Bates' Mark Antony, which London audiences saw at the Barbican in 2000. As if to reinforce the challenge, de la Tour as Cleopatra was disrobed towards the end of the play and performed naked. Doing so would test the nerves of the youngest and shapeliest actress. For a middle-aged woman it was an act of heroism.

The disrobing was also artistically well-judged, for de la Tour carried it off with great natural poise and it showed, more powerfully than any other stage direction or acting trick could have done, that she was not just a queen but also a vulnerable and ageing woman, yet one who could still radiate dignity and command respect, even without any clothes.

There was also something about her which was best summed up in a line by the playwright Nicholas Wright. Wright, whose work has often appeared at the National Theatre, wrote *Vincent in Brixton*. This was an imaginative historical piece based on the bizarre fact that, as a young man, Vincent Van Gogh had been a lodger in Brixton.

Wright's Van Gogh (originally played by Jochum ten Haaf) falls in love with his landlady, a widowed middle-aged woman, played by Clare Higgins. The scene where the older woman is, to her astonishment, seduced by Van Gogh, rates as one of the most touching love scenes of twentieth-century theatre. Wright provides Van Gogh with a line that has a poetic truth, that 'no woman is old so long as she loves and is loved'. The landlady, a dowdy figure despite Higgins's statuesque good looks, visibly glows when she realizes, to her astonishment, that the young man desires her.

Although Dame Judi Dench's blue eyes still radiate sex appeal, the most lusted-after of all our current crop of Dames (with all due respect to Dame Eileen Atkins, whom the much younger Colin Farrell apparently attempted to seduce while on a film set) has undoubtedly been Dame Diana Rigg.

Dame Diana's sex appeal was established at an early stage through the tele-vision series *The Avengers* and in the James Bond film *On Her Majesty's Secret Service*, where she remains, to date, the only Bond girl to have brought 007 to the altar – though she paid for it with her life, when she was machine-gunned shortly after leaving the wedding reception.

Her later career lays to rest the myth of a lack of sexually charged roles for older women. She has played, for example, Medea in the Greek play of that name and Nero's mother (to the Nero of Maggie Smith's son, Toby Stephens) in Racine's *Britannicus*.

There is more to women's roles than sex appeal, of course, though this has historically been the strongest card that any actress can play: another case of the theatre world mirroring the way the rest of society works. This can be a happy reflection as well as a disappointing one as it has given actresses some fabulous roles on stage, just as in real life women have, despite the historical odds being stacked against them, played defining roles in society, whether centre stage as queens or behind the scenes as wives and mistresses of powerful men. *Cherchez la femme* has always been an intelligent injunction for those who want to find the real initiators and wielders of power.

The new political power that women can exert as democratically elected political leaders (Thatcher in the United Kingdom, Merkel in Germany, Meir in Israel, Gandhi in India) doesn't seem to have excited the interest of many playwrights. In the theatre, as in the publishing world of lucrative historical biographies, it is the glamorous, essentially un-democratic women who continue to fascinate – like Eva Peron in Andrew Lloyd Webber and Tim Rice's *Evita* at the Adelphi.

Otherwise, playwrights and audiences seem to prefer non-political women of great talent, preferably with a tragic life. Edith Piaf was one such, as Elena Roger has found recently, and as Elaine Paige and Jane Lapotaire did before her, while a few years ago Sian Philips had a hit with a one-woman show (by Pam Gems, author of *Piaf*) about Marlene Dietrich. Philips, who also made a superb Eleanor of Aquitaine in a touring version of *The Lion in Winter*, sang Dietrich's late-life signature number of 'Where Have All the Flowers Gone?' even better than the Berlin diva herself.

Meanwhile, to summarize, women (Nica Burns and Rosemary Squire) have provided the current and previous presidents of the Society of London Theatre; Nica Burns is one of a handful of major West End theatre owners; Monica Mason runs the Royal Ballet, and women like Judi Dench and (when she can next be tempted back onto stage, where she belongs) Maggie Smith, are as much a box-office draw as men. Theatreland, rather than the business world, is where women can compete with men on equal terms in relation to salaries, while they are also increasingly (if slowly) becoming better represented in boardrooms.

This may have been a slower process than some would like, but the decision to move from dressing room to board room is one that only a relatively few women have been interested in, let alone prepared to make. As Sonia Friedman and Rosemary Squire have proved, there is nothing to stop women becoming theatre producers, and as Lilian Baylis, Daphne Du Maurier and Gladys Cooper also showed, there is nothing new in strong and talented women deciding that they wanted to write or own or manage or produce rather than waft around on stage.

Theatreland will always provide a platform for wafting – and of declaiming, screaming, fighting and scheming – but it clearly offers far more to women than the traditional role of actress, while nevertheless keeping that role, quite correctly, centre stage.

13

An Actor's Life

Actors live very different lives from the general population. By actors, I mean, given the subject of this book, stage actors. Their rhythms are opposite to that of office and most shop workers in that their work takes place in the evening, for a relatively short though intense number of hours. They are busy at weekends, with most shows having a Saturday matinee. Occasionally, as the West End follows Broadway's lead, actors will be expected to perform on Sundays, with no Monday evening performance as a compensation.

Even though the relentless self-publicity of the young Noël Coward began over 80 years ago, his public image of the actor – rising at noon (in Belgravia), swanning around in a silk dressing gown all day before heading to the theatre where, exquisitely dressed in a Savile Row suit, he brings the house down by delivering brilliant one liners – persists. According to this, the actor would emerge from the stage door after the show looking as well-dressed (though in a different suit) and head into the night for cocktails, laughter and some agreeably athletic sex.

An alternative impression was given in Bruce Robinson's film *Withnail and I* (1987), in which Richard E. Grant and Paul McGann play young actors leading an unemployed, subsistence-level existence fuelled by drink and drugs, in a sordid little flat in North London.

The reality is less extreme, though, depending on your taste, just as agreeable. It is an economically uncertain life, with over 80 per cent of actors being unemployed at any one time. The reason for this is that the supply of talent outstrips the demand, even though Theatreland was flourishing, with no 'dark' (i.e. empty) theatres as 2008 drew to a close. This is because the life of an actor has enormous appeal and, if you are good at it and have the luck (and agent) to get frequent work, it provides a fulfilling and well-rewarded way of earning a living. Despite this, only a tiny percentage of actors at the top of the profession can earn enough to be called wealthy, as the economics of staging plays and musicals preclude serious money being paid to all but a handful of stars.

As Richard Pulford of the Society of London Theatre says, it is often the case that the real money to be made in stage productions is through intellectual property: owning the rights to a script, or as producer or one of the artistic team with a share of the gross. While some musicals have generated tens of millions of pounds (*The Phantom of the Opera* and *Mamma Mia!* for example), the millions will go to the writers, composers, producers and some other members of the creative teams with a share in the box-office take, and to the show's investors, rather than the performers.

This doesn't put off those who audition for a drama school place, or for those who cling onto the chance of finally having a breakthrough role. This may have to be, temporarily, through television rather than theatre. There is a very considerable cross-over between the two, as anyone looking in theatre programmes and production credits or the CVs of younger actors will notice. They may not have appeared in Shakespeare but will often have been in *The Bill*.

Stage actors, unlike those who make films their career, need to have the discipline of performing for eight shows a week (six evenings and two matinees), which can seem onerous and is one reason (along with the modest salaries) why in the twenty-first century producers can rarely persuade a star to appear in the theatre for a run of longer than six months.

This was turned from a problem into a virtue by the producer David Pugh, whose first massive hit was Yasmina Reza's play *Art*. This comedy about the nature of friendship and of modern art was a three-hander that was first performed in Paris. Its success was not only a financial windfall for Pugh, it started a fashion for short plays – it was about an hour and a half, straight through without an interval. This left time for audiences to go out to dinner afterwards. Just as art was as important an issue as male friendship in the play, so the experience of talking about the play over drinks and dinner was as much a part of the night out as watching the play in the first place.

Art's long life at Wyndham's and on tour was thanks to Pugh's recasting of the play every six months, judiciously hiring fascinating combinations of well-known actors, with the result that many fans of the play saw it two or more times, in order to enjoy the different dynamic that different casts brought to the piece. This was the theatrical equivalent of the teenage girls who went to see Leonardo di Caprio time and time again in the film *Titanic*, boosting its box-office takings to a record-breaking level.

Stage actors have a very direct relationship with audiences: both the general

The cast of Noël Coward's *Cavalcade* enjoy the Baddeley cake, 1932

public who pay to sit in the auditorium and watch them perform, and the more dedicated fans who wish to see them as themselves, off stage and in the real world. This directness takes several forms.

First, an audience is as much a part of any performance as the acting on stage. There is a powerful relationship, whether in comedy or tragedy, between the performers and the viewers: each feeds off the energy from the other and this is why no two performances are ever the same. A terrible audience – and they do sometimes spontaneously occur, for no obvious reason – can drag a play down with it and provide, in a self-fulfilling prophecy, a dire evening in the theatre.

Conversely, the sense of energy and involvement that an audience can equally mysteriously generate can lift a tired company of actors, performing in a long-running show, and produce the sort of evening that got the reviews that made it a long-runner in the first place.

A laugh – or even comment – from someone in the audience can set off an actor in a fit of giggling: known in the industry as 'corpsing'. This is an occupational hazard that can be set of by the audience, though tends to be more often a case of mutual hysteria among the cast. Laurence Olivier's early career was blighted by his tendency to corpse, until he was cured of it – the hard way – by Noël Coward.

Coward had cast him as the other male part in his play *Private Lives* at the Phoenix Theatre, in 1930. Always a professional on stage, he was infuriated by Olivier's immature habit and warned him that he would do everything he could, including pulling faces at him that the audience couldn't see, and whispering obscene comments to him, to make him laugh. He did this until Olivier was so mortified at the embarrassment that this caused the audience and his fellow cast members that he managed to rid himself of the habit.

Audiences can distract and annoy as well as amuse. Today this generally takes the form of mobile phones going off at inappropriate moments – usually the worse possible ones in terms of dramatic tension – but they can also be the more old-fashioned interruptions like coughing, sneezing, or talking out loud to the people sitting next to them.

Dame Judi Dench, acting in David Hare's *Amy's View* at the Aldwych, was distracted in this way at one performance. Not only did someone at the front of the stalls cough frequently, they did so while ostentatiously waving their hand in disapproval every time that she took a draw on the cigarettes that her character, Esme, liked to smoke. Dame Judi's reaction was an inspired one. Ignoring the fuss while on stage, in the interval she summoned the theatre manager to her dressing room and gave him something to give to the customer concerned.

The theatre manager duly presented the person with a small metal box. Inside were some cough sweets and a note that read 'From one non-smoker to another'.

For most theatregoers, seeing actors on stage is enough but some wish to see them in the flesh, to tell them how much they enjoyed the show, and/or to ask for their autograph. In addition there are autograph hunters (who tend to wear anoraks, hence the term for them) whose interest is in collecting the autograph rather than seeing the show.

This is the most direct form of contact between actors and their public, and there is an unwritten rule that actors stop to sign their autographs or even have their pictures taken – another case of the curse of the mobile phone, as these days most people in effect carry a camera in their pocket.

One exception to this rule was the late actor Alastair Sim (better known for his film roles, such as the cross-dressing role of the Headmistress of St Trinians). Sim had a hang-up about signing autographs, as he thought it was akin to signing away his soul, and many a puzzled young fan was treated to a lecture on the occult significance of signing one's name to a stranger.

Most actors have a more conventional approach to the gauntlet that they have to run – as do dancers and opera stars. During the run of *Ivanov* at Wyndham's in the autumn of 2008, Kenneth Branagh could be seen every day at the stage door, wearing a fixed smile, meeting the modest but determined demands of a group of admirers.

At least today's actors don't have to look particularly good when they go into or emerge from stage doors. Some tend to dress as though they were from an earlier era, like Sir Michael Gambon, who on one occasion had had a drink at an outside table at Koha, the café by the stage door, and was grabbed by the delighted little huddle of signature hunters once they had let Branagh finally get inside Wyndham's.

On that occasion Sir Michael was dressed in an overcoat and what looked like a fedora: every inch the theatrical. This formality, or elegance, was considered essential for leading actors until the social and sartorial changes of the mid 1960s. Stars were expected to look like stars when seen in the street, let alone at the stage door. This is a requirement that has been dead for 40 years, which is a godsend to actors who just want to get out of the theatre and off to the pub or restaurant.

Before looking at where they go, it is worth mentioning a few aspects of what happens inside the theatre and behind the stage.

Theatre is a place of superstitions and habits. The two best-known superstitions are not mentioning Shakespeare's *Macbeth* while in a theatre – it is referred to, instead, as 'the Scottish play'. Various explanations have been offered for why it is considered an unlucky play, but the presence of witchcraft at its centre lends an easy explanation as to why people should be nervous of it.

The 'curse' associated with the Scottish play brought conventional bad luck – bad reviews rather than mysterious deaths or inexplicable accidents – to Bryan Forbes's 1980 *Macbeth* at the Old Vic starring Peter O'Toole. His was an old-fashioned bravura performance, but none the worse for that.

After the critics savaged it – to the degree that a beleaguered-looking O'Toole was shown emerging from the stage door on the evening news referring to the reviews as 'a bit hairy' – it became fashionable to go to the Old Vic and laugh at the production. This was grossly unfair and an example of herd mentality. Yes, there was a lot of blood on Banquo in the banquet scene, but this was an enjoyably Edwardian take on the play rather than the travesty that the critics had made out. It was, though, a case of the ill reputation that surrounds the play being proved right once again.

The other major superstition is that one shouldn't whistle in a theatre. This comes from the more practical history of commands for stagehands to work the ropes that were, before computerization, the way that stage sets were lifted or otherwise moved. To whistle on stage might result in a heavy section of the set landing on your head.

Computerized sets can have their problems too, providing a more modern danger, as one young actor, Adam Salter, discovered at an early stage of the run of *The Lord of the Rings* at Drury Lane, when his leg became stuck in the multi-million pound revolving (and rising and falling) floor of the stage. The accident should have been technically impossible, and the show was immediately cancelled – as were the next couple of performances – by the safety-conscious producer, Kevin Wallace, until lessons could be learned and even further safety measures could be arranged. Salter made a full recovery, rejoined the cast and was a popular guest at the matinee question-and-answer sessions held on stage after curtain call, in which the audience could ask the cast questions about appearing in the production.

Actors' dressing rooms, even in the heart of the West End, used to be surprisingly small and dingy, though they have been improved on over the last 20 years. The most prestigious dressing room is No.1, which also tends to be the largest. Depending on the architecture of the theatre, dressing rooms can be in basements (the Lyric) or virtually in the clouds (the Duchess).

Dressing rooms are little oases for the cast, especially if their part is big enough to warrant a solo rather than a shared room, and it is now commonplace for them to have beds or couches where actors can get some sleep between shows on a two-performance day. Although the National Theatre's dressing rooms are by definition relatively modern and well-planned (having been constructed in the 1970s rather than the 1870s), the best-equipped theatre in terms of backstage facilities as a whole and dressing rooms in particular is the Royal Opera House, Covent Garden. For Royal Ballet principals these are more like modern hotel rooms than the dingy hutches that generations of dancers used to endure.

First night cards of goodwill (but never good luck – that's bad luck in the theatre) are traditional, as are presents between cast members. Flowers tend to be presented on stage only at ballet and opera performances, which is a shame as the pleasure they give recipients and audiences alike are more than worth their cost and the effort of a theatre or company manager to present them.

Until the early 1950s at least there used to be a Theatreland tradition of first night speeches. Ivor Novello, never one to miss an opportunity to stand in the spotlight of his fans' adoration, used to make a brief curtain-call speech *every* night. Nowadays such speeches tend only to be made on very special occasions, or by older actors who grew up with the tradition of wishing the audience a happy new year on New Year's Eve.

While they are performing together, actors form a small family. These can be happy or unhappy families, depending on the personalities involved, but the sense of belonging can be a major attraction of theatre life. As with film sets, theatres also offer temptations and opportunities for love affairs – and for enjoyable gossip by the rest of the cast who happily follow every move and nuance of what the participants in the affair mistakenly believe to be their secret.

The one person who observes – or at least hears – everything, and who represents the shield between the world inside the theatre and that beyond its walls, is the stage door keeper. Stage doors are as varied in size as the playhouses they guard, though the outward size of the theatre does not necessarily correlate with that of its stage door. The modest-sized St Martin's Theatre has a small box for the stage door keeper, as does the neighbouring Ambassadors – but so does the vast Victoria Palace.

The refurbished Coliseum and Royal Opera House both have spacious stage doors with the latest technology, while the Theatre Royal, Drury Lane has a generously large area for the stage door keeper, one of Theatreland's most cheerful characters, Jill Hudson.

Stage doors play their part, along with dressing rooms, in Simon Annand's collection of theatrical photographs, *The Half*, which is discussed in Chapter 1. *The Half*'s inside covers are made up of photographs of a stage door in recognition of its role as the portal into the hidden backstage world that Annand's photographs so vividly convey.

On leaving the stage door, actors will either head home (those with young families or who live a long way out of town) or to the pub or restaurant. Given the salaries they get, it is more likely to be the former than the latter, though wine bars tend to combine the two options of drink and late-night food.

The theatres that give Theatreland its name are also responsible for providing much of the rest of the urban landscape that makes up the area. Theatregoers are catered to by the pubs, restaurant, cafés and sandwich bars than surround the theatres like satellites.

One reason theatres generally don't provide food for customers, along with the lack of space and the extra administration involved, is that there is so much competition in the immediate vicinity. The exceptions are the National, the Coliseum and the Royal Opera House.

Restaurants also profit from theatres by offering relatively cheap pre- and (less often) post-theatre dinner options. These can be combined with reduced price tickets to see the shows themselves, but these tend to be arranged by tour operators or ticket dealers rather than the theatres themselves.

Pubs and wine bars also have theatregoers as a major part of their constituency, as do some specialist shops. These include David Drummond's Pleasures of Past Times in Cecil Court and Dress Circle in Monmouth Street. Dress Circle, which was established some 30 years ago, specializes in musical theatre. The pin board on the left as you enter is a sort of community bill board advertising every new cabaret or musical that is opening in London, while the shelves are full of CDs and DVDs of musicals and singers who specialize in musical theatre and cabaret songs.

Downstairs there is a section of theatre books, and on both floors there is a lot of merchandise for sale – again from musicals, especially *The Phantom of the Opera*, which seems to have created a small industry by itself.

Of the restaurants that have a reputation for attracting actors, the two closest to the heart of Theatreland are The Ivy and Sheekey's. Given its prices and the difficulty of getting a table (such is the demand for them) The Ivy tends to be used for special occasions and then only by the wealthier actors, though they do a very reasonably priced Sunday lunch. The decor is definitely un-theatrical, being rather minimalist and modern, but it is a great place for star-watching – especially for admirers of Joan Collins.

Miss Collins deserves a mention in her capacity as a classically trained actress rather than a celebrity. Fundamentally a film star (and latterly an authoress) she took to the stage in 2001 in *Over the Moon* at the Old Vic, in which she performed with exuberance and flair. Needless to say, the newspapers were more concerned with how she looked rather than how she acted, but to the pleasant surprise of some people who went expecting an equivalent to Peter O'Toole's experience in the same theatre, she was actually very good.

The image of an old-world theatre restaurant is Rules, which advertises itself as London's oldest restaurant, having opened in 1798. The interior is Victorian rather than Georgian, and is full of the sort of plush upholstery, brass, shooting prints and caricatures of nineteenth-century statesmen that any visitor to London, especially from abroad, would expect to find in Theatreland.

The restaurant's theatrical heyday belonged to the nineteenth century rather than the twenty-first, but it still provides a warmly welcoming atmosphere and a sense of Victorian calm and certainty in a changing world – an ideal place to retreat to in a credit crunch. Ideal, that is, unless you happen to be a vegetarian, as Rules' speciality is meat, especially game and beef, both sourced from its own estates in the countryside.

Sheekey's has a busier, bustlier feel to it than The Ivy, and a more modern one than at Rules. The series of smallish rooms, linked by corridors, give an agreeable sense of dining in the restaurant car of an upmarket train – perhaps the Orient Express. Rules is close to the stage door of the Vaudeville and near that of the Adelphi; The Ivy is opposite the neighbouring Ambassadors' and St Martin's theatres, while Sheekey's is besides the Noël Coward and Wyndham's.

Another theatrical favourite is the Old Vic's Pit Bar, which offers food and drinks after the show, and is a popular bar with the cast at the Old Vic and their friends. The Pit Bar, stylishly modern in decor, has its own street entrance at the side of the theatre.

The Pit Bar was commissioned from an actor, George Couyas, whose side-line is interior design, by the Old Vic's owner, Sally Greene. The brief was to create a contemporary and stylish space in the heart of the Old Vic that would subsequently get a late license and find an audience of its own. The Pit Bar has become a flexible and comfortable space for actors meeting their guest, audience members and indeed the general public looking for a taste of late-night Theatreland.

Couyas was also commissioned, by owner Sir Stephen Waley-Cohen, to design the Tudor Room – the VIP bar for the Victoria Palace Theatre. The space was refurbished in 2007 in anticipation of VIPs coming to see *Billy Elliot* and any subsequent shows that will play in that theatre. There was a need for a room that was elegant, exclusive and private in the Victoria Palace Theatre for producers and their guests and it is also hired out for private functions. Among the first meetings held there when the work was finished were (appropriately) discussions about the transfer of *Billy Elliot* from London to Broadway and Sydney.

Returning to St Martin's Lane, opposite Sheekey's and on the other side of Wyndam's and the Coward, is Koha. This café/bar as it calls itself is a wine bar that expanded into the neighbouring building three or four years ago. It is owned and run by three Kosovo Albanian brothers, which makes it another chapter in the age-old story of immigrants coming to London and flourishing. Though the brothers are not a case of rags to riches, they are nevertheless a triumph of enterprise and talent and they provide a relaxed but up-market hospitality that has been taken up by the theatre profession, especially those performing at the neighbouring playhouses.

Koha's interior is continental in feel, not least because the staff are from Eastern Europe. Before its extension the interior was painted a light green. This was an unfashionable and indeed not very attractive colour, but it gave a more old-world European flavour to the place which was partially lost when the green was replaced by the current orange colour.

On a more positive note, the orange helps set off the paintings on the wall. These, which are for sale, are created by the youngest of the brothers, Naim, who has exhibited at The Hospital Club, the private members' club in Endell Street, Covent Garden, which has an art gallery space. He has also exhibited, and won prizes, in Amsterdam.

The presence of the pictures – which range from darkly disturbing abstracts through colourful and cheerful ones to more conventional though distinctive pastoral scenes, gives a further level of individuality to what is already a very unusual venue. Its reputation as a congenial place to meet has spread beyond the next door theatres: during the recent run of *Ivanov* the director Tamara Harvey was seen examining the model box of a theatre set in one of the two alcove window tables that face the north side of Wyndham's.

Outside Koha there is a row of tables and chairs, which further help create a continental atmosphere in the summer, and which are still resolutely placed in the courtyard even in winter. The smokers are grateful for them, and the management has provided heaters under the awning so their customers can have a cigarette break without freezing.

Downstairs there is another floor area, which is often let out for private parties. As it has not just a modern sound system but an ancient piano, it is also occasionally used for small-scale rehearsals of musical theatre pieces. The feel here is not so much Eastern Europe as St Petersburg – not because there is anything specifically Russian about it, but the low ceiling, the colourful cushions and an air of secrecy are reminiscent, even though they don't look exactly the same, of the feel of the basement room where Prince Felix Yusupov entertained Rasputin before assassinating him in a doomed attempt to save the Russian monarchy three months or so before it was swept away in the February Revolution of 1917.

Another basement venue that actors enjoy is a restaurant, Joe Allen's, in Exeter Street. Joe Allen's has been feeding hungry actors after a hard night's work since 1977. And one of the main attractions – along with the late hours (last orders at half-past 11), the unpretentious food and the (usually) friendly staff – has always been, since those earliest evenings, Jimmy Hardwick on the piano.

Jimmy is more than the house pianist. He is, in many ways, the soul of the place. He knows and is to known to all of Theatreland's stars – and many of Broadway's. When the latter come to London they head to Joe Allen's after a show – whether as performer or audience – and Jimmy will not only recognize and chat to them, he will play the theme music from their best-known show as they take their seat.

Taking your seat, if Jimmy knows you, can be a lengthy process, as he likes to chat, but given his fund of showbiz anecdotes and his eye on who is doing what, where but never *whom*, as he's far too discreet, chatting to him is a rewarding process that's well worth the time.

Every so often he disappears for a week or two, usually to the Canaries. When he comes back he is tanned almost black. This is wildly disconcerting the first time you see him, but once you are used to the process it is less of shock.

Trevor Nunn has a favourite table, where he often eats with his wife, Imogen Stubbs, against the wall, whereas Sheridan Morley was usually seated on the other side of the room, a few feet from Jimmy. Christopher Biggins is a regular, as are several other familiar faces, including Julia McKenzie.

Another frequent visitor is the American singer and actress Lorna Dallas, who spends much of the year in London. She is known as an interpreter of classic musical theatre composers from both sides of the Atlantic, especially Jerome Kern and Ivor Novello. She put her concert and cabaret career on a very temporary hold when she played one of the victims of the 9/11 hijackings in Paul Greengrass's award-winning film *United 93*.

The decor is simple (brick walls, plain tables, paper tablecloths) but very theatrical, as the bricks are covered with posters from scores of shows. There is another Joe Allen's in New York, which opened first, in 1965, but the London one seems to have more atmosphere, even though Broadway takes showbiz rather more seriously than London often seems to.

The London restaurant has a green awning over the doorway. While descending the stairs you are faced with a wall which displays the posters of most of the major shows in the West End, after which you reach the cloakroom, where coats, bags etc. are left, before the duty manager (usually a woman) greets you from behind a stand-up desk that is a mixture of a concierge's desk and a church lectern. Having had your booking confirmed (it's always best to book) you are then allocated a table and, if you're in the right area, you get to say hello to Jimmy before reaching your table.

The kitchen is visible from the dining area, while the waiters move around quickly and (usually) efficiently, some of them managing to do so as if they were wearing roller skates, weaving through the gaps between the tables. Although the place is busy during normal restaurant hours, by definition the real theatricals don't arrive until after 10 p.m., as they will be on stage when most diners are eating.

There is some table hopping, and a lot of hugging and kissing when groups of thespians recognize each other, and a lot of surreptitious glancing when someone arrives with a companion who is obviously not just a friend but a date.

Given that it is far more affordable than The Ivy, Sheekey's and Rules, is open later and is geared to the hours that actors work, Joe Allen's can claim to be the actors' restaurant. It would be even more so if there had not been a flurry of other places to go opened in the last decade, with non-stuffy private members' clubs like Teatro and Century (both on Shaftesbury Avenue) along with Soho House and its satellites.

These other venues attract some younger actors who might otherwise head for Joe Allen's bar or restaurant area, but the latter continues to generate a unique sense of belonging to the community, which Theatreland, despite the social and cultural changes of the last 25 years, still is.

14

Let's Do the Show Right Here! – How Shows are Staged

Putting a show on in the West End is a complicated process, but a simplified version of it gives an idea of how shows get from script to stage.

The key figure is the producer. Theatre producers have been given a comic and slightly sleazy public image thanks to Mel Brooks's stage musical *The Producers*, which played at the Theatre Royal, Drury Lane.

Kevin Wallace, the producer of *The Lord of The Rings*, the show that followed *The Producers* into the Lane, discussed the role of a producer in the education section of *The Lord of the Rings* website – a section that was one of the most detailed of any major West End show, reflecting the large number of students and school groups who came to see it, thanks partly to their already having been fans of the books and/or Peter Jackson's film trilogy. Wallace's creative team also described their jobs, as did others working in the theatre, both backstage and front of house.

Given the unprecedented range of skills that were brought into the theatre, the website was comprehensive in its discussion of what was needed and how it fitted together, but the general process is true of any show, depending on the scale of the enterprise.

A producer is far more than someone who finds money to put on a show. He or she will be the originator of the project, who has to put together the creative team who can make the idea a reality. The original idea may be the producer's or it may be brought to them by someone else. It is, however, the producer's professional expertise and judgement that decides whether and how the project takes off.

Having decided to start, there is a somewhat chicken-and-egg range of issues to be arranged. The rights to the piece are an essential first step, but some rights holders (the original author/composer, or perhaps representatives of their estate if the author is dead but the work is still in copyright) may want to know who will direct the play and who will star in it before they give their agreement to the project going ahead.

The most important single choice that a producer will usually make, unless the piece is entirely star-led, as in a classic play fronted by an A-list Hollywood celebrity, is the choice of a director – and even here the actor or actress would only accept the role if he or she were to have complete trust in whomever the producer was suggesting as a director.

The director will then, with the producer, put together a creative team. Depending on the show, this will include a music director, a sound director, a lighting director, a casting director, a designer (sometimes clothes and set designers are separate, sometimes one person will design both), a choreographer and, if there any fight scenes, a fight director, too.

Each of these people will have responsibility for a specific area of the production, but by definition their responsibilities will overlap and in every interview with any kind of creative, the teamwork that is involved in staging a show is stressed.

A producer, meanwhile, will have had to raise the money to finance the production. Raising this is a crucial part of the job and relies on the producer's contacts as well as, on occasion, his or her ingenuity in finding new sources of investment.

Investing in theatre is notoriously risky, as only a small percentage of plays or musical go into profit. As Richard Pulford of the Society of London Theatre has said, this means that despite the usual division of theatre into subsidized and commercial, all theatre is in effect subsidized, as every show needs to raise money, and does so from individuals or companies who are aware that the chance of earning a positive return on their investment is slim.

It is for this reason that theatre investors have traditionally been known as angels – they will only get their reward in Heaven. What investors do buy into is not only the chance of being part of a rare long-runner that will make them serious money over many years (i.e. a long-running musical) but the opportunity of being part of the theatre process: of meeting the producer, going to the opening night show, being invited to the after-show party, feeling an inherent part of the magic of theatre.

Significant supporters of the Donmar Warehouse for example, will enjoy behind-the-scenes access to the theatre's work, including meeting cast and creatives. Similar backstage access is one of the attractions of the various Friends groups that are such an important feature of London's major opera and ballet companies.

One way of arousing potential investors' interest is by staging what are called 'backers' showcases'. This is when a producer, director and cast will, by arrangement with a friendly theatre owner, use a stage or similar performance space to put on a rehearsed performance of a new work with professional cast. This is usually done as a concert performance, wearing everyday clothes, and the performers appear for free or a token payment, either because they are friends of the writer or production team or because they feel it is helpful for their career to be associated with the potential new production.

One such showcase in late 2008 was for a new musical, *Mathilde*, by Conor Mitchell. An early 30-something composer from Northern Ireland, Mitchell is a hugely talented composer of modern music theatre and has recently worked with the National Theatre. His award-winning musical *Have a Nice Life* was one of the hits of the 2007 New York Music Theatre Festival, in a production directed by Pip Pickering.

The *Mathilde* showcase was at the Vaudeville Theatre, where the cast included Sally Ann Triplett (Reno Sweeney in the National's *Anything Goes*) and Samuel Barnett (*The History Boys* at the National, *Dealer's Choice* at the Trafalgar Studios), both of them high-profile performers.

However he or she arranges the finance, any producer has to capitalize a show, that is, produce enough money to pay all the costs in getting it from page to stage. They will also have calculated how much is needed in terms of running costs. These should be no more than 50 per cent of net revenue from ticket sales. Once a show's capitalization has been repaid it goes into profit, and these profits tend to be split in a ratio of 40 per cent to the producer and 60 per cent to the investors. The producer will also charge a management fee, which counts as one of the fixed running costs.

Producers come from a variety of backgrounds within the theatre, as do directors, but they have to have sharp financial minds as well as the ability to pick teams of people who will work well together and material that the public will want to see in the first place. Becoming a producer has traditionally been a haphazard process driven by ambition and interest rather than any sort of training, with mentoring being done in the job, with budding impresarios learning the basics of their job through working in the office of an established producer.

This has now changed, with the Society of London Theatre offering a bursary scheme to help young people with a proven interest in, and experience of, theatre, who feel that producing is an area they would like to explore. They are given a training course and are assigned to a mentor as they prepare to produce a play of their own, using the lessons and the bursary to help launch the production. This scheme has been understandably popular and is usually over-subscribed. It represents a far-sighted attempt by the industry to help nurture some of those who will be responsible for putting on the next generation of plays and musicals.

The director is the person whose overall artistic vision for the piece is responsible for how it looks, sounds and feels, and what aspect of the script is stressed most. Every director will find something different in every script, whether new or ancient, and will also draw different performances from actors. As such they are the key interpreter of the work, the conduit between it and the audience.

The director must focus the audience's attention on the action on stage and tell the story that is being presented as clearly and effectively as possible.

Writers may have been involved at the very start of the process, if a producer has seen the manuscript of a play he wants to produce, or they may be brought in to work on adapting a book or film (or, in the case of *Cats*, a series of poems) for the theatre.

There is a public misconception that a play's script is printed and then brought to the stage, when actually a new script can be radically changed in the course not only of preliminary discussions with the director and producer but, more frequently, in the course of rehearsals. Modifications to a script, as it takes shape during rehearsals, will continue right up to opening night and occasionally afterwards. This is especially true in musicals, where it is not unknown for lyrics to songs to be changed many times, along with the structure of the show and where the songs appear in them – many is the actor who has laboriously learnt a song, in several versions, only to have it cut before opening night.

Set designers shape the world that the characters inhabit on stage. This is usually restricted, by budget as much as by convention, to the proscenium arch that frames the stage in a traditional playhouse, and to the stage area itself. On occasion the set comes off the stage and into the auditorium, too. This happened to great effect in *The Lord of the Rings* at Drury Lane, where set and costume designer Rob Howell created an extraordinary mass of branches that spread over the arch and onto the walls of Drury Lane.

This immense tree created an atmosphere of mystery and of vast, dark forests. It gave an immediate visual impact, which helped take the audience out of the West End and into the action on stage, before the curtain had risen. The effect was aided by the presence of actors dressed as hobbits being on stage in front of the curtain and mingling with the audience members taking their seats.

Musical supervisors are responsible for the shape and sound of the score, and will sometimes conduct the orchestra as well, though this is a role that is often divided between colleagues. The musical supervisor may also be responsible for orchestrations, or they may work with someone brought in specifically to orchestrate the score.

The choreographer is responsible for dance routines, but can also be used for more general direction of movement, to help actors suggest their characters through body language as well as the text. Choreographers have trademark styles, but they can also be very versatile. Peter Darling, who was responsible for the hobbit dances (an especially athletic one taking place in the Prancing Pony inn at Bree), had previously choreographed *Billy Elliot* for Stephen Daldry.

Lighting and sound designers work with the director and other members of the creative team. Lighting can create a story as effectively as any set, and can help the audience move with the actors from one scene to another, with or without a set change.

Sound is similarly evocative, and there is great technical skill, especially in the larger theatres, in ensuring that the sound generated on the stage or in the orchestra pit (and sometimes by members of the band in rooms offstage and away from the auditorium) reaches every level and area of the theatre at the right time. This not only means that everyone, wherever they are sitting, will hear the best sound possible, they will hear it at the right time, as allowance will have been made for the time it takes to leave the actor and reach, say, the back of the balcony. The desired impression, given that we tend to hear visually, as it were, is that if we are looking at a singer on stage we seem to hear the sound leave their lips rather than coming from a set of loudspeakers far above them.

A fight director's job is by definition a very specific one, but even here there is great scope for individuality and creativity in the application of experience and technical skill to produce a convincing result. Unlike on films, theatre fight directors generally work without gory special effects, whether the fight they are creating is a fist-fight in a domestic family drama or a battle with swords and halberds in a one of Shakespeare's history plays.

In film and on television the absence of blood and bruises on an actor whose character had just been in a fight would be completely unbelievable to an audience and the illusion that the actors, directors and cameramen had striven to create would be broken. The opposite tends to be true on stage, where the application of a lot of blood (especially in a mass battle scene, as in *The Lord of the Rings* or *Richard III*) would be absurd, Pythonesque even. It would also be wildly impractical as the stage would need to be swabbed down before the next scene could continue. Such is the power of theatre to stimulate the imagination, however. Audiences soon buy into the stage conventions, which is why stage fighting can be as exciting as the far more graphic versions that we are used to seeing on television and film.

Casting directors approach the agents of the people they are interested in for specific roles, and let agents in general know about casting requirements so agents can put forward those of their clients who they believe have a chance of being cast. As with any creative decision the director and producer have the ultimate choice of casting each role.

Sometimes 'general' auditions will be held – especially for dancers. This is a form of audition that attracts some people who have no hope of getting cast but who like the experience, the feeling of belonging to a process, even though they will make sure they are never at the front of a group of hopefuls, which is where the real dancers will want to be. This is a strange phenomenon but offers a harmless form of therapy.

It is a casting director's job to keep an eye on new talent as well as established actors. 'Understudy runs' are one way of doing this. The term refers to the standard practice of running a performance of a play, during the afternoon of a non-matinee day, where the lead roles are played by the understudies. This gives them a chance to play the role at least once, in costume and on stage and in front of an audience, albeit not the paying public. The audience will, however, include families and friends and crucially, agents.

Understudies have a somewhat thankless role, in that no one really wants to see them, and many an actor, seizing their chance to go on when a principal has fallen ill or been otherwise indisposed, has had the experience of hearing the audience groan out loud on hearing that their favourite actor or actress will not be appearing on stage that night. For David Tennant's understudy in *Hamlet*, that must have been a particularly heavy burden to bear, as the Royal Shakespeare Company's production sold out due to the demand to see Dr Who on stage.

Another classic way of spotting new talent is at the showcases that drama schools present with their final-year pupils. These can be modern or classic plays or musicals, depending on the courses. One such example recently was by the Central School of Speech and Drama, one of London's leading drama schools, whose MA Classical Acting students gave a performance of *The Merchant of Venice*.

Three students stood out: Saif Alfalasi (who on the strength of his double performance as the Prince of Morocco and Lorenzo was immediately cast in the TV series *Trinity*), Konstantinos Kavakiotis (as Shylock) and Howard Morgan (as Lancelot Gobbo). As their names imply, actors in London drama schools come from an international background, or from British families of foreign origin, as well as from the more traditional ranks of the English middle classes.

Although actors from ethnic minorities have, over the last ten years, had a field day in British television and, up to a point, films, too, they have traditionally been less visible on stage, though that too is changing, and not just in modern plays. Adrian Lester, for example, played the young King in Shakespeare's *Henry V* at the National Theatre, in a 'colour blind' production and the trend is for this to be increasingly common.

Once a show is finally cast, a pivotal role is played by the company manager. His job (it is generally a he) is to be the producer's representative in the theatre and to ensure that each performance runs as smoothly as possible. It is the company manager who makes sure that each part is covered, that understudies are in place where necessary, and who juggles the holiday and sick-leave rotas, which in a large musical is no easy matter.

Company managers are not just organizers, they are sounding boards for any discontent within the company and the point of reference between the company and the theatre. It is the company manager, just before each show starts, who tells the theatre manager when the company are ready for the lights to be lowered, the door into the auditorium closed and for the show to begin. After every performance the company manager will send a show report to the producer, keeping him up to date with how the actors are performing and how the show was received, noting whether there were any technical problems and so on.

Between casting and the performance, there is the rehearsal process. Rehearsals are usually not initially on the stage of the theatre at which the show will be performed. There are a number of rehearsal spaces and studios in central London, including the Drill Hall in Bloomsbury and the Dragon Hall in Covent Garden. On the South Bank the National has its own rehearsal spaces, while the Jerwood Studio in Southwark is also much used by commercial theatre companies.

Very large musicals, including *The Lord of the Rings* and *Oliver!* have rehearsed well outside traditional Theatreland, in 3 Mills Studios, a massive complex in Bromley-by-Bow by the site of an old mill, whose water and local swans make a pleasant contrast with the grim motorway and subterranean walkway from the tube station. The complex of rehearsal rooms includes a vast stage area where large-scale casts can get a feel for the sort of space they will be performing in on stage.

After final rehearsals in the actual theatre, with a lot of technical as well as artistic fine-tuning, there will be a dress rehearsal and then (sometimes on the same day) the first public performance will take place. Opera and ballet companies will often let people into their dress rehearsals, especially if the run of performances is already sold out, as they frequently are when a major star has been cast.

As well as letting an extra audience see the show, albeit only a rehearsal in which the singers will often hold back from full power to save their voices, this is a way of involving the companies' Friends organizations. This is the start of previews, which are full performances for a paying audience, but which take place before the press night – also variously referred to as the first night or opening night, even though the show will have been running 'in preview' for one or even two weeks.

Tickets for previews are sold at a slight discount to reflect that the show is still being broken in, though the public still expect to see a fully prepared and professionally delivered show. It is at previews that not only actors settle into their parts, the stage technology is also given a chance to go through any teething problems before the press night.

Cards and presents are swapped by cast members on the opening night, and there will be a party after the show. The scale and location of the party will depend on the generosity of the producer – or rather their use of investors' money as the party will be paid for out of the production budget.

The first night party for *The Lord of the Rings* was held at the Royal Courts of Justice in the Strand. The exterior of the Courts looks like a cathedral, and the building is frequently mistaken, by tourists, for St Paul's cathedral, leading them to get off the bus several stops before the real St Paul's which is on Ludgate Hill, at the other end of Fleet Street, four bus stops away.

The route from Drury Lane to the Royal Courts of Justice was lined by good-looking young men and women holding candles, while the Courts themselves – vast stone hallways – were atmospherically lit and full of equally well-chosen staff bearing a seemingly endless selection of food and drink while, later in the evening, a jazz band struck up for anyone interested in dancing.

While this was one of Theatreland's most spectacular after-show celebrations, the most consistently stylish first night parties are given by Bill Kenwright, who hires five-star hotels or similarly up-market venues and provides sit-down meals rather than just canapés that have to be grabbed and consumed while standing up and balancing a drink in your other hand.

Other parties are held in bars – like that for the musical *Carousel*, which opened at the Savoy and had a party at a bar on Trafalgar Square – or on stage. Drury Lane's saloon is an ideal place for a theatrical celebration, and is used not just for a first night party or an event during the run of a show, but for the traditional Baddeley Cake ceremony on Twelfth Night.

This tradition dates back to the eighteenth century, when Robert Baddeley (c.1732–1794), who had been a pastry cook, joined David Garrick's company at Drury Lane. After a long career at the theatre he left in his will a sum of money to provide for the purchase of a cake, washed down with punch, for the cast of whatever play happened to be on at the Theatre Royal on future Twelfth Nights.

The ceremony, with the cake decorated to reflect the current show (a challenge during long runs like *Miss Saigon*) has continued ever since with breaks only on the very rare occasions of there being no show running on Twelfth Night. The cast, plus guests, gather in the theatre's Grand Saloon to hear a brief speech about Robert Baddeley, then to raise their glasses of punch and toast their benefactor before enjoying the cake.

Whether the same cast return the next year is down to the public – and to the theatre critics whose initial reviews of a play can help ensure a long run or drag a show off the stage within weeks – which is a cue to look at the role of theatre critics in the theatre industry, the subject of the next chapter.

15

Theatre Critics: Sheridan Morley and his Colleagues

The late Sheridan Morley was one of the best-known London theatre critics of the twentieth century. He had a perfect start to this career, having been brought up in a highly theatrical family – his father was the stage and screen actor Robert Morley, while on his maternal side his grandmother was the actress, Edwardian pin-up and inter-war impresario, Dame Gladys Cooper.

Morley was named, not after the eighteenth-century playwright and theatre owner Richard Brinsley Sheridan (as many people assumed), but after a character in a play – *The Man Who Came to Dinner* – in which his father was starring when he was born.

Sheridan worked, in the course of a 40-year career, in television, on radio – where his mellifluous voice combined easiness on the ear with a warm and un-hectoring authority – and in the old Fleet Street of *The Times* and the long-running magazine *Punch*. Yet his heart belonged to Theatreland, and he was never happier than when in the Covent Garden theatre restaurant Joe Allen's after seeing the first night of a West End play or indeed musical – he was one of the few major theatre critics to praise *Les Miserables* when it opened in the mid-1980s, and his judgement was to be vindicated by its continuing long run, first at the Palace Theatre and latterly (and even more successfully) at the Queen's, on Shaftesbury Avenue.

Morley was unusual in many ways. A bear of a man, his impressive bulk suggested at first view that he might be a bit of a bruiser, but he was sweet-natured, generous and gentle, with a well-honed sense of humour and an infectious, guttural laugh. Although very much a ladies' man, and theatrical without ever drifting towards camp, he was very gay-friendly and had a tendency to address all and sundry, regardless of age, sex, or sexual orientation, as 'Darling'. This trait was, he cheerfully admitted, due to short-sightedness and an increasing inability to remember names as he got older, as much as any inherent 'luvviness'.

Morley's commitment to London theatre was never in doubt. What was, though, was his style of reviewing, which delighted his many readers but was known to irritate his critics, who found his habit of referring to past productions and long-gone stars of the inter-war years irrelevant and backward-looking.

What really upset many people, however, was his habit of falling asleep during a production. When this was followed by a bad review, actors, directors and writers were naturally indignant. How could he criticize a play he had slept through? They had a point, though the fact he had gone to sleep in the first place was itself a judgement on the quality of the piece he was there to review.

Morley's nodding off was like a little ritual, or a short ballet, in which every move was carefully choreographed. First, the head would begin to nod, then sink gracefully onto his massive chest – above the even larger stomach. Next, the breathing would become slightly more pronounced, though never loud. After this, there would invariably come a slight click or clatter as the pen that he, like his colleagues in the stalls, had brought into the auditorium to write notes fell to the floor. Finally, the notepad itself would drop, often producing enough noise to wake Sheridan, as well as to alert those who had been concentrating on the actors rather than on him, that he had fallen asleep. An awakened Morley would then retrieve pad and paper as if he had just dropped them by mistake, and immediately start scribbling away.

For an actor in a smaller theatre, the sight was disconcerting at best and infuriating at worst if the first night review was a critical one. Yet the review, when it came, would be as good if not better as any by more physically alert critics, of whom Benedict Nightingale and Michael Billington continue to be among the most distinguished.

Morley's professional relationship with his colleagues was cordial, but complicated by the fact of his belonging to theatrical aristocracy by birth, and his enthusiastic embrace of a very old-fashioned theatrical lifestyle, one that belonged more to the world of 1950s actors than to the modern lives of profes-sional journalists, who tended to catch the last train home rather than revel in late-night conversations at Joe Allen's or The Ivy.

Morley's lifestyle included large houses in London and his parents' Berkshire country home, plus swimming pool, to provide a weekend getaway. He was a generous host, employed a driver as well as a secretary and a cleaner and sent flowers and cards like other people send text messages or emails.

Although this detracted from his street cred, he never had any to speak of and would not have welcomed it in any case – he belonged not to the street, but to the Cowardesque balcony, from which he could look out across the Mediterranean (or Chelsea Harbour, at least) to the yachts where those whose lives he admired, knew about, and often chronicled, enjoyed their leisure.

Sheridan had arguably the best private collection of books on the theatre in England, many of which he wrote – whether collections of his reviews or the dozens of biographies he wrote or co-wrote. This cascade of anecdotes had been started in 1969 with the first biography of Noël Coward, who was also to be the subject of his last such book.

In 2000 he published his long-awaited official biography of Sir John Gielgud, having waited until Gielgud had finally died before producing the book. Gielgud combined an actor's typically low opinion of theatre critics with a unique ability to drop 'bricks' – gaffes that punctured the egos of whomever they were aimed at.

Phoning Sheridan one day, to find out just how far he'd got with the biography, Gielgud commented, absent-mindedly, 'Do you know, they've just unveiled a statue in America to a theatre critic! Extraordinary! Oh my God, *you're* a theatre critic!' – and slammed the phone down.

Gielgud's forgetfulness about Morley's job description was forgivable, as in addition to his reviewing work, Morley not only wrote books and broadcast on radio and television, he also wrote a highly successful play, *Noël and Gertie*, about the relationship between Noël Coward and his favourite leading lady, Gertrude Lawrence – the star who appeared opposite him in *Private Lives*, and whom he would always remember, as she appeared on stage in that play, in a white Molyneux dress – the epitome of inter-war glamour.

Morley also appeared in cabaret, at Pizza on the Park, at the Jermyn Street Theatre, on cruise ships and in numerous other places around the world. He was an effective and engaging introducer of performers like Steve Ross, the legendary New York cabaret star, and Michael Law, whose Piccadilly Dance Orchestra brought back, for several years, some inter-war style to Noël Coward's old haunt, the Savoy Hotel.

The high point of his involvement on stage was when he directed a revival of *Song at Twilight*, one of Noël Coward's last plays. This was performed, first at the King's Head, Islington and then transferred to the Gielgud, with Vanessa Redgrave replacing the New Zealand-born Nyree Dawn Porter – once referred to by Coward as the three worst actresses that country ever produced.

Although the play on her three-part name made a good quip (and Coward never seemed to mind the pain that was caused, so long as the quip was memorable), Nyree Dawn Porter had been stunningly beautiful as a young woman (when she starred in the 1960s television series *The Forsyte Saga*) and gave an assured performance as Carlotta in the King's Head production.

Despite this, Vanessa Redgrave brought something far deeper and more involving to the role when it transferred. She also brought the interest of the press, especially as this was to be the first time she had appeared opposite her brother, Corin, on a West End stage.

Morley's direction of the production, which marked the centenary of Coward's birth in 1899, was informed by his unrivalled knowledge of, and love for, Coward's work, but his direction of the Redgraves (and a supporting cast that consisted of Corin's wife Kika Markham and the strikingly handsome Mathew Bose) was given with a very light touch.

The analogy that he himself used in a number of interviews was that the role of directing them was like that of an air traffic controller – he cleared a landing path for the aircraft, pointed out the landing strip, but let them find their own best way of getting safely down on the ground.

As noted above, Morley was not content with directing theatre as well as reviewing it and broadcasting about it – he also established himself as a successful playwright with *Noël and Gertie.*

This two-hander (plus pianist) played all over the world, from Hong Kong to the South of France to the United States, with a West End run at the Comedy Theatre and at least one subsequent production at Jermyn Street. It was a celebration, not only of Coward's career but also of the relationship between the Master and his favourite leading lady, Gertie Lawrence. They had met as child actors, when they shared a railway compartment on the way to yet another theatre. She was Amanda to his Elyot in *Private Lives*, and always had a special place in his heart.

Towards the end of his short but enormously full life (he died aged 65 in 2007), Morley suffered not just from the depression that had dogged him throughout his adult life, but also the effects of a stroke, which robbed him of much of his trademark energy, and added an extra challenge to his health. Despite this, he continued to review, and came nearest to his old self when standing in the aisle in the stalls on a press night, swapping gossip with his colleagues.

Were his ghost to appear anywhere, however, it would not be in a West End theatre, but a Covent Garden gentleman's club – the Garrick. Here, in the clubhouse designed as a place where gentlemen and actors (the two rarely being synonymous) could meet and enjoy each other's company, Morley loved to lunch or wine and dine his friends, surrounded by the Garrick's marvellous collection of theatrical memorabilia and portraits.

One of the most striking of these is on the ground floor room to the right (as you go in) of the entrance hall. Here, under a vast and suitably impressive portrait of his grandmother, Dame Gladys Cooper, Sheridan spoke eloquently, even movingly, of his love of theatre in general and of his interest in the career and world of Sir John Gielgud when he gave a talk to booksellers prior to the publication of his Gielgud biography. Food, drink, stage memorabilia, family connections, reminders of a vanished glamour, a golden age of the West End, in the heart of today's Theatreland together create the perfect setting for Sheridan Morley's spirit.

Morley was very much a one-off, and his absence, to anyone who knew him, is palpable at every first night. However, the rest of the band are still (at the moment) very much there, as theatre critics continue to be an essential part of the ritual of opening a show in the West End. There are, of course, relatively few of them – the most important being those who write for the major newspapers, whose reviews still come out the following morning, wherever possible.

One of the most influential critics, given the size of his paper's readership, is Nicholas de Jong of the *Evening Standard*. The paper's lead reviewer, he has, like Sheridan Morley, also tried his hand at writing for, rather than just about, the stage. Another Morley connection is the subject matter of this play – Sir John Gielgud.

De Jong's play *Plague Over England* (directed by Tamara Harvey), about the anti-gay campaign by the authorities in 1953, was a critical success despite, rather than because of, his normal job: critics may have a certain fellow-feeling when sitting in the stalls together, but they know they cannot be seen to be giving 'soft' reviews to a colleague. De Jong's success had to be earned the hard way, which must have made his critical triumph all the more rewarding.

Benedict Nightingale hasn't written for the stage yet, but his son, Christopher, has composed for it: he was musical director and co-composer on the stage version of *The Lord of the Rings* at the Theatre Royal, Drury Lane in 2007.

Michael Billington has restricted himself to writing about the stage in books rather than coming up with a play or score but, as he recalled in the November 2008 edition of *Whatsonstage* magazine, he spent a month at a leading London drama school, LAMDA (the London Academy of Music and Drama), directing third-year students in a triple bill of three works by Harold Pinter: his plays *Party Time* and *Celebration* and a rehearsed reading of his lecture, *Art, Truth and Politics*.

In the article Billington argues that critics should be encouraged to be more versatile rather than slammed back into the convenient 'theatre critic' box. For him, the main joy of the experience was the sense of collaboration with the students on a joint exploration of the plays. This is understandable, as the role of theatre critic is an essentially lonely one. You know your fellow theatre critics, who are technically your rivals, you know the producers, theatre owners, agents and publicists who tend to be found at every major theatre first night, and you know the theatre managers who greet you with a wary eye, wondering if you will help make or break the show, but you write on your own.

Despite this understandable concern and although Billington, Nightingale and a number of their contemporaries are well-respected by the public and in the theatre world, it is undeniable that none of them have the critical or commercial clout that used to be enjoyed by the likes of Kenneth Tynan, James Agate or Harold Hobson. The latter two will have barely been heard of by most people today, though in the early- to mid-twentieth century they were towering figures who could make or break a production.

Tynan was a brilliant critic whose unorthodox and anti-establishment style perfectly caught the changing face of British culture from the mid 1950s through to the late 1970s. He was to be Laurence Olivier's literary manager at the National Theatre and wrote the nude revue *Oh! Calcutta!* that was a symbol of the permissiveness of the late 1960s (and the end of theatre censorship), but despite this versatility it is as a theatre critic that he made the most impact and for which he will be most remembered.

His most important single review, that helped make theatre history in that it launched a play that changed the face of modern British drama, was for the young John Osborne's play *Look Back in Anger*, which opened at the Royal Court Theatre in 1956.

Other critics had been lukewarm about the play: it was Tynan's extraordinary review, in which he claimed he could not love someone who did not like *Look Back in Anger*, that made people flock to see it. John Gielgud had seen it and disliked it. He was, however, sufficiently intrigued by the vehemence of Tynan's reaction to the play, and his remarkably personal championing of it, that he decided to see it again – and was converted. Sir John's revised opinion helped champion the play among people who would not otherwise have gone to see it, but who respected his opinion.

Today's theatre critics can only dream of such power. One reason is, with all due respect to current journalists, that there is no one writing today who regularly brings such extraordinary passion to reviewing. Intelligence, yes; experience, yes; engaging style, yes; but not, it seems, the spark that made Tynan's reviews required reading.

Given this, do theatre critics still matter? How many newspapers, or indeed magazines, have theatre reviews on their covers? How many people buy a paper for the theatre reviewer, rather than for sports coverage or political commentary? When was the last time a theatre critic was interviewed on the flagship television news programmes?

The last question relates to the broader issue of the role of theatre in public

Sheridan Morley's grandmother, Gladys Cooper, seduces Ivor Novello in *Enter Kiki*, at the Playhouse Theatre in 1923

affairs. News stories invariably recount details of sports matches, of the transfer of footballers from one club to another and so on. How often do they record an understudy's taking over at the last moment when some theatre knight or dame has fallen ill? How often does a new play's first night get covered – unless it features Madonna or a major Hollywood star?

And yet, reviews *do* still matter – to producers, to casts, to the theatre-going public. And though we live in the internet age, which means that every person who sees a show can write about it and post his or her thoughts online, the fact remains that by far the easiest way for the public to get an idea of what a show is like is to look (in a paper or online) at what the professional theatre reviewers make of it.

These critics would be even more attended to if they could bring themselves (as not all do) to record not just how they felt about a particular drama or musical, but how the rest of the public reacted.

For a theatre critic's job is to give the reader a picture of what it was like to be present in the theatre on the first night. This should, therefore, mean not just a description of, and commentary on, the set, the lighting, the acting, the script and the direction, but also the impact that all this had on the audience.

Theatre is a communal event, in which the atmosphere in the auditorium is a crucial part of the artistic experience. Every performance of every play is subtly different, not so much because actors have off days, or choose to vary their performance from one evening to the next, but because every audience is different, has a different energy, reacts differently to what happens on stage and therefore affects and alters that performance.

The way the audience reacts should, therefore, be a part of any critic's review. Did he or she hate the performance? Fine. Say so. But also record the fact that, as they sat glowering, at the curtain call the rest of the house was on its feet, cheering and whistling a beaming line-up on stage.

Whether a reviewer is fair or not, it remains the case that what they write matters. Good reviews are quoted in press releases, on posters, on displays on the walls of the theatres. They generate interest and enthusiasm, they raise a cast's morale, they encourage people to go to the theatre and if the play is indeed a good one then they will have contributed to the most important element in any show's success – word of mouth.

16

The Actors' Church

Given that the church and the theatre are alike in many ways, it is entirely fitting that actors' should have their very own church. This is St Paul's, Covent Garden, whose portico, facing onto the west side of the Piazza, was the setting for the first meeting between Eliza Doolittle and Professor Henry Higgins, in *My Fair Lady*.

The church was built in 1633, at the time when the whole area was being transformed into a smart new residential district, to the north of the Strand, which had traditionally been the location for the mansions (between today's Strand and the Thames) of the nobility.

Any residential area required a church, but the architect, Inigo Jones – who was also a theatre designer specializing in masques, a form of Court entertainment – was asked to build something cheap and simple. 'Perhaps the ecclesiastical equivalent of a barn?' he was asked. 'I shall give you the finest barn in Christendom', he replied, and proceeded to do just that. Other than the classical portico on the Piazza, this could indeed be a grand stone barn rather than a conventional church.

The design of the interior is similarly simple, with the added advantage of being light and airy. It is not a beautiful church, nor a very interesting one, but its simplicity has an appeal, and means there is plenty of room on the walls for plaques and other inscriptions to, and mementos of, past theatrical luminaries. While St Paul's is known as the actors' church the walls commemorate a wide variety of theatrical professions, including ballerinas, lighting designers and playwrights.

Although the feel is one of theatre rather than screen, there are also plaques (wooden ones, at the west end of the church) to stars of screen as well as of stage. Vivien Leigh is one who easily glided between the two disciplines, but Boris Karloff, for example, will always be thought of exclusively in terms of his career as a star of horror films – especially *Frankenstein*. Television stars are here too, like Richard Beckinsale, the good-looking young star of *Porridge* and *Rising Damp*.

Given its associations, and its location in the centre of Covent Garden, St Paul's is often used for theatrical funerals and memorial services – as well as, happily, for weddings. Among the latter was that of Aled Jones, the boy soprano who had an enduring hit with the song 'Walking In the Air' (from *The Snowman*) and who, some years later appeared as Joseph in Lloyd Webber and Rice's *Joseph and the Amazing Technicolor Dreamcoat*.

The current incumbent of St Paul's, the Revd. Simon Grigg, has an easy way with him, which is ideal for memorial services, which, unlike the inevitably sad funerals, are supposed to be occasions for celebrating a life's work rather than mourning a life's passing. He presided at the memorial service for Graham Payn, the long-term lover of Noël Coward, who survived the Master by some 30 years.

Speaking to the congregation, Mr Grigg welcomed them to 'this theatre – I mean this church!' and his infectious sense of humour was exactly right for the occasion. Given that Payn had first been linked with Coward over 50 years earlier and that Coward himself had died in 1973, there was a strange sense of dissociation about the memorial service – as if one had somehow stumbled back in time to something that was of an earlier era. There was a similarly strange sense to the funeral of President Reagan in 2004.

Reagan belonged to the 1980s, not to the 2000s. He had been, in effect, dead for years, due to the mental ravages of Alzheimer's disease, so the funeral rites, however noble and deserved, seemed to be some 20 years too late. The world had moved on, as it had after Coward, though at least Coward, who lived through the theatre, has continued to display his talent to amuse in theatre productions all over the world, and will do so long after anyone who knew him has themselves had their memorial service.

The etiquette of theatrical memorial services – and even funerals – is different to that of other such events. Some thespians seem to see St Paul's church (whether they are planning a service or taking part in one) as just another theatre space, albeit a rather formal one.

When friends and colleagues speak about the deceased, let alone sing a song or recite a poem in their honour, the congregation – which on these occasions could as accurately be described as an audience – will applaud. This would be deeply frowned upon by normal congregations, but, given that applause would have been the life blood of the deceased, and still is of those gathered to commemorate and celebrate him or her, applause seems somehow fitting, despite the religious setting in which it is heard.

Outside, between the church and Bedford Street, is St Paul's Churchyard. This takes the form of a modest but attractive garden. A lawn, divided in two parts by a central path and surrounded by trees and shrubs, provides a welcome green oasis in the heart of the very urban Covent Garden. Office workers and young lovers use the garden during the day, especially in the lunch hour. The garden is locked every evening, often fairly early on, so it also maintains a sense of tranquillity, even mystery, given that for so many hours of the day it is deserted.

As with any such area and given its historic location, it is tempting to think of benign ghosts being present, perhaps of some of those whose names are inscribed on the many memorial benches which line the central pathway and other paved areas round the side of the church. If that is so, they will be joined by those of the pets of local residents who have the unofficial privilege, if they ask the rector, of burying them deep in the churchyard grounds, underneath the bushes.

Theatre cats have a long tradition in the West End, for obvious pest-control reasons, and the species were the inspiration for T. S. Eliot's poems, which Andrew Lloyd Webber and Cameron Mackintosh turned into the massive critical and commercial international success that was *Cats*.

17

Selling the Show

However good a play, however big the star, shows still need to be sold. This is done through press and public relations work and, in the case of the bigger shows, through marketing. The two are of course closely related and are both vehicles for letting the public know about the show and in the best possible way.

Theatreland's dominant marketing company is undoubtedly Dewynters. The company is based in a large building that takes up much of the west side of Leicester Square and has an impressive art deco entrance. Under the direction of Anthony Pye-Jeary, Dewynters handles the accounts for many of the West End's musicals, including recent blockbusters like *Oliver!*

The company has always worked closely with the producer Cameron Mackintosh and is responsible for the eye-catching posters promoting his shows on buses, in underground stations and elsewhere. Designs that are originated here are also found on the usual range of lucrative merchandise – t-shirts, mugs, posters, etc. – that are sold in the theatres where the musicals are playing.

Dewynters also produce programmes and souvenir brochures. These are the responsibility of producers of shows rather than the theatres in which they appear, and they too can be a useful source of income – one reason why they have become noticeably more expensive over the last decade.

Programmes are not just a souvenir of the show, they are a useful source of information about it, with their cast and creative team biographies, brief history of the theatre in which they are sold, and an article or two on the play itself.

Theatre programmes vary wildly in the size and quality of articles that they provide, and the range here is dependent on the show (some are more inherently easy to write articles about, or around, the subject matter the shows deal with) and on the amount the producer is prepared to pay to commission a writer to provide them.

The subsidized theatres (the National, the Royal Opera House, the Coliseum) are generally able to produce the most informative articles in their programmes. This is partly because they have the money to spend on such things, but more importantly there is a sense, given they receive public subsidy, that they have a remit to educate as well as entertain, so they have to provide as much information about the background to the play/ballet/opera as possible.

That is not to say that commercial companies don't provide good notes as well. The programme for *The 39 Steps*, for example, has an article on the writer John Buchan, another on the three film versions of Buchan's original novel, and a piece on 'The cult of the great British hero', looking at *The 39 Steps'* Richard Hannay and some of the other fictional gentlemen-adventurers who followed after his appearance in the pages of Buchan's thriller in 1915. The stage play is discussed in greater detail in Chapter 25 of this book.

Programmes are important social records as well. Looking at old programmes in the collection of the Theatre Museum or the Mander and Mitchenson Collection, the adverts that they contain give a vivid glimpse into the world in which they were produced.

Programmes from the 1930s show the flourishing trade in restaurants that seemed to cater mainly for theatre-going customers. As plays tended to start rather later than today (hence the title of Noël Coward's *Tonight at 8.30*) customers could eat before shows with less haste than they need now.

Other regular adverts were for cold cream, endorsed by leading actresses who would enthusiastically recommend the use of lashings of the stuff, and for cigarettes. This was the golden age of cigarette smoking, sandwiched between the Victorian disapproval that saw men banished to smoking rooms, wearing smoking jackets so the smell of smoke wouldn't emerge from the rooms with them and the current health-led campaign against the perils of passive smoking, let alone the active kind.

Today's programmes also include adverts for restaurants or bars, but tend more to cross-promote other West End shows, as well as clothes or, on occasion (depending on the show) private schools. The adverts tend to be more specific to the show – *The 39 Steps* programme, for example, has a back-cover advert for an apartment near where John Buchan wrote the original novel.

However informative they may be, programmes are in effect after-the-event: they are bought by people who have already seen the show, as they are only on sale at the theatre, or in the National Theatre's case, at the theatre bookshop. Some commercial theatres also sell them at the box office, but the point is that it is only personal callers at the theatre who are presumably going to see/have seen the show who will buy one.

So how are the public attracted to the show in the first place? The primary role falls to the press representative, or 'rep'. His or her (women have now achieved a much higher profile in this part of the theatre industry) role is to make sure that publicity photographs of the cast are taken (for use in promotional material), that information about the show (basic details such as its name, which theatre it's on at, when it opens, performance times, ticket prices) are included in the appropriate listings (newspapers, magazines, websites, etc.) and that articles or interviews relating to the show appear wherever possible.

The appearance of the latter depends to a great deal on the show having high-profile actors, as most papers and magazines tend to be personality-led rather than content-led. The fact that David Tennant was playing Hamlet, for example, was what saw a flood of articles and profiles in the press ahead of the play opening at the Novello in December 2008, rather than the fact that the Royal Shakespeare Company were bringing *Hamlet* to the West End.

Theatre publicity is one area that has been relatively slow to change for the times. Throughout the twentieth century the boxes that were ticked by press reps tended to be the same, with the occasional addition of a new magazine or newspaper. For decades the twin pillars of theatre publicity were *Time Out* and the *Evening Standard*, both aimed at Londoners and visitors to London and therefore more targeted than the (nonetheless influential) nationally distributed newspapers.

With the advent of the internet this has now changed. The two most influential websites are arguably www.whatsonstage.com and www.lastminute.com. The latter took over www.theatrenow.com, a classy website set up by a consortium of the theatre producers and industry insiders that had a large readership and growing ticket sales, based on special deals with theatres, and made money from the publicity that the site's articles and interviews generated. The new owners changed the name and eventually dispensed with any substantial editorial and now concentrates just on ticket sales, of which it has a very high turnover.

The owners of www.whatsonstage.com not only maintain a website that is packed with editorial about Theatreland, they also publish a free monthly magazine of the same name, available at most theatres, with news, profiles, interviews and commentary on the current state of Theatreland.

Radio has been with us since the 1920s, has survived the rivalry offered by television and is an increasing rather than diminishing resource when it comes to theatre promotion. Capital Radio and LBC are both influential in sending listeners to the theatre and are targeted by press reps, especially if they have a star willing to head into the recording studio.

Television offers the *Newsnight Review*, where a panel of usually literary figures, chaired by a regular *Newsnight* presenter, head off to see a play and a film or exhibition, or read a book, and then comment on it on air on a Friday night. There is also the South Bank Show, whose profiles of arts figures can include theatrical ones who have a show about to open.

These two flagships of the BBC and independent television sail a lonely path through the airwaves, as there is no regular theatre programme on mainstream TV. Theatre only gets mentioned on the news if there has been a disaster (Peter O'Toole's Old Vic *Hamlet*) or a major Hollywood star has caused a sensation. One such was Nicole Kidman (then married to Tom Cruise) in *The Blue Room* at the Donmar Warehouse. Appearing opposite Iain Glen, she was vividly described by the *Daily Telegraph*'s theatre critic, Charles Spencer, as 'pure theatrical Viagra'.

Given that more people attend live theatre every week than attend football matches, it is culturally curious that sport should be given a regular slot on the national news programmes, whereas theatre never is. This means that the transfer of a major player or an injury that keeps another from an important match may well make the BBC's Ten O'Clock News or ITV's News at Ten, whereas a Titania's indisposition or a particularly well-reviewed opening night performance of Pinter's *The Caretaker*, or the opening of a run of Alan Ayckbourn plays fails to get a mention.

The one exception to this has been the popularity of reality-TV shows that let the public vote on who should play a leading role in a forthcoming West End musical. This formula, which began looking for a Maria in *The Sound of Music*, continued with clothing a Joseph in a Technicolor dreamcoat before deciding who would play the role of the cheerful cockney barmaid Nancy in *Oliver!*

It was during the run of *Any Dream Will Do*, looking for a Joseph, that criticism of what was seen by some as using public (licence payers') money to promote a private commercial operation – a revival of Lloyd Webber and Rice's biblical musical at the Adelphi Theatre – began. As the search for Nancy continued, Kevin Spacey, the artistic director of the Old Vic, publicly wondered why a similar television programme could not be dedicated to straight rather than musical theatre.

Whatever the artistic merits of casting a role through an extended public audition, the programmes made for exciting and involving television and helped promote theatre to a wider audience, which was by definition good for Theatreland. It also meant, as the various contestants sang their hearts out before a panel of judges made up of Theatreland figures like actors Denise Van Outen and John Barrowman, as well as veteran producer Bill Kenwright, that on Saturday night, prime-time British television was broadcasting a string of musical theatre songs rather than the endless procession of police and hospital dramas that otherwise populate the small screen.

Even if this does shine the spotlight on a handful of musicals, to their inevitable financial advantage, there seems nothing wrong in that. The reason they have been adopted by television is that, apart from the sense of drama generated by the contest for the roles, the roles themselves are in exciting large-scale musicals whose songs are a fondly remembered part of many people's childhoods and will attract family audiences to the shows.

This is in no way more sinister than showing football matches between leading clubs, thereby giving both the game and the clubs enormous publicity. Given the difficulty of getting television to take theatre seriously, any programme that promotes it and encourages more people to try it should be applauded.

Shows with a lower profile do not have access to such exposure, but despite newspaper circulations supposedly being on the decline, the number of pages and supplements to existing newspapers seems to have expanded enormously in the last ten years and today's Saturday papers are almost as bulky as Sunday ones used to be. This means there is a plethora of pages to be filled, which offers opportunities to press reps who are prepared to be proactive in finding outlets for publicity for the plays they represent.

One area that producers have realized can be a major help in selling tickets is education. Yes, they pay lip service to the altruistic delights of introducing young people to the theatre, but the bottom line is that coachloads of schoolchildren coming to see a musical make for a lot of ticket sales.

As a result canny producers have expanded their links with schools and colleges, offering not just ticket discounts but education packs, whether online or in print, which the students can access before or after seeing the show. But again, however genuine their commitment to creating a new generation of theatregoers by introducing them to the delights of stage musicals, the bottom line is always revenue.

The final stage of selling shows is one of the oldest and simplest: getting theatre critics into the theatre and providing as hospitable a climate as possible within which they view the show.

This generally takes the initial form of carefully prepared smiles of welcome from the press reps and their assistants, who stand behind press tables (it really is that old-fashioned) to hand out tickets in envelopes to the assorted ladies and gentlemen of the press. This can lead to the other meaning of 'press', with journalists bumping into each other while resisting the onward flow of normal theatregoers anxious to get past them and into the bars before the performance starts.

The press corps are offered interval drinks and, if they are lucky, a selection of sandwiches (the egg sandwiches at the *Carousel* press launch were delicious).

As one of the drawbacks of all save the subsidized theatres and opera houses is that there are no sandwiches available for sale to the general public before the show or in the interval, those on display in the area roped off for the press tend to be looked at enviously by everyone else. If there were ever to be a riot in a theatre it would be not over the bar prices or the sight-lines of customers' seats, but because someone finally snapped and clambered over the rope towards the sandwich tray.

Whether the press like a play or not naturally depends on the performance, and can be surprisingly hard to judge from the body language in the interval – they are all too busy stuffing themselves with whatever food is available, or being polite to anxious theatre executives trying to jolly them along. Immediately after the curtain falls those critics sitting on the aisle tend to get up and rush out. In the case of the major national newspapers, they still need to send in their reports more or less immediately, so they can appear in the papers the next day.

That they still do so (as does the *Evening Standard*, which has a marginally longer lead-in time, given that it appears in afternoon and evening editions) adds to the sense of excitement generated by a first night. It is a tradition for actors to claim they never read their reviews but it is a claim that should in most cases be taken with a large pinch of salt. Even if the claim is true, the rest of the cast will read the reviews and make sure that everyone in the company is aware of exactly what they contain.

18

What about the Audience?

However hard a press rep works, whatever the theatre critic then makes of the show, however inventive a producer is at finding ways to generate follow-up publicity or to offer special ticket deals, it is the audience who ultimately decides whether a show works or not. It is their arrival at the theatre and experience of the performance that is the whole point of the entire industry. Whether it is critical praise or financial profit that drives anyone in Theatreland, nothing is possible without the audience.

So what is the experience of going to a West End theatre like, and how has it differed from theatregoing in the past? Is there anything about it that needs to change? What stands in the way of such change?

The experience of watching a play or musical has not fundamentally altered for over a century, other than in technical advances, which have made unobtrusive but significant improvements in sound and light possible.

Audiences are still segregated by ticket price, and though these days they may go in through the same foyer (though some theatres, like the St Martin's, home of *The Mousetrap*, still have separate entrances for the cheap seats) once they are inside they have their own bars, lavatories, mini-foyers and even if they enter through the same doors, they will be disgorged into the street through different ones.

One major distinction between theatres is that of alcohol in the auditorium. Some theatres will let you take it in in plastic glasses, others refuse to allow it in at all. Patrons can be upset even at the restriction on glass, and an assistant manager at the St Martin's once had a glass of wine thrown over him by a belligerent customer when he asked him to swap the glass for plastic before taking his drink to his seat.

A new hazard, for actors and audience alike, is the advent of mobile phones. Some theatres resort to playing ring tones loudly through the speaker system before the lights go down, and accompany this with an exhortation to turn off the mobiles.

Some such messages verge on the nannyish, with extra instructions about double-checking that the phones are indeed off, and even asking patrons to check once again on returning to their seats after the interval. These announcements can be almost as intrusive, in their way, as phones themselves. Almost.

The press night of *Carousel*, at the Savoy Theatre in December 2008 had one of its most dramatic moments ruined by just such a phone call. Billy Bigelow (Jeremiah James) had just killed himself after a botched mugging, and his still-warm body was being mourned over by his wife Julie (Alexandra Silber) and by Nellie, played by Lesley Garrett.

Garrett, who made her name at English National Opera, was gearing herself up for her show-stopping number, 'You'll Never Walk Alone', which is meant as a consolation to the grieving Julie. The actresses were just registering despair to a deeply sympathetic, teary-eyed audience when a mobile phone rang out. Then again – and again, before eventually being turned off or switching to the answer phone.

There are another nuisances, of course. Patrons who fall asleep and snore loudly. Patrons who rustle sweet papers – which could be stopped by theatres cancelling the policy of selling noisy sweets at their kiosks in the first place. It is surprising that no such voluntary ban has come into place.

Patrons also talk to each other during performances. This used to be taboo, and it was said that anyone who tried to do so while sitting in an auditorium full of Wagner fans would be lucky to emerge alive. Nowadays it is almost commonplace.

This is partly a class thing, in that it tends to be people up in town on a Friday or Saturday night, often at musicals, who talk as if they are at home. This is also true of patrons who don't normally go to the theatre but are keen to see a movie star on stage – especially if he or she is in a play that was once a film. Kathleen Turner in *The Graduate* and Josh Hartnett in *Rain Main* both attracted this demographic.

It is also a generational thing. Today's audiences of all ages, but particularly the young, have grown up in the age of the television rather than of live performance. They are used to commenting to their friends and relatives round the set, and have little or no empathy for, or interest in, the other members of the audience.

This sort of behaviour can happen even in the most expensive seats. People who can't behave properly at a theatre take great exception to being hushed by anyone, and those who have forked out £60 or so for their seats seem to feel even greater entitlement to speak their mind than those in the balcony.

Patrons who misbehave can be of any class, and some of the more bizarre stories of audience behaviour have emerged from the stalls at the Coliseum. On one occasion an usher noticed that a woman was taking a large bag with her into the auditorium. This itself would normally have been frowned on, but in this case the bag was cradled in the patron's arms rather than being carried by its handles. It was also moving.

On approaching the woman, the usher could see a small dog inside – the bag was open a little to give the animal some air. Not quite sure what to do, the usher simply stared the patron in the eye – she had been looking furtively behind her – and said, loudly and firmly, 'Woof! Woof!' The woman took the hint, turned round and left the theatre.

Another patron at the Coliseum once complained to the astonished duty manager that the female lavatories were a disgrace. Her problem? That the washbasins were too high for her to comfortably bathe her feet in them.

Occasionally patrons will get aggressive. This tends to happen at lowbrow musicals, but has also occurred at the Coliseum. Back in the 1980s the theatre manager had a policy of only hiring firemen (who doubled as a security presence during performances) who were very tall and powerfully built – a policy that calmed several otherwise excitable and potentially dangerous customers.

There is an old tradition of violence in theatres, but that was associated with the eighteenth century, a period of lawlessness and public drunkenness that seems to be returning after the sober and lawful public behaviour that characterized the later Victorian era and the great majority of the twentieth century. There were riots at Covent Garden (in the building on the site of the current opera house) when prices were substantially increased after the theatre had been extensively refurbished.

Not that the twentieth century didn't have its moments too. The Coliseum was the scene of a fist-fight on stage in January 1933, at the final curtain call of the musical (about the eighteenth century lothario) *Casanova*.

The part had been played alternately by two actors, who hated each other. The fight broke out when the actor who was not performing on the final night was invited (at the insistence of the theatre owner) to join his colleagues in taking a final bow. When he did so, it was in costume, as Casanova. This infuriated the other actor, who had to be pulled off him by a sobbing leading lady. The spat reached the front page of the *Daily Mail*.

Verbal violence is a related issue. Mary Ellis, Ivor Novello's leading lady first in *Glamorous Night* (1935) and then in *The Dancing Years* (1939), was livid when Roma Beaumont (aunt of the film director Sir David Puttnam), a new star and the female juvenile lead in *The Dancing Years*, stopped the show with her number

'Primrose'. As the applause carried on, each new wave of it replacing the previous one, Ellis stood in the wings, waiting to come on for her next scene, out of sight of the audience but in view and earshot of Miss Beaumont, snarling 'Get off! That's enough! Get off!'

More common is for audiences to express themselves vocally to actors – which raises the question or whether or not to boo. Booing used to be far more common at theatres than it is today, as Tony Field recalled in an article for *The Stage* in November 1991, when he described an extraordinary scene between Sophie, a well-known member of the Gallery First Nighters Club (who saw every show from the cheap seats) and William Douglas-Home, the playwright brother of conservative peer and later Prime Minster, Alec Douglas-Home.

The occasion was the first-night curtain call of Douglas-Home's play *Ambassador Extraordinary*, at the Aldwych Theatre in 1948. In response to sustained booing a defiant Douglas-Home shouted, 'The time will come when you will have to listen to what this play tells you'. To which Sophie replied 'Rubbish, young man!' The playwright tried to fight back: 'I don't mind being heckled, Sophie'. As ever, she had the last (and better) word: 'You are not being heckled. You are being judged!'

Booing only very rarely occurs (unless it is cheerfully ironic, as when a villain takes a curtain call) in commercial theatre. It is much more common at the otherwise rarefied environment of an opera house, for opera lovers seem either to feel more passionately about performances or to be simply more difficult to please and more expressive in letting director and cast know their feelings.

The most extraordinary first night in the last quarter of a century, in terms of audience reaction, must surely be English National Opera's *Mazeppa*. This romantic story of a Cossack rebel was given a very modern make-over, with the curtain coming down on characters dressed like Mafiosi. This was provoking enough – although having characters (whatever the opera, whatever the period it was written or set in) dressed and behaving like 1950s Mafia was an all-too regular characteristic of English National Opera in the 1980s, though did work very well in director Jonathan Miller's Mafia version of Verdi's *Rigoletto*.

Mafia overcoats would not have caused the boos on their own. What caused the most sustained, stormiest – and most exhilarating – jeers and catcalls anyone present that night is ever likely to experience, was that the characters on stage were, as the curtain fell, hacking each other to death with chainsaws, as a deluge of blood was sprayed across the set.

The other side of the coin is the question of when to applaud. Here there is an unwritten convention that still holds across Theatreland. Audiences do not applaud in the course of a drama – however good a performance, however powerful a speech. Nevertheless, they do applaud at a particularly good speech – or even one-liner – during a comedy, when they feel that something even stronger than laughter is deserved.

Audiences applaud not just at the end of scenes in ballet but many times during them if (as with, for example, *Sleeping Beauty*) there are a series of 'turns', with displays of virtuoso classic dancing by a succession of performers within a scene. In this case each dancer gets his or her share of applause once they have finished their routine.

As a result, regular attendees of the ballet, however small and frail they may look, develop enormously strong wrists, which they need to sustain the amount of clapping required to do the dancers justice. This is especially true of the curtain calls, which can seem – even to the greatest fan – interminable.

In the mid-1980s Rudolf Nureyev used to tour, and brought his ballet company to the Coliseum for a summer season. By then he was unable to dance properly, let alone in the dazzling way he had over 20 years earlier when he arrived in London after his dramatic defection at Paris airport. At the time, his insistence on continuing to 'star' in classic ballets, where he more or less walked around the stage (albeit very elegantly) seemed absurd and demeaning. In retrospect, given we now know he was suffering not just from advancing years but also from the ravages of AIDS, his determination to keep going seems not ridiculous but heroic.

What cannot be excused, however, was his relentless milking of applause, which kept audiences in their seats long after they should have emerged into the warmth of a summer's evening in St Martin's Lane and headed for the nearest bar or restaurant. Nureyev would keep coming back for yet another curtain call even if only the most desultory clapping was all that an exhausted and by now irritated audience could manage. On one such occasion it looked as if he had finally disappeared when one devoted (or perhaps deranged) fan slapped his or her hands together in a final gesture of adoration. Somehow, through the thickness of the Coliseum's curtain, Nureyev's antennae picked up the noise, as a bat's must the sound of an insect victim, and he re-emerged, wearing a surprised but triumphant smile.

Opera audiences and the singers who entertain them enjoy a modified version of ballet etiquette when it comes to applause. Here the audience also applauds during a performance, but only after an impressive rendition of a well-known aria. Curtain calls, as at the ballet, are more vocal than with most theatre audiences, with cheers and cries of 'Bravo!' at the men and 'Brava!' at the women (by those who want to show they can speak Italian). Singers love several curtain calls too, but they have the grace to leave the stage earlier than dancers do.

Ballet and opera audiences have historically been more likely, too, to give a standing ovation, but this has changed in the twenty-first century, with an increasing number of theatre audiences (generally at musicals, especially lowbrow ones) enthusiastically rising to their feet, while yelling and whistling.

One reason for the increasing trend to stand at the curtain call is that audiences can't bear the cramped leg room a moment longer. As already mentioned in this book, both of London's opera houses and a number of her theatres (with Cameron Mackintosh leading the way for commercial theatre owners) have undergone extensive refurbishment and improvement, but it is still the case that the majority of Theatreland's theatres were designed and built when the average person was several inches shorter than we are today.

Theatre owners and producers are faced with the fundamental problem that to make every seat substantially larger and more comfortable, with increased leg room to match, would be wholly uneconomic. Given human evolution and the continuing trend for people to become taller (and often wider) this is a problem that will eventually have to be resolved, but in the meantime audiences have come to accept that a level of comfort they would find intolerable in a cinema is simply part of the theatre experience. The fact that according to the Society of London Theatre a substantial percentage of theatre visitors travel by train may explain why people are inured to this level of discomfort: at least theatres don't charge for seats then, having sold too many, expect patrons to stand.

There are some standing places in theatres (and again this is more of a feature in opera houses) but these places are by definition very cheap and are only for the hardy. Shakespeare's Globe has bucked the trend by making a (historical) feature of patrons standing, though at the Globe they are in front of the stage and very much part of the action, whereas at the Royal Opera House they are at the back of the auditorium, out of view. The retro-poverty chic of Shakespeare's Globe has its charm, and is an ingenious way of packing people into the playhouse at minimal expense.

By way of compensation, the Globe is very good at providing an interesting range of refreshments, unlike most theatre bars, which supply over-priced wine and spirits in cramped conditions. The Trafalgar Studios, at the top of Whitehall, by Trafalgar Square, used to be the Whitehall Theatre before being renamed and divided in two auditoria, the main one of which has an unnervingly steep tier of seats that has *The Sound of Music* aria 'Climb Every Mountain' springing to mind if you are unlucky enough to have a seat near the top. The wine here seems even more expensive than elsewhere (or so it feels when one goes to pay), but at least the quality reflects the skill of whoever chooses the theatre supplies, as it is among the best wine served in Theatreland.

Ivan Putrov in *The Prodigal Son* – a Ballets Russes classic

The main problem with theatre bars is not the cost of the drink. Nor is it the lack of nourishing snacks. It's the lack of staff. Given the pittance that front-of-house workers earn, theatre owners should, as a general rule, hire more staff to serve at the bars. Intervals in theatres are never longer than 20 minutes and are quite often only 15. It's different at Covent Garden, especially in triple bills of ballet, where the intervals can last as long as the performances, but then at the Royal Opera House, enjoying the surroundings and entertaining clients is for many people the whole point. In most other theatres, however, intervals are a chance for the loo or for a drink and a chat.

Women suffer from the relative shortage of ladies' lavatories, especially as the turn-around time for visits is longer. That this is a historical architectural hangover from Victorian times when less women would go to the theatre (these days they make up a majority) and those that did would not, if they were ladies, be expected to go to the bar, is no comfort to today's female theatregoers. Nor is the little gem of cultural history, explained in a survey by the Theatres Trust, that such female lavatories as were provided were for the use of wealthier patrons and were therefore not intended for use by more than a small proportion of the audience.

So for women patrons even more than men, the shortage of available time in an interval makes a quick and efficient service at the bar an essential part of an enjoyable trip to the theatre. The employment of a less than ideal number of staff detracts from this enjoyment, as does the modern insistence on using electronic tills. Things were much better when old dears were employed with just dishes for the change. They may have been able to fiddle the odd pound here and there but that was a minimal cost compared to the greater turnover of drinks sales that they invariably managed, compared with today's hesitant youngsters, shackled to their temperamental machines.

The other area of the theatre experience that was also better in the not-so-distant past was going to a box office. It used to be the case that you could phone the box-office number for a theatre and actually be put through to that theatre's box office and speak to staff who knew something about the building and the play or musical or opera that was being presented inside it. Today you are almost always directed to a call centre somewhere and, even if it is run by a theatre chain, the staff are not sitting in the theatre whose tickets they are selling.

Yes, today the buying of tickets via the internet has revolutionized the process, not least because producers seem far happier, for some psychological reason, to offer very cheap deals on the internet rather than in the press.

Yes, computers also enable producers and their accountants to break down box-office figures in a great variety of ways, some of which may even be helpful to them. But when box offices were staffed by little old dears (of both sexes) who used paper seating plans and marked off reserved or sold tickets by pen, there were fewer double bookings and purchasing or collecting tickets by hand was as convenient and often much quicker than it is in the age of the computer.

The Coliseum was the last major theatre to computerize, long after everyone else had, yet its box office was easily as efficient as its more technologically advanced equivalents in the rest of Theatreland.

One reason the Coliseum finally switched over was the difficulty for the staff in coping with the vast range of different prices, dependent on the deals on offer, that were being presented to the public. In the internet age the way of doing business means that computers have become necessary. That this is a sign of the times does not make it necessarily a good thing – any more than the modern banking practices that have cost ordinary people tens of billions of pounds in the last year or so must be better than the older, more stable, risk-averse practices, just because they are modern.

One modern Theatreland development that is definitely not an advance is the habit of charging customers a booking fee, even if they are simply phoning the box office. Only callers in person, at the theatre itself, are not charged two or more pounds for the privilege of buying a ticket to see the show – and this at a time when top-price seats at West End musicals can be £60 per head. If the theatre industry wants to show that it is feeling its customers' pain and wants to make the experience more affordable, cutting these booking charges would be the decent thing to do.

19

Preserving the Past/Ensuring the Future

Theatreland's past is evident in more than the old bricks and plaster of its playhouses. Inside the theatres there are often busts or other mementos of the actors and actresses who have played on stage within their walls. These are seen by theatregoers who have bought tickets to see plays rather than the general public. The latter are catered for by a handful of statues on the outside, and, on the inside, by collections such as that at the National Portrait Gallery (known to its regulars as the NPG), which holds a vast stock of paintings, cartoons, drawings and photographs.

It is outside the NPG that one of the few public statues in Theatreland of theatre figures (rather than the usual collection of generals and members of the royal family) stands. The person commemorated is Sir Henry Irving, who has the distinction of being the first actor to be knighted – by Queen Victoria, in 1895.

Prior to this, actors – and especially actresses – were seen as being morally suspect and socially unacceptable – hence Richard Brinsley Sheridan's desperation to be seen as a politician rather than a playwright and theatre owner. At a stroke of the Queen-Empress's sword, this all changed. Irving's knighthood meant that acting could now be seen as an artistic endeavour rather than mere entertainment. In an age when stockbrokers and solicitors were seen, by the landed gentry, as one step above tradesmen, actors were still far from being gentlemen, but they were now ranked as highly as artists, sculptors or composers of serious music.

The best part of Irving's career was spent at the Lyceum, a large playhouse in Wellington Street, Covent Garden, near the junction between the Strand and the Aldwych. Here, from the early 1870s to the end of the century, he was the leading actor-manager of his generation, heading a company that produced the spectacular stagings that Victorian audiences loved.

Irving's most famous role, in a career that had many highlights, was as

Matthias, the central character in the melodrama *The Bells*. The plot is about an old man whose wealth is based on a murder of a rich merchant that he committed many years before. Now, years later, at a family celebration, the guilt that he has suppressed for decades bursts out, as he imagines that he hears the sleigh bells that heralded the arrival of his victim all those years ago.

The Lyceum was condemned to be pulled down in a road-widening scheme introduced by the London County Council in 1939. At a farewell gala performance that year, John Gielgud (whose great-aunt Ellen Terry had been Henry Irving's leading lady on stage and, it was reputed, in his bed as well) gave a suitably theatrical curtain-call cry of 'Long live the Lyceum!'

One of the few happy side-effects of the Second World War was that the London County Council had more important things to worry about than widening the roads, and the Lyceum plan was quietly shelved, not only for the duration of the conflict, but after it too.

The theatre may have been spared, but it went into a period of decline, and was for many years used as a dance hall. The dances held here were very popular, but were not what the architects had had in mind, and Irving's ghost must have been looking very stern as young couples gyrated to rock and roll.

Eventually the theatre was bought by Andrew Lloyd Webber, who restored it at great expense and re-launched it in 1996 – a fact marked by a panel on one side of the portico that fronts the building and is one of its most impressive features. The show re-opened with a gala performance, in front of the Prince of Wales, of the show that Lloyd Webber moved into the theatre – a revival of his early hit (with Tim Rice), *Jesus Christ Superstar*.

At the back of the restored Lyceum, carved in stone, are three names: Irving – Sir Henry Irving of course; Terry – Irving's leading lady, Ellen Terry; and the name of Irving's business manager. The business brains behind successful actor-managers rarely get a mention in the history books, let alone immortalized in stone in a central London street, on the outside of one of the capital's largest theatres.

The reason for this man's inclusion is that he decided to try to earn some extra money – despite having a very good job – by writing a novel. He did so, and the book, published in 1897, was *Dracula*. Bram Stoker, its author, is now far more famous than his sometime employer – a fact that would astonish not only Irving but his contemporaries, and which is in itself a statement about the transience of fame.

It is also a commentary on the inevitably fleeting nature of theatrical reputations, built as they are on transient performances that vanish with each curtain call. Literary reputations, by contrast, may change depending on public taste in fiction and different social or sexual mores, but at least the work itself is there, permanently, to be read and experienced by anyone as easily a century after it was written as on the day it was published.

The closest Irving has got to immortality is the statue, standing on a tall plinth which looks as if it was designed to keep vandals away from the great man. It also means that there is a certain distance between him and his admirers. These, in the form of the Irving Society, meet each February to mark Irving's birthday and congregate round the base of the statue.

A brief speech is made, a wreath is laid, with the help of a ladder, often supplied by David Drummond, the owner of London's best theatre memorabilia shop in nearby Cecil Court. After this short ceremony and a round of applause, the devotees set off for a gentle stroll (many of them are past the first flush of youth) through Covent Garden to the Club for Acts and Actors in Bedford Street.

This club, which has a hall (plus a small stage and piano) downstairs, and offices and a bar upstairs, is a throwback, in the nicest sense of the word, to the 1930s. You expect to see, on the panelled walls of the hall, a picture of King George VI and Queen Elizabeth, if not George V and Queen Mary. It also has about it something of the air of the drill hall that was the central point of the action in the long-running TV series *Dad's Army*. It looks as if Captain Mainwaring might appear at any moment, with a cross look and an exclamation of 'You stupid boy!'

In this suitably old-world hall the Irving Society holds its annual general meeting after the wreath-laying. This event includes a lecture, and past speakers have included Frances Hughes, an ex-headmistress and theatre expert who is arguably the best lecturer on theatre in London today. Her knowledge of her material is extraordinary, and she delivers it, without notes, in an authoritative but sprightly manner.

Another good speaker who has appeared here is, appropriately, Professor Jeffrey Richards, an expert on British cultural history who has numerous radio series and documentaries to his name as well as a string of books, including one on Henry Irving's acting career.

Other lecturers have included Sir Donald Sinden – who acted, as a young man, with a veteran actor who had been, in his youth, part of Irving's company – and Richard Briers, who is still best-known for his role in the 1970s TV sitcom *The Good Life*, but who is an accomplished stage actor whose theatre career was given a new lease of life through his association with Kenneth Branagh, who brought out of him a superb performance in *King Lear*, among other Shakespearean roles.

Henry Irving was one of the few men whom Oscar Wilde, the late Victorian playwright, author and wit, hero-worshipped. He thought Irving was a great artist, and watched him on stage whenever he could. His own stage career, as playwright, was a glittering one which ended in complete humiliation and despair.

Wilde, like Irving, has a statue in Covent Garden too, on its very edge, just off the Strand, near Charing Cross. The statue, by Maggie Hambling, is called 'A Conversation with Oscar Wilde', and shows the author's head and shoulders – and an arm, brandishing the inevitable cigarette – emerging from a coffin, which is designed to encourage passers-by to sit and, as it were, have a chat with Wilde on the way to the nearby railway station, or indeed to the theatre.

Wilde has many fans, for many different reasons, and in March 2008 about 120 of them, in two groups of 60, one in the morning and one in the afternoon, gathered at Wilde's statue. They were there not for a conversation with Oscar, but for a brief talk about by him the author, broadcaster and West End performer, Gyles Brandreth. Brandreth's musical, *Zipp!* in which 100 musicals were presented in the course of ninety minutes, played at the Duchess Theatre in 1999.

As much a polymath as Stephen Fry, Brandreth is also the author of a series of detective novels, set in late Victorian London, with Oscar Wilde as the hero, on the track of the perpetrator of various criminals whose activities affect him or his circle of friends. To promote the second in the series, *Oscar Wilde and the Ring of Death*, Brandreth was giving a Wilde's West End walking tour of Oscar's London, in which the Maggie Hambling statue was an essential stopping point.

Wilde's life and works are well known, but Brandreth made some interesting points about him, including that he was a regular traveller on the London underground, frequently going from Sloane Square (the nearest tube station to his house in Chelsea) into the West End. Brandreth reminded the audience that Wilde was happily married with two children before he discovered, or at least gave way to, his gay side, and that his sons suffered terribly from his disgrace. They were forbidden to talk about him at home and their mother changed their surname, to Holland, to distance them from their father's legacy. Vivian Holland, the older surviving son, married relatively late in life, and his widow was still alive when a commemorative window was unveiled in Westminster Abbey in 1995, to mark the centenary of the opening of Wilde's last and greatest play, *The Importance of Being Earnest*.

It was fascinating to be in the Abbey, to see and hear John Gielgud, who played in *The Importance of Being Earnest* on stage though not in the classic screen version in which Dame Edith Evans gave her definitive performance of Lady Bracknell, booming out the line (those who know the work will forgive the pun) 'A handbag!' in that uniquely deep, vibrato voice. What was most striking about

Oscar Wilde, playwright, author and wit

the group of dignitaries who proceeded down the aisle towards the window was the inclusion, among them, of Holland's widow, because it meant that there, in Westminster Abbey, in 1995, one was in the presence of Oscar Wilde's daughter-in-law!

The NPG has many pictures of Oscar Wilde, and of a whole range of other theatricals. Its acquisition policy means that even the youngest actors, writers and directors have had their images purchased and displayed, and the gallery has a policy of frequently changing the display of contemporary portraits on the ground floor.

A recent display included a photograph of Michael Boyd, the artistic director of the Royal Shakespeare Company, who looked out from the frame with his trademark rumpled charm, while a much larger photograph of Dame Judi Dench, wearing white, stared down rather fiercely from an adjoining room.

In person she has surprisingly sexy eyes – their piercing blue helps –for a woman in her 70s, but there is something about actresses that keeps the sex appeal going long after one might expect it to have gently moved away. The late Moira Lister, who began her career in England during the war, having braved the U-boats to sail from her native South Africa, still looked ravishing in her 80s. Not just well-preserved, or showing interesting traces of a past beauty, but still genuinely beautiful.

Acting is not always a beauty treatment, but there is something in the theatre tradition of 'Dr Theatre' – the almost miraculous way an actor who looks (and feels) like death seems to summon up reserves of energy when they walk through the stage door, and can get through a full-length play once they walk out of the wings onto the stage and in front of an audience.

This aspect of theatre life was brilliantly caught in Ronald Harwood's play, *The Dresser*. Produced at the Queen's Theatre, this starred Freddie Jones as 'Sir', a wartime actor manager very much in the mould of Sir Donald Wolfit, with Tom Courtenay as his devoted dresser.

Although *The Dresser* is set in the Second World War and strongly conveys a real sense of period detail, it is also a timeless piece about theatre: the backstage jealousies and tensions, the unnecessary tantrums and scenes, the selfishness, the ambition – and yet also the majesty and magic. Harwood's 'Sir' is also an extreme case of the power of theatre to enable a very sick man to somehow get through the toughest Shakespearean roles – though in this case the effort finally kills him.

Harwood has denied that 'Sir' is exactly modelled on Sir Donald, but he is a figure with many similarities to him. Wolfit, too, was an over-the-top (for today's taste) actor but, like 'Sir', he toured Shakespeare through wartime England, sometimes with a very inadequate supporting cast, given so many of the younger or fitter men had been called up to serve in the armed forces. On the other hand, this masked a tendency that Wolfit had not to be too choosy about his supporting actors as this meant that he – who was a first-rate Shakespearean – shone all the more when compared with them.

Despite his talent and the knighthood that was an entirely deserved recognition of it, Wolfit was professionally looked down on by fellow knights Laurence Olivier and John Gielgud. In their lifetime Olivier pulled away from any other rival to be the acknowledged head of his profession, though this must have grated with the slightly older Gielgud whose star had risen before Olivier's.

Despite this, Gielgud, with his Terry ancestry, had a strong sense of theatre history, and presented Olivier with a sword that had been handed to him by a leading actor of a previous generation. Olivier accepted the sword with alacrity. When, years later, asked to which rising young actor he intended to hand it on, Olivier snapped 'No one! It's mine!' It was that attitude that enabled Olivier to push himself in front of his nearest rivals and breast the tape before them in the competition to be regarded as the greatest living actor.

Olivier has plenty of pictures in the NPG, and a statue by the National Theatre, but it would be fascinating to see a joint sculpture of Olivier and Gielgud – perhaps with Ralph Richardson and Michael Redgrave, with Wolfit lurking behind them – like a theatrical version of the statues of the Burghers of Calais that stands in the park outside the House of Lords, opposite what used to the headquarters of the Church Commissioners at No.1 Millbank.

Alternatively, one wonders what has happened to the *Spitting Image* puppets that showed the aged Gielgud and Olivier forever reminiscing about their theatrical past while continuing their sublimated rivalry with each other into old age. The puppets, or copies of them, would sit very well in one of the modern display areas of the NPG. It is good to admire and be inspired by great figures of the past, as the founders of the gallery intended, but it is also healthy to have a sense of humour about them, too.

Two organizations that have the job of preserving Theatreland's past and ensuring its future are the Theatres Trust and the Society of London Theatre (SOLT). The latter is located in Rose Street, a little alley between Garrick Street and Floral Street in Covent Garden. Its office, to which it owns the freehold, is in a modernised building next to an ancient pub, the Lamb and Flag. It was in the tiny alleyway at the side of the pub that, in 1679, the playwright John Dryden (*Marriage a la Mode, All for Love*) was beaten almost to death by thugs allegedly hired by the Earl of Rochester, who thought Dryden had been the author of a lampoon on his lordship's character.

SOLT exists to protect and promote the interests of theatre owners and producers rather than battered playwrights, but in a wider sense it represents Theatreland as whole: in liaising with government about laws and regulations that affect theatre practice, in representing the industry overseas, in working with tourist organizations at events like the London Trade Fair and in promoting the cultural attractions that the capital offers to visitors from abroad.

SOLT's other ventures include the valuable service of running the TKTS reduced-price ticket sales booth in Leicester Square, which offers the long lines of customers cheap seats for selected Theatreland shows, and the national theatre token scheme.

SOLT publishes an annual report which, in the last couple of years in particular, has been very upbeat. Chief executive Richard Pulford is a well-dressed and aesthetic figure who is the only major Theatreland figure not only to be invariably seen in a suit and tie, but who also habitually wears a hat. This, combined with his penchant for a cigarette, gives him a very old-world appearance, though his mind and his job are both very much up to date.

The reasons for his patent optimism are borne out, in the small print, by the latest annual report, called *Pleasing Audiences* – it's nice that the annual report, like any West End show, has its own title. Pulford's report shows that in 2007 audience numbers reached 13.6 million, 10 per cent higher than the previous year. Gross receipts were up 18 per cent on 2006 with a figure of almost £470 million. As a result, the theatre industry paid £70 million in VAT.

Pulford is confident that, as in the past, any recession will encourage the public into the theatre rather than away from it. Terrorist threats are only temporary in their impact; the number of foreign visitors to London theatres is increasing; and the recent collapse of the pound can only help that trend, as staying in London and seeing a musical or play is increasingly affordable for tourists.

Pulford sees SOLT's primary role as maintaining a kind of order in Theatreland, by providing an established basis for staging shows in mainstream London theatres. As an umbrella organization, SOLT provides a structure within which the industry can work as well as representation that gives individual members a clout in dealing with unions or government that they – apart from the economic giants Andrew Lloyd Webber and Cameron Mackintosh – simply wouldn't have.

SOLT also extends its influence to the European Commission through its membership of a Europe-wide agency (of which Pulford is currently the President). This allows for SOLT to input on a wide variety of European measures, on such matters as working time, noise in the workplace and copyright.

SOLT's members are drawn from subsidized as well as commercial theatre, but Pulford sees the two as opposite sides of the same coin.

'Out of every ten "commercial" shows in the West End, only two will make their money back, only one will make a profit. The other seven lose money to some extent. No wonder they call investors angels. Some treat investment in theatre as a tax loss. Most enjoy above all the glamour of association with the theatre and those who work in it.'

Nevertheless, the theatre industry as a whole generates a huge amount of money and Pulford agrees that his own organization is in a healthy financial situation, not least thanks to its Theatre Tokens scheme. Theatre brings vast amounts of money into London: not just in terms of the ticket sales mentioned above but also in the wider expenditure that a visit to the theatre generates, especially for hotels, taxis, bars, cafés and restaurants. Given that 40 per cent of visitors to London claim that the theatre was their main reason for visiting, the contribution that the art form makes as an industry is staggering.

This was one of the main arguments for government support, to the tune of some £250 million that the Theatres Trust campaigned for in a 2004 report, *Act Now! Modernising London's Theatres*. The Trust argues that London's theatre stock was a historic resource and an economic powerhouse but that the financial realities (and planning regulation restrictions) of the twenty-first century are wholly different from that of the nineteenth and early twentieth centuries when they were constructed.

Act Now! gives an excellent background to the social and economic history of these theatres while explaining the economics of theatre ownership today and how the massive expenditure needed to bring an 1890s theatre up to the standards of comfort and convenience required by a modern audience cannot possibly generate a return in capital value, let alone revenue, that would bear any relation to the money spent.

The report fell on deaf ears, though Rosemary Squire attributes the failure to secure public funding for modernizing the theatres' facilities was due to the channelling of huge sums of money to the Olympics, and that, post-2012, it might be possible to reach some sort of compromise that would at least help today's theatre owners to make some improvements.

That would certainly be a welcome relief to theatregoers as they swelter in summer, in buildings that lack any sort of air conditioning, first because it wasn't invented when the theatres were built and secondly because listed buildings (as all but a handful of Theatreland's stock are) require vastly more money to install an air conditioning system than would a purpose-built new one.

The Theatres Trust, unlike SOLT, which is a private company, is a public body – The National Advisory Board for Theatres – with a board of trustees drawn from the theatre community and from architectural experts. It plays a vital part in protecting the theatrical heritage not just of London's theatres but of the whole country's. Located in modest offices in the Charing Cross Road, between the Garrick Theatre and Wyndham's, it produces a magazine that is far more than a dry run of statistics: it has a wide range of articles, lavishly illustrated, about theatres that it has helped protect or restore, as well as more general issues to do with theatre architecture.

The Theatres Trust may be about preserving theatres but it is not a dinosaur. It has a relatively young staff, a can-do attitude and has been prepared to accept, in some cases, that a theatre does not have a viable use as a theatre any more, and that it can therefore be allowed to be replaced. These cases are not always that simple: it is now common practice to seek a compromise when larger buildings are concerned, to see if, say, a studio theatre can be included in a mixed-use redevelopment of a large theatre site.

The Trust's current success in protecting our theatrical inheritance was born, phoenix-like, from the ashes of an earlier disaster – the failure to save the St James's Theatre from demolition.

The St James's was an attractive and fashionable Victorian theatre where Oscar Wilde's last first night, that of *The Importance of Being Earnest*, was performed, in 1895. The St James's had been run previously by Gilbert Miller, an American theatre impresario who spent much of his life in Europe, and who turned the St James's into one of London's most successful playhouses, shifting the balance of theatrical power further west from the Theatre Royal, Haymarket, on the other side of the nearby St James's Square.

After Wilde's arrest his name was removed from playbills. Disgracefully, George Alexander, Wilde's leading man in *Earnest*, was one of those who celebrated the playwright's public humiliation with a lavish dinner.

The last in a line of actor-managers at the St James's was Laurence Olivier who, with his wife Vivien Leigh, appeared in several plays there including alternating performances of Shakespeare's *Antony and Cleopatra* and George Bernard Shaw's *Caesar and Cleopatra*. Leigh, who had the looks to play Cleopatra but was perhaps too well-bred and English to convey the full Eastern sensuality of the Queen of the Nile, also filmed her Shavian Cleopatra, opposite Claude Rains's Caesar.

Rains entered Hollywood heaven when he played the cynical, corrupt but charming Captain Renault, the Chief of Police in *Casablanca*. One of the best scenes in a film that is packed with iconic moments is when the Nazi officer who is pursuing Paul Henried's Victor Laszlo, the Resistance leader, orders Captain Renault to close down Rick's Bar. Rick is the not-as-cynical-as-he-seems owner of the bar, which has its own band and a very profitable (and crooked) casino.

When Rick, played by Humphrey Bogart, asks why the bar is being closed, Renault announces, with fake indignation, that he is deeply shocked to learn that there has been gambling taking place on the premises. Just at that moment the croupier, realizing the night's gaming is over, hands Renault his winnings.

Rains seems every inch the suave Frenchman, but at the start of his acting career he was a regular performer in West End theatres, where he was advised that if he wanted to get on he should lose his East End working-class accent and adopt something more cultivated. He did, then left Theatreland for Hollywood, but would return periodically to the stage in London and to give lectures to drama students about their art.

Returning to Vivien Leigh – always a pleasure – she was horrified to learn that the St James's landlords wanted to close the theatre and redevelop the site as offices. She led a vociferous and well-supported campaign to preserve it, marching in protest through central London and even being forcibly removed from the public gallery in the House of Lords, where she made an outburst in order to get further publicity for the cause.

Although she lost the battle, and the St James's was duly demolished, her protest did not fall on entirely deaf ears, for Parliament decided to give statutory protection to Theatreland's building stock. No longer would it be possible for a landowner to simply decide that he wanted to pull down a theatre and put up something else in its place. Given that according to the Theatres Trust some 15 theatres have been earmarked for demolition since 1950, this safeguard has been crucial in maintaining the number and variety of theatres that are enjoyed by audiences today. The fragrant ghost of Vivien Leigh is no doubt smiling at them from a dressing room mirror.

20

Theatre Ghosts

Ghosts are generally associated with anger or sadness and in either case there is a sense of regret. This is true of theatre ghosts too, though as a breed they seem to exhibit, beyond the grave, an interest in what is going on in their old theatres – an interest that has a surprisingly cheerful and good natured way of expressing itself. Joseph Grimaldi, the clown who frequently performed at Drury Lane, is said to materialize from time to time and offer performers a ghostly hand when they aren't quite sure where they should be standing.

Theatreland's most relaxed ghost has to be that of William Terriss, a matinee idol and star of what were known as the Adelphi melodramas – a series of plays at that Theatre. It was on his way to his dressing room at the Adelphi that Terriss was murdered, on 16 December 1897.

There is a green plaque, unveiled by Sir Donald Sinden, which commemorates the fact of Terriss's death, though it rather coyly refers to his 'untimely death' rather than the brutal stabbing that finished his life at the Adelphi's stage door. The murderer was an out-of-work actor called Richard Prince. He had a grudge against Terriss, who had been forced to fire the troubled man from his company.

Although Terriss had been justified in doing so, given Prince's behavioural problems, he had taken pity on him and arranged some financial support for him. This generosity didn't register with the embittered man, who decided to take his revenge for what he saw as Terriss's persecution of him.

Terriss's ghost has been reported on many occasions, but not at the Adelphi. Instead, a man answering his description has been seen in and around the Covent Garden underground station. Why would a leading actor want to stride around a tube stop rather than a theatre?

The answer, it transpires, is that there used to be a very good patisserie at the station, where Terriss would buy pastries and cakes to eat in his dressing room. If you are going to be called back to earthly realms because of the suddenness and violence with which you left them, then surely it must be much more agreeable to return to a patisserie than to the place where you were murdered.

Even the most sceptical theatregoer can enjoy a ghost story at the Fortune Theatre in Russell Street. Built in the mid-1920s, the Fortune is small, discrete and, unusually for a West End playhouse, has a façade that incorporates concrete. The theatre partly shares its site with a church – the Church of Scotland. The church's congregation may have been less than amused by the theatre's first production: a play called *Sinners*.

The Fortune was where, in 1961, the Cambridge Footlights launched their West End run of *Beyond the Fringe* and in the process helped make the names of Alan Bennett, Jonathan Miller, Peter Cook and Dudley Moore. Cook and Moore were to work together as a comic duo, becoming British television favourites later in the 1960s, after which Moore made a career for himself in Hollywood, with films like *Arthur* and *10*, while Cook took pleasure from co-owning *Private Eye*, the satirical magazine that has cast unwelcome light on the murkier doings of the British establishment for over 40 years.

There is little that is light in *The Woman in Black*, the play that has been at the Fortune since 1989, having played at both the Strand (now the Novello) and Playhouse theatres earlier that year. *The Woman in Black* changes casts approximately every six months. Adapted by Stephen Mallatratt from the original novel by Susan Hill, this is the most terrifying horror story that anyone is ever likely to see in a theatre.

That is one reason for its longevity. Another is that it is wonderfully simple and cheap to produce: there are only three in the cast (two, officially, but someone does have to play the ghost) while the set and props are an empty stage, a large wicker basket and precious little else.

The plot involves a middle-aged solicitor hiring a young actor to help him recreate the events of his (the solicitor's) life. In doing so we see the events that have literally haunted the older man ever since. Many years earlier, it transpires, he had been paid to wind up the estate of a client, an estate based in a desolate house on a bleak and eerie coast. In the course of this, without giving away too many details, he sees a ghostly figure: the Woman in Black. Anyone who sees this ghost suffers (often via their nearest and dearest) a terrible calamity.

The play, which has no blood or gore, is literally horrific. There are a couple of points at which the audience scream out loud, and one at which they also jump up in their seats, from fear. One scene in particular will give anyone who sees it that strange, cold prickling feeling at the back of the neck that you only get when seriously scared of something spooky.

The Woman in Black is popular with school groups (girls' schools provide especially loud screams) and with theatregoers – the production has deservedly won several awards.

Waiting for ghosts to appear is a notoriously hit and miss affair, and most theatre ghosts (apart from the Man in Grey at Drury Lane) can only be seen inside the theatre, late at night, when the public are not allowed to be there. The Coliseum is said to be haunted by a First World War era soldier who would take his girlfriend there (when it was a variety house) when on leave. His body presumably lying somewhere in Flanders, his spirit likes to return to where he found light, warmth and humour when he was alive.

Her Majesty's Theatre, where *The Phantom of the Opera* has been playing since 1986, ought to be haunted by the ghost of the much loved comedian, Tommy Cooper. Cooper was a man who made you grin from ear to ear as soon as he walked on stage, and was a favourite at the Royal Variety Show. He was also a major draw on television, and it was for a television programme that he made his final appearance on stage.

The theatre was at that time (1984) going through an awkward patch, and rather than staying dark had hired itself out for a regular TV programme, *Live From Her Majesty's*. Cooper, who had heart trouble, was appearing as a headline attraction, when he suffered a fatal heart attack in front of the audience. Used to his routine, where he pretended that tricks had gone wrong, they assumed that he was only pretending to be ill, and roared with laughter. Realizing that something had indeed gone terribly wrong, the stage management carried him off to a room at the side of the stage, where he died. A macabre end to be sure, but for a comedian of his stature to pass away to the sound of laughter has a certain fitness to it.

If Cooper does decide to materialize at Her Majesty's, he will have company. The theatre's builder, Sir Herbert Beerbohm Tree, who had an apartment at the top of the building where he lived with his wife, is known to haunt the place.

Before giving an example of this, a popular anecdote about Sir Herbert bears retelling. A happily married husband and father who had always had a keen eye for the ladies, in later life he developed an interest in young men, too. Lady Tree, an actress in her own right, took an understandably dim view of this and let her feelings be known – though she was too well-bred to actually have a row about it.

So when Sir Herbert invited a gorgeous young actor up to the flat for dinner one night, Lady Tree played the perfect hostess. She couldn't have been nicer. The killer punch, leavened with humour, was saved for the very end of the evening. Rising from the table to leave the men, as was the habit of those days, so they could have port or brandy by themselves late into the night, she was half-way through the doorway when she turned and said, firmly: 'Remember, Herbert, it's still adultery!'

Given that Her Majesty's was very much Sir Herbert's, it's not surprising that he chooses to stay there as a ghost. He has been seen on many occasions, but the most authenticated – and spookiest – was when he made his presence known, without actually appearing.

John Causebrook, who in the 1980s was theatre manager at Her Majesty's, was walking across the stage one night, having cast a proprietorial eye around backstage before leaving for the night. Having done so, he was walking across the front of the stage, heading for the exit. Theatres are always rather creepy places late at night when no one else is around. Perhaps it is the contrast between how they are then rather than how they should be – full of people, sound, music, light and *life*. Perhaps it is just the primitive fear of being alone in a dark place. Whatever the reason, they can, however much one likes them as venues, be places one would rather not be, alone, after everyone else within shouting range and rescue has left.

Causebrook reached the middle of the stage when there was a sudden sound from the auditorium. Not just sound. A movement. One of the seats, in the visibly empty auditorium, in the circle, moved down, as if someone was sitting in it – but there was no one there. Causebrook froze, then pulled himself together and walked a few more steps. The seat went back up, as if its occupier had moved and a couple of seconds later, further in the direction that the manager was moving, another seat was tipped down.

With great presence of mind the by now seriously spooked manager looked directly at the seat, across the footlights, and said loudly: 'Good evening, Sir Herbert!' The seat rose, as if Sir Herbert had risen to acknowledge Causebrook's greeting and, satisfied that he was still recognized as an essential presence in his theatre, disappeared. Causebrook continued locking up without further disturbance then headed out to the pub for a well-deserved drink.

For anyone who doesn't want to smuggle themselves into a theatre late at night (an action not to be recommended in any case), the easiest way of seeing a ghost in the West End, and of being enjoyably frightened rather than given a heart attack, is to pay for a ticket to *The Woman in Black*. The advert for the movie *Alien* said that in space no one can hear you scream. At the Fortune it is reassuring to know that in the theatre, *everyone* is screaming. If you are going to be afraid – very afraid – then it's best to be so in company.

21

The Eternal Debate: Drama or Musicals?

Journalists writing for the general public rather than theatre audiences seem to make a habit of writing articles about there being too many musicals in London. The subject crops up again and again, with the occasional variation on the theme being a piece suggesting that at last straight plays are fighting back – until the next article about the pendulum swinging in favour of musicals again.

Despite this there is a serious question of balance that the theatre industry often debates and a widespread belief that musicals may indeed be taking over. It is reassuring to read the 2007 report of the Society of London Theatre, *Pleasing Audiences*, where the chief executive points out that although in 2007 there were 45 different musicals on offer in the West End, there were also 108 plays.

Though many musicals enjoyed packed houses, the biggest buzz of the year was not a musical but a play: Daniel Radcliffe, of the *Harry Potter* films, starred as a troubled young man in a revival of Sir Peter Shaffer's *Equus*, a play based on a real story about a youth who blinded horses. True, Radcliffe was not only Harry Potter made flesh on the stage, that flesh was also naked, as the play requires his character to appear without clothes. This certainly added to the run on tickets when the play was announced.

The advantage that musicals have is that many of them have been running for years, so the public knows what it is getting, knows it will have a good time. Even newer musicals tend to be based on songs that are already known – *Mamma Mia!* is entirely based around ABBA's existing hits, for example, and *Carousel* has 'You'll Never Walk Alone', which has been a popular football anthem for years and is one of musical theatre's most recognizable songs.

Those who worry about the balance might argue that although there are generally more plays on offer than musicals, that is largely thanks to institutions like the National Theatre with its large annual repertory of plays, but that doesn't alter the fact that the plays are being produced and generally selling well – the National has a regular audience who are prepared to experiment with new or rarely seen dramas.

When a revised version of *Buddy* took over the little Duchess Theatre it did ring alarm bells among the straight play brigade, but the clanging cash tills at the Duchess, where the show has been well received, drowned them out. Straight play supporters should have drawn comfort from the lines of Arthur Hugh Clough's 'Say not the Struggle Naught Availeth', the rousing nineteenth-century poem that suggests that even when things look terrible, one should not despair:

> For while the tired waves vainly breaking
> Seem here no painful inch to gain
> Far back through creek and inlet making
> Comes, silent, flooding in the main.

Translated into a Theatreland context this means that though the Duchess may temporarily have been 'lost' to a musical, the Duke of York's, another small playhouse that has been captured by musical theatre in recent years (*Rent*, for example) is once again showing a play by one of Britain's most distinguished playwrights, *No Man's Land* by the late Harold Pinter.

Similarly, though some small playhouses have tended to host musicals, they too will often have a run of straight plays in-between. One such example is the Vaudeville, on the Strand.

The Vaudeville stages plays from time to time, and was where *The Female of the Species* opened in 2008. This was a very funny take on modern feminism, with a central character (a famous, talented, book-writing champion of feminism) that was widely believed to have been based on Germaine Greer. Starring Dame Eileen Atkins, *The Female of the Species* poked fun at the wilder shores of feminist theory without ever negating the fact that this was a comedy about women, by a woman playwright, starring one of our leading actresses, with women also playing the strongest of the supporting characters on stage.

At the time of writing, Michael Grandage's production of *Piaf*, starring the Argentinian actress Elena Roger, has brought a very different female icon to the Strand, via the Donmar Warehouse, and returned the Vaudeville to musical theatre, which has been its traditional staple. Julian Slade's *Salad Days*, for example, opened here in 1954, and enjoyed a long and prosperous run. A young Cameron Mackintosh, on being taken to see it, fell in love with musical theatre, with dramatic long-term effects on the industry. (*Salad Days* was was revived for a shorter run in 1996.)

Most musicals at the Vaudeville have a less extraordinary impact on the future direction of London theatre. One cheerfully slight but memorable musical was Kander and Ebb's *70, Girls, 70* which opened at the Vaudeville in 1991 in a production that starred the irrepressible and much loved Dora Bryan.

A more serious issue than the fluctuating number of theatres showing plays as opposed to musicals is whether musicals are in some way a lesser, in the sense of less serious, less lofty, form of theatre than straight plays. This has always been a strange distinction to make, but it has been perennially discussed, nonetheless.

Music can produce heightened emotion, whether of joy or sadness, far quicker than can the spoken word, though poetry can arguably soar as high as the highest note. Given this, musicals should be able to speak to the human soul as easily if not more so than straight plays.

The counter-argument to this is that musicals may be all very emotional – after all so is opera, so is ballet music – but the subjects they treat are more flippant, more superficial than those addressed by plays. True, there are a lot of light and frothy plays – Matthew Warchus's award-winning production of the farce *Boeing Boeing* (at the Comedy Theatre, suitably enough) could not be argued, even by its greatest fans, to be a thought-provoking inquiry into the nature of man, but then what musical is? Well, *Les Miserables* deals with some very heavy issues, including crime and punishment, the nature of redemption, the need for political freedom, the enduring power of love and the way that even the hardest heart can be moved by the presence of pure goodness.

Musical theatre performers have suffered from a snobbery within the industry because of the old assumptions about what musicals can and can't do, and *The Lord of the Rings* was immediately up against just such a snobbery – even though there are dozens of songs, written by Tolkien, throughout the whole of the three books. The story makes it very clear that music was integral to the cultures of Middle Earth, so why not do a stage musical?

Actors who can sing and therefore carve out a career in musical theatre do find it very hard to make the transition from musical to straight theatre, and the nearest they often get to it is the Christmas panto. One reason is very practical: if you are blessed with a very good singing voice then why not use it? Why try for parts in straight plays, with all the competition involved, if you have an inbuilt advantage in going for a musical theatre role? This natural tendency to specialize has been reinforced by the relative popularity of musicals, which means there is plenty of work for a good singer.

Musical theatre performers can justifiably argue that, far from being some sort of junior league compared with the Shakespearean specialists, the range of skills required for a career in musical theatre means they should, if anything, be seen as more qualified than actors in plays. The need to teach the range of skills required for musicals was one of the inspirations for the creation of the Liverpool Institute of Performing Arts.

Musicals are in any case not some single juggernaut of an art form. Just as the new Craig Revel Horwood production of Andrew Lloyd Webber's *Sunset Boulevard* is a complete contrast in scale to the first production at the Adelphi, so *Chicago*, which opened at the same theatre in 1997 and played there for years before transferring to the Cambridge, is wholly different, with its almost non-existent set (comprising a bandstand, some chairs and few feathers), from the lavish sets and lighting of *Oliver!* at Drury Lane or the period recreations of *Blood Brothers* at the Phoenix.

Blood Brothers is one of the longest-running shows in Theatreland. This is so not as much because of Willy Russell's music, though 'Easy Terms' has real emotional punch, as does the show's hit song, 'Tell Me It's Not True'. The real strength lies, as it does at the heart of any stage show, whether spoken, sung or danced, in the strength of the story.

Russell's' *Blood Brothers* is a modern (well, 1950s) Liverpudlian version of a Greek tragedy – complete with a (sinister) narrator, who fulfils the role that the Chorus did in Greek drama. The device of twins separated at birth is one with a very Greek resonance that was also mined for dramatic effect by Shakespeare. Russell's reinvention relocated it from palaces and ports to a 1960s working class urban environment to great effect.

Les Miserables has a more historic setting – Paris in the 1830s – but it also has the epic sweep and dramatic power of its source, one of the great masterpieces of French fiction, the massive novel by Victor Hugo of the same name. *Les Miserables* shows, just as *The Lord of the Rings* did, that even the biggest epics can be staged. Indeed, until relatively recently and the advent of the amazing computer-generated special effects that we now take for granted it was only possible to put epics on stage rather than the screen, as they would only look convincing when told through a theatrical medium.

The huge advantage *Les Miserables* enjoys is its songs. It has a superb score, with the exception of the deeply irritating 'Little People' which is meant to be comic relief that later generates an extra layer of poignancy when the child who sings it is shot, but it merely serves to hold up the action. *Les Mis*, as it is affectionately known, works best in its ballads, like the incredibly depressing but equally beautiful 'I Dreamed a Dream'.

That *Les Mis* is a modern classic and one of the best of them now seems obvious, but when the show first opened, at the Barbican, its producer, Cameron

Mackintosh, had taken a great risk and Sheridan Morley was in a minority of established critics in thinking that the show had legs.

The show that has the longest legs of them all, and enjoys a continuing record that can surely never be beaten is *The Mousetrap*. A drama – indeed a thriller – rather than a musical, it owes its position, 30 years ahead of *Les Mis* and *The Phantom of the Opera*, to the continued fame of its writer, Agatha Christie, and to the sheer momentum that over half a century of dogged performances has generated.

Visiting *The Mousetrap*, in the quaint old St Martin's Theatre, is like entering a time capsule and being transported back to the 1950s. The look and style of the piece is exactly that. A hangover from the year Elizabeth II became Queen, it is based on a radio story written for the occasion of the 80th birthday of Elizabeth's grandmother, Queen Mary.

Christie's plot, which must remain a mystery, as every audience is sworn to secrecy (which, amazingly, they keep), is in some ways very old fashioned – especially in the way she clearly equated being gay with being a disturbed neurotic – and the fundamental situation – a group of people in an isolated place under threat from an unseen but clearly present enemy – is, like the twins in *Blood Brothers*, an ancient archetype.

The one single drama that could be called the archetypal play, the one that most people think of – or least have an image of, with a man in Elizabethan costume holding a skull in his hand, is the Shakespearean tragedy *Hamlet*.

This is not only the most instantly recognizable of plays, it is one of the most performed and enjoyed in the whole of English theatre. The recent productions by the Royal Shakespeare Company with David Tennant (and understudy Edward Bennett) and the Donmar with Jude Law show its continuing appeal and its ability to attract the most bankable and watchable actors of every generation.

Although Law and Tennant have attracted massive publicity thanks to a film career and *Dr Who*, respectively, as well as both men's highly individual talent, one of the best Hamlets of the last quarter of a century was that of Paul Rhys, at the Young Vic. David Lan, the director, translator, administrator and general polymath who is artistic director of the Young Vic has made it, the younger relative of the Old Vic, into a centre of innovation and excitement.

Lan has also been at pains – well, pains is perhaps not the right word for someone who so clearly enjoys his work – to ensure that the Young Vic has reached out to the relatively deprived and multi-ethnic area in which the theatre is situated, and to do so in a non-patronizing and very effective way. The local population and theatregoers more normally seen north of the river have visited the Young Vic so often because of the consistent standard of productions that

John Gielgud as Hamlet, 1934

Lan has commissioned or directed himself, and of these, Paul Rhys's Hamlet stands out.

Rhys brought a quiet dignity and a sense of real poetry to the role as well as a sense (not always captured by actors in the part) that this was a Prince. This is a crucial part of the plot that is always damaged if not lost altogether if the sense of class, of rightful and ordained place in society, so important in the England of Shakespeare and his audiences, let alone in Hamlet's Denmark, is lost.

Rhys has had a lot of competition in the role, with actors including Samuel West and Stephen Dillane in the part, as well as Alan Cumming, Daniel Day Lewis and Ben Whishaw, whose strikingly youthful Hamlet, under Trevor Nunn's direction (featuring Nunn's wife, Imogen Stubbs, as Hamlet's mother), made Whishaw an overnight star. Day Lewis's performance was at the National, where in the course of the run he had a nervous breakdown. Seeing what he thought was his father, during the scene where Hamlet speaks to his father's ghost, Day Lewis walked off the stage and out of the production.

If the role of Hamlet can have that effect on an actor, it's no wonder it continues to fascinate audiences. The basic plot is that of an Elizabethan and Jacobean revenge play: a young(ish) man has to avenge his father's murder. In Hamlet's case his father was King of Denmark, and Hamlet is avenging his own usurpation, for the throne has passed not to him, as the son and heir, but to his father's brother. This man, Claudius, has compounded his crime against nature and the natural ordering of society in the form of the succession to the throne (let alone regicide) by marrying his dead brother's widow. That this is a love match as well as a political union is all the more revolting to Hamlet, whose feelings for his mother are themselves tinged if not with incest then at least with neuroticism (Agatha Christie probably thought he was gay).

Hamlet has a play within a play (called The Mousetrap, which Christie borrowed) and the role of theatre as a mirror to corruption and light to show the truth makes Hamlet all the more attractive to theatre lovers.

The play also has poison, a dramatic swordfight, pirates (albeit offstage) and the graveyard scene with its musings on mortality and the transience of youth and beauty. It also has the most famous debate (which Hamlet has with himself) on the validity of suicide as a way of coping with an unbearable burden. The wealth of material makes reinterpretation (is Hamlet mad or just pretending to be, for example) possible several times in each generation and just when one thinks everything than can be mined from it has been, along comes another one. The role lends itself to being played well by such wildly different personalities and physical types as John Gielgud and Richard Burton, or Ben Whishaw and Simon Russell Beale.

Millions of words have been expended on *Hamlet*, in learned books and articles and doctoral theses down the centuries since it was its first production but none have been able to sum it up as vividly, succinctly and accurately as it was by Jack Buchanan in *The Bandwagon* – Hollywood's 1953 tribute to life on stage (itself based on a stage musical by Arthur Schwartz and Howard Dietz): 'A ghost and a prince meet – and everyone ends in mincemeat.'

A postscript to a discussion of the balance between musical and drama should be a mention of another theatrical art form: cabaret. Kander and Ebb's show *Cabaret*, which had a recent revival at the Lyric, Shaftesbury Avenue with James Dreyfus as the Master of Ceremonies, claims that life is a cabaret. That may be a little optimistic, but it is certainly true that all of life can be found in the range of songs that a great cabaret performer has at his or her disposal.

London's cabaret scene has never been as vibrant – or self-satisfied – as New York's, though it has on many occasions imported one of the greatest cabaret performers of all time, Steve Ross, to play at Pizza on the Park and Jermyn Street. Both these venues have been mainstays for many years, though Pizza on the Park's basement cabaret room (and restaurant) has not regularly programmed shows for some time. The room remains open for private bookings, however, with occasional performances and short runs, so it is still technically available, as is Jermyn Street Theatre.

The ornate art nouveau dining room of the Café Royal hosted cabaret before its recent temporary closure for refurbishment. One of the stars who regularly performed there once a week was Holly Penfield, an American singer-songwriter who divides her time between California and London.

Penfield, who has also regularly performed at The Green Carnation bar and cabaret room in Greek Street, Soho, on Monday nights, has a highly sexual act (without removing her clothes). This is an integral part of her stage persona and her rapport with (mostly young and often gay) audiences, but her main appeal is in her voice.

Whether singing one of her own compositions, like the torch song 'What Would Love Do?' or a classic like 'Both Sides Now' or 'The Trolley Song' her powerful, highly expressive voice has made her a must-see for any visitor to London with a taste for cabaret.

There are, sadly, relatively few other places where cabaret can be regularly seen since the Theatre Museum's Paintings Gallery was shut. The Donmar had a summer season of cabaret under Sam Mendes that was discontinued when Michael Grandage took over. Cameron Mackintosh (riding to the rescue as usual – if he ever has a statue in Theatreland he should be shown on horseback) provides a wonderful room for cabaret – and showcases – in the downstairs bar area of his refurbished Prince of Wales Theatre. This is the space to watch for new cabaret talent, but until someone special emerges, Miss Penfield remains the woman to watch.

22

Ballet – And a Little Opera, Too

Two of Theatreland's largest and most impressive theatres have been given over to opera and ballet, the two other lyric art forms that are recognized as being inherently part of the London theatre scene by their inclusion in the Society of London Theatre's annual Olivier Awards categories.

The two buildings are the Royal Opera House (ROH) and the Coliseum, the renovation of which has already been described in Chapter 8. The ROH stands on Bow Street, but it is, since its refurbishment ready for the new millennium in 2000, vast enough to also face south to Russell Street and east across Covent Garden piazza and James Street, as well as north to Floral Street.

Floral Street's name recalls Covent Garden's historic role as London's central fruit and vegetable market, which also sold flowers. The association continues inside the ROH, where the largest public room is the Floral Hall, an enormous conservatory-style structure, which was used for storing flowers until the market was swept out of Covent Garden and south of the Thames to Nine Elms.

The Floral Hall is now named after Paul Hamlyn, the multi-millionaire publisher and philanthropist. Hamlyn's name replaced than of Alberto Vilar, a wealthy financier and generous donator to numerous arts organizations but whose financial commitments proved to be larger than the means at his disposal to fulfil them.

Hamlyn, who died in 2001, established a charity that provided free tickets to children who would not otherwise have been able to afford to go to a performance at the ROH. These occasions saw a wonderful contrast between the children's arrival – all noise and exuberance – and the performance itself, when the auditorium would be in total silence as they sat, enraptured, as Romeo and Juliet danced beneath the balcony or a mass of swans glided mournfully across the stage in *Swan Lake*.

The ROH can be entered from two points: the modern frontage on the piazza, and the old entrance on Bow Street, entering strait into the foyer of the theatre, which was built in the 1850s. Opposite the Victorian façade stands the impressive bulk of Bow Street police station, the first purpose-built police station in the West End. At its side is Bow Street Magistrate's Court. Both are now closed, but for many years anyone approaching the opera house, to buy a ticket at the box office, or heading for the stage door to go to work, could tell – by the presence of paparazzi staking their pitches on the pavement, or reporters and their sound assistants checking that the microphones or cameras were working – that a celebrity was due to appear in court later that morning.

The police station had, until its closure, a unique feature. Every police station in England has a blue lamp outside it – as does the main station in Theatreland, by Charing Cross. The tradition of having this sign as a symbol of the presence of the police was recognized in the 1947 film *The Blue Lamp*, in which a young Dirk Bogarde, playing a hoodlum, shoots Jack Warner, playing a decent, old-fashioned 'copper'. The film was a hit, and Warner made such an impression that his character was resurrected for what proved to be a long-running TV series, *Dixon of Dock Green*.

Bow Street police station was the only one in the country to have not blue but clear glass in its lamp, providing a white light to passers by. The reason for this is that Queen Victoria, visiting the theatre and seeing the blue lamp at this new building, demanded that the colour be changed. 'Why, Your Majesty?' she was asked. 'Because it looks improper' was the royal reply. Assured that the building was a police station rather than a brothel – which would in any case have had a red light – she nonetheless insisted: 'Change it!' It was duly changed and retained its individuality until the day it closed.

There have been various suggestions as to an appropriate use for the building, including its being taken over by the ROH, but when last heard of, the latest plan was to turn it into a five-star hotel. If this does happen then the suites at the front of the building will have superb views of the opera house.

This would be fitting as the architects (Dixon Jones) who designed the changes to the building during the extensive refurbishment, have made the most of the vistas from and within the building itself. The most obvious alteration was to enable every customer to enter the opera house at the same point, and to travel to every level of the auditorium from within the building, by escalator, lift or stairs. The escalator, which runs along the side of the Floral Hall, takes you up from close to the champagne bar to the top level, the amphitheatre. This level, with the cheaper seats, used to be only accessible by a long set of stone stairs, accessed from a side entrance in Floral Street.

Once the amphitheatre was reached there was a fairly restricted drinks service, and though there was a certain camaraderie of the poor and the committed – those who attended at least once a week, and therefore needed to sit in the cheaper area – you nonetheless felt that you were tucked away from the wealthier section of the audience, and that you were getting a different experience from them.

That has now changed, and not only is the long sweep of the amphitheatre bar an attractive one, with a good range of snacks served, but there is a smart restaurant, too. There is also one of the best-kept secrets in London: the terrace. This wooden-decked area, reached from glass revolving doors between the restaurant and the bar, is an L shape that has tables and chairs, and from which you can look over the roof of Covent Garden market and the piazza around it to Nelson's Column, the London Eye and other landmarks.

The rooftop scene is both very British and strikingly continental. On the one hand, you half expect to see, as in *Mary Poppins*, a row of Victorian chimney sweeps dancing their hearts out across the rooftops. On the other hand, given the Italianate design of the piazza and the age of its surrounding streets, there is, especially on a summer's evening, in the interval between ballets and with a glass of chilled white wine in your hand, something very European about the view.

The amphitheatre is open during the day (unless there is a special event on) for the public to have coffee, drinks and snacks. Given that hardly anyone other than Royal Opera or Ballet regulars seems aware of this, it is a perfect place to meet a friend for a coffee or a light lunch. In the summer, sitting outside on the terrace, with a coffee and a newspaper (in the absence of a friend) with the sound of music wafting up from the piazza several stories below (provided by street buskers, including some Chinese regulars who play familiar tunes on a strange instrument that gives the melodies an attractively haunting air) you really could be abroad. In financially challenged times, you can get the experience of a city break for the price of a cup of coffee and a Danish pastry.

The amphitheatre has a final surprise to offer: a viewing platform that overlooks the Floral Hall. Situated opposite the bar, this is a window onto the hall that projects slightly into the wall behind the main bar, and gives a charming view of the moneyed patrons on the floor of the Hall or (another ROH speciality) dining at tables that are themselves on a terrace that runs along three of the four sides of the Hall, and where diners can eat their courses before the show and in its intervals.

From the floor of the Floral Hall, looking upwards, the viewing platform seems to be suspended in air, as the wall from which it projects is of mirrored glass, so it is as striking a design to those looking at it as it is to those standing in it looking down.

People watchers looking from it into the Floral Hall will often see ex-cabinet minister and arts pundit Michael Portillo dining here, as he is a regular at the ROH. So, too, are the National Theatre's director Nicholas Hytner and the Donmar Warehouse's Michael Grandage. Both of them are dance fans, and Hytner first came to public attention with his production of Handel's *Xerxes* for English National Opera at the Coliseum in the 1980s.

The old Crush Bar, which used to be the most fashionable place to be seen at the ROH, is now used as a dining area. As mentioned earlier, between it and the Floral Hall is a plaque in memory of the late Princess Margaret, the Queen's younger sister, who was a devoted patroness of the Royal Ballet. Her interest in the ballet was shared by Princess Diana, who not only enjoyed watching dancers, but on one occasion took to the stage herself, for Prince Charles's birthday, when she surprised – and appalled – him by making a surprise appearance to perform a dance routine with Wayne Sleep, the diminutive but dashing Royal Ballet star.

Dancers have a relatively short career, as their bodies simply can't, after their mid-30s, perform as well as they should – something recognized by the government, which accepts pension schemes for dancers that kick in (as it were) at 35. Sleep made the cross-over from classical ballet to West End dance shows, and has subsequently appeared in West End shows like *Chitty Chitty Bang Bang* at the London Palladium, where he played the Child Catcher.

Another Royal Ballet dancer who has moved from classical dance to West End musicals is Adam Cooper. Admired by regulars at the ROH, he surprised them when he left the Royal Ballet for Matthew Bourne's Adventure in Motion Pictures dance company, which performed in theatres more usually known for plays, rather than in exclusively dance venues.

This led to a wider audience for Bourne's work, but the real change came when he reworked the ballet classic *Swan Lake*. Bourne kept the score but changed everything else, turning the story into a powerful study of the loneliness of a young prince with a scheming mother and a life driven by duty rather than love. Feeling suicidal, he is about to throw himself into a lake when the swans appear.

Bourne's genius was to tap into the power that swans radiate as well as their grace. He reinvented them: no longer were they ethereal creatures danced by ballerinas. Now they were athletic, menacing, wild creatures, danced by men. Adam Cooper played the chief swan, and just as ballerinas double between the good Odette (the girl turned into a swan by a magician in the original story) and the bad Odile (who looks identical to Odette but is an incarnation of evil), so Cooper played both the white (good) swan and the dark (bad) stranger who appears, like Odile, at a Court Ball.

Bourne's version is witty and clever and is especially skilful in its comments on the royalty who are a staple of plots on stage and the most valued members of any theatre audience. It is also unbearably sad at the end, when the prince, having been labelled mad by his mother's manipulative chief courtier, is, alone in his bed, attacked by a flock of swans.

Adam Cooper's white swan tries to protect him but is himself killed in the process. The prince dies of grief, his body found by his now contrite (but far too late) mother as the spirits of the swan and the prince ascend to heaven. This final scene must rank as among the most tear-jerking in modern British theatre, and when it was played out on Cooper's last night in the role the old adage 'not a dry eye in the house' was for once literally true.

Cooper, who was trained as a musician, singer and actor as well as a dancer, has moved from dancing (which he still does, as he enters his late 30s) into choreography. Most recently (in December 2008), he earned consistent praise for his choreography from the theatre critics at the first night of *Carousel* at the Savoy Theatre.

Matthew Bourne has continued to bring his own imagination to standard ballet pieces, as with his *Nutcracker!* which is a regular seasonal favourite at Sadler's Wells and, with Lez Brotherston's darkly inventive stage designs, has proved a popular alternative to the inevitable productions of *The Nutcracker* by the bigger ballet companies.

Bourne's own cross-over into musical theatre has included *Mary Poppins*, which opened at the Prince Edward Theatre in Soho before transferring to Broadway, and Rupert Gould's production of *Oliver!* which opened, after previews, at the Theatre Royal, Drury Lane, in 2009.

One of Bourne's most inventive projects was one commissioned by Nicholas Hytner at the National Theatre. This was *Play Without Words*. As its name implies, it was text-free performance, based on Harold Pinter's screenplay for the early 1960s Joesph Losey film *The Servant*, which co-starred Dirk Bogarde in the title role and James Fox as the younger upper-class man who employs him.

A sinister story about role-reversal in which the initially deferential servant comes to exert an unhealthy influence on his master before completely taking over his life, *Play Without Words* had several dancers playing the lead roles, with simultaneous versions of the story taking place in front of the audience as the action developed.

Bourne, who worked as an usher at the National as a young man, has made another dance theatre piece from a film, *Edward Scissorhands*, and from Oscar Wilde's book (itself filmed) *The Picture of Dorian Gray*. He remains the leading example of someone from the ballet world who has seamlessly moved over into mainstream musical theatre.

Firmly still in the ballet world, at the ROH, is a ballerina who has moved from dancing not to choreography but to senior management. Ballerinas have traditionally swapped dancing either for marriage, or for teaching the next generation of dancers. Rarely do they move into arts administration, but Monica Mason is the notable exception to this. Born in South Africa, she spent her distinguished career as a dancer with the Royal Ballet, starting aged 16. Her roles included the Chosen Maiden in Kenneth MacMillan's version of Stravinsky's *The Rite of Spring*.

Having served as assistant director of the Royal Ballet to Sir Anthony Dowell (who had been one of the Royal Ballet's greatest stars in his own time as a dancer), she carried on in that role under Ross Stretton, an Australian whose brief tenure as director was marked by controversy, not least because he wanted to bring in not just new dancers but to jettison much of the Royal Ballet's regular repertoire in favour of something radically new.

Stretton's acrimonious resignation saw Monica Mason promoted to director, a post where she has been singularly successful. Now Dame Monica (an honour she received in 2008 but which was long overdue), she has led the Royal Ballet into a much happier, more productive and more artistically rewarding place than she found it.

Given they share the same building, there has always been a certain rivalry between the Royal Ballet and the Royal Opera, with a sort of seesaw as to which company is the most chic at any given time. For the last few years the Royal Ballet has had more of an air of excitement about it, but that wasn't the case in the past, especially when superstars like Placido Domingo and Luciano Pavarotti were in their prime.

The 1980s were an exciting decade for the Royal Opera, as indeed they were for English National Opera, and the Royal Ballet, despite retaining its international status, seemed to be overshadowed by its sister company. That changed, and will no doubt do so again as public taste, new creative talent (composers, choreographers) and the emergence of a new generation of singers and dancers tips the balance one way or another.

The Royal Opera is, in any case, in a healthy state at the moment. Its director, Antonio Pappano, combines a sense of authority with a genuine bonhomie – an attractive combination, especially when he is conducting.

On the subject of health and the opera, opera singers and the management of the theatres they appear in have a uniquely irritating habit, when ill or under par. There will be a frozen silence as a representative of the opera house or opera company walks on stage – usually in an ill-fitting suit – to make an announcement.

In the opera world this will often be on the lines of 'We regret to announce that Miss X or Signor Y has a terrible throat infection . . .' and then continues '. . . but will continue to sing the role of Z tonight and hopes you will understand'. Why? Why should we put up with a below-par performance? Either they are fit to sing or not. If they are fit enough then the announcement is superfluous, prompted by vanity rather than health. If not fit, then the understudy should get a chance – they can be even better than the main attraction, not least because they have so much to prove.

It is as if someone from the Royal Ballet were to announce that Margot Fonteyn (had she still been around) had broken her leg earlier that night but would stagger around the stage, dragging it behind her, rather than let the understudy go on. This only happens in opera and only an opera audience would put up with it.

The appointment of Antonio Pappano (British but of Italian extraction and who spent much of his earlier life in the United States) and the South African-born Dame Monica reflects the international nature of both opera and ballet. Both companies tend to draw their brightest stars from abroad, which makes home-grown stars all the more popular to the British press. Bryn Terfel for the Royal Opera and Darcey Bussell for the Royal Ballet have both been sources of pride for their nationality as well as their talent. More recently, Edward Watson, a flame-haired principal with the Royal Ballet, and Rupert Pennefather, a handsome rising star within the company, have both been greeted as English performers among the best of international talent that the Royal Ballet can attract.

The best-known example of the latter was Rudolf Nureyev, whose appearances at the Royal Ballet from the early 1960s made him a superstar. His reputation was partly thanks to his spectacular ability and the charisma that he exuded, on stage and off it, but his appeal was also due to the chemistry between himself and Margot Fonteyn, the Royal Ballet's prima ballerina. Their partnership was one of the artistic phenomena of the 1960s and helped popularize ballet to wider audiences than would normally have been interested in it.

A large photograph of Nureyev, which was used as part of a dance tribute to him on the stage of the ROH, has been kept in the wings ever since, as a tribute to him. This was a spontaneous gesture, and made not by the management but by the stagehands – a touching recognition of the effect that he had on those, at every level, with whom he worked, as well as on the public.

That public, whether at the ROH for the opera or the ballet, tend to be far better dressed than at most theatres. This is partly because there is still a sense of occasion about ballet and opera performances that encourages rather more formal wear than usual; partly because the Royal in the theatre's name and the vast gold monogram of EIIR on the curtains that divide the front of the stage from the auditorium provide a sense that the monarch is, or could very well be, present at the performance.

Partly, however, it is also due to the wealth of the audience. Top-price tickets for a Royal Ballet performance are £85. For the Royal Opera than can rise to £120 or more. People who can afford those prices tend to work in the City or the Law, and when the men come on to the theatre from work they are still wearing suits, while their wives and women friends like to use the occasion to dress to match.

The result is an atmosphere not of snobbery, as some would accuse, but of comfort and elegance. While it is right that you should be able to go to the theatre in jeans and a pullover – and in some smaller, less formal theatres, like the Donmar, that seems the most appropriate outfit – it is equally enjoyable to be able to dress up for a performance, knowing that the great majority of the rest of the audience will also be wearing their best. The result is not so much elitism as elegance, and there is a role for that in the auditorium as well as on stage.

Whether a production is classical or modern, the most important aspect of it is the rapport between performer and public, the sense that, though we are physically sitting in our seats, we are emotionally on stage – not just with the characters but actually as them.

We suffer the agonies of Madam Butterfly as she decides that the best thing for her little son's future is to give him up to his absentee American father and his new American wife. We feel Tosca's terror and rage as she surreptitiously takes a knife from the dinner table, and prepares to stab the Secret Police chief, Scarpia, through what passes for his heart – and we feel her sense of despair and defiance as she hurls herself from the ramparts of the Castel Sant'Angelo as she robs Scarpia's troops of their chance to avenge his death.

Puccini made a speciality out of humiliating women on stage. True, others may have written the libretti, but the composer was clearly attracted to stories in which beautiful women were atrociously treated by men and had everything they ever loved wrenched from them. *Madam Butterfly* is a prolonged exercise in psychological sadism, while *Tosca* has literal sadism in the form of a torture scene, where Tosca's lover, Cavaradossi, has a spiked metal band screwed ever tighter on his head, in an attempt to force him to reveal an escaped political prisoner's hiding place.

Sir Kenneth MacMillan, one of the two great twentieth-century choreographers with the Royal Ballet (the other being Sir Frederick Ashton) also made a career out of heroines being ill-treated. His *Anastasia*, for example, graphically shows the Romanov princess, in an asylum, recalling the horrors of the Russian Revolution, while his 1970s classic *Manon*, taken from a French novel, is about the very brief rise then dramatic and indeed fatal (after being imprisoned, transported to the colonies and raped) fall from grace of the eponymous heroine.

However grim the storyline, *Manon* shows why MacMillan was so highly prized by the Royal Ballet, and why his early death, in 1992 was such a loss. The only positive thing about his demise was that it was swift (a heart attack) and took place at the ROH, during a performance.

Manon was a regular part of the repertoire in the 1970s and early 1980s, and still returns periodically. In 2008 Ivan Putrov, one of the Royal Ballet's most photogenic principals, made his debut as Des Grieux, the young student who becomes the lover of Roberta Marquez's Manon.

Marquez was suitably flighty and immature as the convent girl who suddenly experiences the temptations of the adult world and in the final act she brilliantly conveyed the sense of a broken spirit without being in any way histrionic. Her portrayal of a young woman whose brief experience of the world has ended in degradation and despair was not only expressed through Macmillan's choreography but also her acting: her eyes were as expressive as her body language.

Ivan Putrov brought a boyish charm to the part of Des Grieux, along with the elegant classicism that is his trademark. His looks as well as his dancing have earned him a following, as has his willingness to experiment in dance as well as play the traditional roles. He has worked with Sam Taylor-Wood, the artist whose video of David Beckham sleeping was a major draw when exhibited at the National Portrait Gallery.

In Taylor-Wood's short film *Strings*, Putrov, almost naked, hangs suspended above a small group of musicians playing classical music. He moves gently and gracefully, like some sort of angel or spirit, responding to the music and musicians. In London the film was shown in the same gallery as Taylor-Wood's striking exhibition of photographs of famous actors crying. Putrov has years of dancing left in him but given his expressive acting ability as well as his technical skill as a ballet dancer, it would be natural for him to move from the dance world into theatre or film when the time comes.

Along with Marquez and Putrov, the production also starred Brian Maloney as Lescaut, Manon's brother who pimps his sister to a rich old man. Manon slips from under the rich man's nose to elope with the young and handsome Des Grieux. The older man is led to Manon by Lescaut and tempts her away from true love with lavish presents. As in all proper tragedies, the heroine's character flaw is at the root of the disaster that overtakes her: had she stayed with Des Grieux instead of being seduced by furs and diamonds, the horrors that were to come would never have materialized.

Des Grieux manages to meet up with Manon who persuades him to try to cheat at cards so he will have enough money to support her in the style she now

Ivan Putrov in *Le Spectre de la Rose*

enjoys with her lover. The cheating is discovered and the couple are arrested and sent to Louisiana, then a French colony, where they are separated. She is raped by an official before Des Grieux bursts in, kills her tormentor, then escapes with her to the swamps where, her life passing before her eyes, she dies.

MacMillan is the master of soaring love duets, of which the bedroom scene between the young lovers is a classic example. Another such is the balcony scene from *Romeo and Juliet*. In a gala evening commemorating the Royal Ballet's history, the excerpts from the earlier years, from the 1930s, 40s and 50s were attractive but not emotionally involving. When the programme moved into the 1960s, with the *Romeo and Juliet* balcony *pas de deux*, the atmosphere in the theatre completely changed, with an emotional connection between audience and dancers that was absolutely electric.

Another Royal Ballet dancer turned choreographer who deserves a mention is Sir Robert Helpmann. One of the stars of the pre-war English ballet scene, Helpmann earned the unusual distinction of a ground-breaking obituary in *The Times*, which mentioned that he had been an active and energetic homosexual, making the fact explicit – describing him as 'a proselytising homosexual' rather than simply implying his sexuality in the usual way though phrases like 'he never married'.

Helpmann created a short ballet version of *Hamlet* which was premiered at the New Theatre (now renamed in Noël Coward's honour) during the Second World War. This piece, with lush, dark, threatening designs by Leslie Hurry, was less than an eighth the length of the Shakespeare play but managed, despite seemingly insuperable odds, to tell the story as powerfully as the play does.

This *Hamlet* has remained in the repertoire of the Royal Ballet but has not been performed for a quarter of a century. Dame Monica has expressed an interest in reviving it, and it was unfortunate that it was not scheduled for late 2008 or early 2009, to coincide with either David Tennant's version for the Royal Shakespeare Company at the Novello or Jude Law's for the Donmar Warehouse's West End season at Wyndham's. It would have been fascinating for theatre audiences to have been able to compare the two versions, and might have provided a useful cross-over impetus between audiences for theatre and ballet. Too many of the former see ballet as a specialized art form that mainly consists of stereotyped images of dancers in period costume striking poses to Tchaikovsky, when the reality – as MacMillan's *Manon* demonstrates, not to mention more modern pieces by Christopher Wheeldon and Wayne Macgregor – is of a highly sexualized, thrillingly physical form of theatre which, as Helpmann's *Hamlet* shows, can tell even the best-known theatre stories in a fresh, exciting and artistically equal way.

At this point, a favourite Helpmann anecdote – one that ties in with his honest obituary. Helpmann in later life appeared on screen (as the Child Catcher in *Chitty Chitty Bang Bang*) and also on stage. He was very good in Shakespeare – among his roles being Oberon, opposite Vivien Leigh's Titania in *A Midsummer Night's Dream* at the Old Vic in 1937. Leigh had an elaborate headdress as the fairy queen, and when the pair were presented to Queen Mary after the performance, Leigh's headdress became caught in Helpmann's hair, so the two had to back out of the royal presence like a pair of Siamese twins.

As well as appearing in London – and Sydney – he toured extensively, in England and in his native Australia, which he had left as a young man to further his career in London. One evening, his tour, which had exhausted all the major theatres, was in a backwoods settlement, where he would be performing to the locals in the open air (or a tent – there are several variations on the anecdote, though the punch line is the same).

Helpmann's dressing room was the umpire's changing room in the nearby cricket pavilion, and it was here that a young assistant was sent by a frantic management when the great man was dangerously late to take his place for the start of the show. The assistant found the actor perched on a chair, under the only working light bulb in the pavilion. In one hand was a small mirror; in the other was a stick of make-up that he was applying to his face.

The chair was very precariously placed in order to catch such light as there was, and the assistant was terrified that Helpmann would lose his balance – as most people would – and break his leg before he reached the makeshift stage.

'Are you alright, Sir?' he asked, nervously. 'Do be careful!'

'Oh, I'm fine!' came the reply. 'I've been doing my make-up in the strangest places for years now. But what really worries me is – how on earth do the umpires manage?'

Helpmann and Margot (later Dame Margot) Fonteyn were founder members of what was to be the Royal Ballet, but the oldest dance company in England is not, as many people assume, the Royal Ballet, but Ballet Rambert. Now known as Rambert Dance Company, to reflect its role as a touring company that specializes in modern dance rather than classical ballet, Rambert is led by its current artistic director, Mark Baldwin.

Baldwin spent many of his years as a dancer with Rambert, when he sported a rather French-style shock of dark hair, which has now been replaced by a far more cropped style. What has not changed is the inventiveness and elegance that he brings to his choreography, the most recent example of which is *Eternal Light* which, in Rambert fashion, has toured as well as having appeared in London, at Sadler's Wells.

Rambert's headquarters has for some years been in Chiswick. There has been a long campaign, not helped by the complexities of planning law, for the company to build a new home on the South Bank, behind the National Theatre. If this finally comes to fruition it will provide a purpose-built headquarters that would include the most modern physiotherapy rooms and dance studios as well as an administrative centre for a company that will continue its historic role of touring, to present modern dance to the widest and most diverse possible audience throughout the country. It will continue, when in London, to perform at Sadler's Wells.

Located in Islington, Sadler's Wells theatre was bought by Lilian Baylis, the redoubtable owner of the Old Vic, as a north London base not just for plays (her first season opened with John Gielgud as Malvolio in *Twelfth Night*) but also for the opera and ballet companies that she saw as sister companies to her Old Vic theatre troupe: all three would present the best possible examples of their art form to the widest audience at the most affordable prices.

The theatre's name comes from a spa on the site, owned by a Mr Sadler and whose finances were based on the eponymous well whose water supposedly had healthy qualities. There is a plaque to that effect, on the site of the well, in one of the two entrances from the theatre foyer into the stalls.

The Sadler's Wells theatre that Baylis bought and promoted has been pulled down. This may have disappointed purists and theatre historians, but for once the demolition of a historic theatre was richly justified, as the seats were easily the most uncomfortable in London (though the dress circle at the charming little Comedy Theatre in Panton Street leaves a lot to be desired in terms of leg room).

The new building erected in its place is a vast improvement and a good example of the use of glass – and hence of light – in a modern theatre. The result is a sense of modernity and minimalist elegance: an ideal setting for much of the modern dance that the theatre hosts. Visiting companies tend to stay for a run of only a couple of weeks or so, with longer runs over the Christmas/New Year period, which means that audiences get to see a wide variety of companies and styles.

Flamenco has been popular, with flamenco festivals seeing several companies bring their own interpretation of this art form. Perhaps the most remarkable experience that Sadler's Wells has offered in the last three or four years was a season of Kabuki, the highly stylized Japanese theatre that is a mixture of theatre, dance and mime. Sadler's Wells remains, as it always has been, an outpost of Theatreland that showcases London theatre's cosmopolitan sister art of dance.

23

Tony Field: A Life in Theatre

A spry, smartly-dressed man walks up St Martin's Lane from the Coliseum to an office doorway, sandwiched between two restaurants: Browns and Beotty's. Browns is, as it were, a child of the 1980s: a popular, unpretentious yet smart restaurant, catering mainly for the younger end of the market and a meeting place for 20- and 30-somethings. Beotty's, by contrast, is a London institution: a Greek restaurant that has been situated here, in Covent Garden (rather than the more traditionally cosmopolitan Soho) since the 1950s.

Tony Field, who looks about 70 but is in his early 80s, has been a Theatreland fixture as long as Beotty's, but has, throughout his career, had an affinity with, and ability to motivate, the young. His career was centred on over a quarter of a century (1957–1983) as finance director of the Arts Council, but has also involved the creation of LIPA, the Liverpool Institute of Performing Arts, which was set up by ex-Beatle Sir Paul McCartney, to provide a training ground for talented young performers in musical theatre.

Field had first been approached with the idea for such a school by the pop singer turned theatre and film star Tommy Steele, but it was not until Paul McCartney decided to try to save his ex-school from falling into complete disrepair that Field's energy and administrative ability were brought to bear on creating an enduring academy that could give young people a thorough grounding in acting, singing and dancing for a future in musical theatre. As Chairman he presided over the raising of £18 million to provide studios and classrooms for the refurbished school.

Tony Field's own background is musical: his father ran his own band in the 1920s, while his mother took him not just to see his father at work, but to a huge range of theatre and music performances – something that was to stand him in good stead at the Arts Council.

Field started his career as an actor, but despite an early break, his first experience of life in London was sleeping rough on the Embankment and in railway stations, as he was unable to find any steady employment in the theatre. Putting his theatrical ambitions on hold, he decided to train as a chartered accountant, as it not only provided a good, steady income but also because he found the work genuinely interesting and proved to have a head for figures.

Although he has said on many occasions, when speaking to students, 'If you had told me, when I was 16, that I would be a chartered accountant, I'd have shot myself!', he was eventually able to bridge the gap between finance and the stage, when working as finance director for an entrepreneur whose business interests were to include the Comedy Theatre, in Panton Street, between the Haymarket and Leicester Square.

Having been acquired and refurbished, the theatre needed programming, and Field was asked to do so. Running a West End theatre might have satisfied most accountants' artistic ambitions, but Field was keen to take this further. At the time, the Lord Chamberlain was still censoring plays and musicals on the London stage (and indeed throughout the country). This was a leftover from 1737 when the then government took deep exception to a satirical play that poked fun at politicians. The government passed a law making it a requirement that all scripts for public performance be presented to the office of the Lord Chamberlain (a senior royal courtier) for approval.

In the strange way that England often had, of combining a surprising degree of political liberty with an astonishingly repressive social policy, the Lord Chamberlain continued to be a deadening hand on London theatre until 1968 when his lordship's office was finally stripped of its outdated powers.

Until then, and certainly when Tony Field was first active in theatre production, the only way to get round this censorship (showing homosexuals on stage, for example, was banned, as was nudity – unless, as at the Windmill Theatre in Soho, the girls on stage simply stood as *tableaux vivants* and were not seen to move) was to open a theatre club, with private membership.

Field did so, co-creating the New Watergate Theatre Club, named after the seventeenth-century water gate that stands, in rather depressed isolation, in Victoria Embankment Gardens, near the Embankment tube.

The water gate marks the northern part of the Thames, in the days before the mid-nineteenth-century embankment of the river pushed it southwards and created the space not only for a highway, gardens and buildings but, crucially, for the Victorian sewers on which London still depends.

The water gate is a stone structure that was an elegant and impressive docking point for visitors to the Thames-side mansion of the Duke of Buckingham. The

Duke would have enjoyed many of the gay plays that were staged at the Watergate club centuries after his death, because he was, as a young man, the object of the homosexual passion of King James I (1603–1625) and the emotional attachment of James's heir, King Charles I (1625–1649).

Buckingham's extraordinary career as royal favourite, soldier and politician, which ended in 1628 when he was assassinated by a disgruntled sailor, is commemorated in the streets that mark the site of his palace, and which are each named after a part of his title: George Street, Duke Street, Of Alley and Buckingham Place. All that is left now is the water gate, which would be more profitably moved from its land-locked position to the banks of the Thames, where it belongs.

The New Watergate Theatre Club presented a wide range of otherwise banned plays, including the first UK productions of *A View from the Bridge*, *Cat on a Hot Tin Roof* and *Tea and Sympathy*. Field's practical experience of producing there and at the Comedy, whose complete refurbishment he also oversaw, gave him a sympathy for fellow producers when he became finance director of the Arts Council.

That sympathy included an admiration for a very young impresario called Cameron Mackintosh. He asked Field if, in his capacity as finance director, he could persuade the Council (who at the time took a dim view of musicals) to help fund a tour of *My Fair Lady*.

Field cannily referred to this as a musical version of the George Bernard Shaw classic *Pygmalion* and the Council, who saw Shaw as the sort of serious playwright they approved of, agreed. The production was a success. Mackintosh next asked for help with *The Sound of Music*, but Field balked at the idea of suggesting this to his colleagues. Very well then, asked the young impresario. What would Field like to see on stage? Field mentioned *Oklahoma!* which Mackintosh agreed to produce. Field managed to sell it to the board by saying that Mackintosh wanted Arts Council help in staging an American folk opera. The Arts Council finally drew the line at what seemed complete madness – a musical based on T. S. Eliot's poems about cats.

Whilst at the Arts Council, Field created and established the Theatre Investment Fund and the TKTS scheme in Leicester Square.

Among Tony Field's other activities in Theatreland he was on the board of Theatre Projects, a firm that designs and builds theatres all over the world; he was a visiting professor at Harvard and the initiator of Britain's first arts management course, at City University. In addition to these, since leaving the Arts Council he has moved back into producing and investing in plays and musicals in London and around the country.

The range and length of his activities make him an ideal contributor to the theatre industry newspaper, *The Stage*, whose editor, Brian Attwood, has used him as a commentator on theatre trends and issues for many years. Field's way with a pen (which he still insists on using when he writes anything – all his articles have to be typed up and emailed by an assistant) has earned him a place in the affections of *The Stage*'s readers over the years, and Technology Entertainment Press, a publisher specializing in books on the technical aspect of theatre, produced a selection of his articles in *Pages From Stages* in 2004.

As a newspaper, *The Stage* has inevitably come under some criticism over the years, and others have considered trying to launch a rival, but it has always remained the industry standard, a place people can advertise their acts in, or look for work, post notices of auditions and offers of individual jobs, often in technical or front-of-house roles in theatre buildings. It continues to be read by those in the industry and though it also covers British television, it is still primarily associated with the theatre, as its name implies.

Tony Field's most recent producing work included, in 2007, a revival of the American musical *Babes in Arms*, at Chichester. The show was a huge success, with reviews that most producers can only dream of, but despite these and a cast headed by Judy Garland's daughter Lorna Luft, the production was unable to find an available West End theatre to transfer to.

The wait for an available building that producers sometimes have to endure is not unlike planes having to circle in the air over Heathrow, but they cannot afford to circle for long and in any case the casts who made the shows a success will inevitably split up as actors, directors and other members of the creative team head off in search of other, guaranteed work. When this happens the producer is faced with the dilemma of simply abandoning the show to the cuttings albums or of storing the sets and costumes and hoping to resurrect the production with as many of the original team as possible, at some point in the future.

At the time of writing, *Babes in Arms* is still technically available for a West End production, but meanwhile Tony Field and John Causebrook are ploughing on with other projects, both potential and realized. This explains the purposeful way with which the silver-haired Field walks up the street to his office, ready to find a new playwright (one of his pet projects) or actor, or to revive another classic.

It is something of a tradition to quote Stephen Sondheim's lyrics, 'I'm Still Here' from his musical *Follies*, when talking about a still-active survivor of an earlier theatrical era. In Tony Field's case something less defiant (because age does not weary him, nor the years condemn) and less elegiac would be more appropriate: 'Open A New Window' from Jerry Herman's *Mame*, perhaps, as, finally reaching his office on the fourth floor, Tony Field opens a new window, opens a new door – and gets on with the business of theatre.

24

Little and Large:
Two Theatre Collections

At the junction of Russell and Wellington Streets, within view of the colonnade of the Theatre Royal, Drury Lane on one side and the administrative offices of the Royal Opera House on the other, there stood, until 2007, the Theatre Museum. The façade is still there, though the interior will presumably be redesigned and given a new use.

What form the interior takes does not matter; what does is that Covent Garden, the historic starting point for modern Theatreland, no longer hosts at its centre a museum for the performing arts. True, the Theatre Museum still technically exists and its head, Geoffrey Marsh, moved with it from Covent Garden to South Kensington, but it is a scandal that the theatrical capital city of the world, which happens also to be one of the richest handful of cities on the planet, was apparently unable or unwilling to maintain a collection of theatre (and ballet and opera) where it belongs: surrounded by theatres.

Geoff Marsh is an engaging man who is passionate about his work. Slim and boyish looking, he bears more than a passing resemblance to David Tennant, the actor who has played Dr Who for several years and who at the time of writing was about to appear at the Novello Theatre, playing the title role in *Hamlet* for the Royal Shakespeare Company.

Marsh even wears a Dr Who-style scarf – which is appropriate in a way as the Theatre Museum's storeroom is rather like a time machine in which, hanging on clothes racks or resting on shelves, literally millions of artefacts (including a million-plus photographs) are each like a little tardis which, when viewed, speed you back through time to another era.

Marsh is particularly good when giving a private tour of these Theatre Museum archives, which are in a vast building in Olympia, shared with the British Museum. The theatrical relics cover almost every aspect of London's theatre history, from publicity posters to souvenir postcards of once-famous and now long-forgotten stars.

Among the most entertaining are adverts from 'trade' newspapers, looking for porters to carry actors' luggage around on tour – and to be available to play small parts when required or pianists needed for singers' rehearsals. A different era – literally, as *The Era* newspaper was a major conduit between advertisers and would-be performers. One such advert was looking for 'Extra ladies, tall, showy and young'. If they fitted the bill, they were asked to present themselves to the perfectly named Mr Valentine at his office in Maiden Lane. If anyone did answer his call to arms, let's hope they took a chaperone.

The huge rooms at Olympia, with their acres of shelving, contain innumerable theatre programmes, diaries, posters and handbills (ranging from Victorian trapeze artists to a gig by the Sex Pistols in Oxford Street in 1977) and office paperwork – including an invoice, recorded in the accounts book of the St James's Theatre, for the cost of providing police officers outside the theatre to protect it from the machinations of the half-crazed Marquess of Queensberry, whose relentless attempt to ruin Oscar Wilde finally succeeded a few weeks after *The Importance of Being Earnest* opened at the St James's in 1895.

The collection includes many mementos of Diaghilev's Ballets Russes, including the original costumes worn for Stravinsky's *The Rite of Spring*. This was an extraordinary ballet, premiered in Paris in 1913 and then brought to London, where it was more politely received than it had been in France – there was a riot in the theatre there on the opening night.

The reason for the outrage was the modernity of the piece, despite it being set in the distant past, in ancient Russia, where a village gathers to celebrate a pagan ritual to welcome in the spring. Stravinsky's score, which still thrills nearly a century later, was hard enough to stomach for balletomanes and society figures who had come to expect gloriously romantic, if highly-sexed productions from the Ballets Russes.

Worse even than the score for the original audiences was the choreography. The Ballets Russes had revolutionized ballet as an art form. This was down to Diaghilev's genius (he had trained as a musician as well as being an art entrepreneur) and especially his ability to bring together the most talented people in a variety of arts and make them work together.

His greatest protégé, who was also his lover, was a young dancer, from Kiev, Vaslav Nijinsky. Nicknamed the 'God of the Dance' by besotted Parisians, he had transformed the role of male ballet dancer from being a mere supporter of a ballerina into the sexually charged, athletically astonishing centre of wildly exciting, stunningly-designed dance spectaculars.

Nijinsky had already shocked audiences with his choreography for *L'Apres Midi d'un Faun*, to the languid music of Delibes. In that ballet he played a young faun who, entranced with a nymph, picks up a scarf that she has left behind, takes it back to the forest ledge on which he was sleeping, and rubs himself against it until he has an orgasm. This was deeply shocking – which helped the box office, as it has throughout history – but at least the music was lovely, the setting was a classical one, inspired by ancient Greek vases, and Nijinsky himself, over whom both sexes swooned, was centre stage.

For *The Rite of Spring*, he was choreographer rather than star – that role was in any case a female one, the Chosen Maiden – and so his many fans were disappointed that he was not there in front of them. Where he was, was in the wings, screaming at the dancers as they tried to keep time to Stravinsky's almost impossibly difficult rhythm, which was unlike anything they had had to do before.

Nijinsky chose to go against all the conventions of classical dance. Feet were turned in rather than out. Dancers moved in jerky, angular ways rather than with a classic sweep and grace. The whole effect was primitive, raw and frightening. It was artistically astonishing and a cultural turning point for European dance, but a disaster on the night.

Whether the English audiences were more open-minded, or whether they wanted to do whatever would most upset the French, or because, more prosaically, they now knew what to expect, thanks to feverish press reports, (whereas the audience in Paris had been taken entirely by surprise) for whatever reason, the audiences at Covent Garden were polite rather than abusive. No wonder Nijinsky seemed to prefer London to Paris, and eventually moved to England to live.

By then however he had gone mad, which happened gradually until he finally tipped over the edge, after the First World War. His estrangement from Diaghilev, caused by his making a spur-of-the-moment marriage to a young Hungarian aristocrat who had had herself hired by the Ballets Russes for a tour of South America later in 1913, had ruined his career, as Diaghilev promptly fired him.

Without the structure and support of a whole company working for and with him, Nijinsky, whose mental instability had begun to show during rehearsals for *The Rite of Spring* and was partially exacerbated by the hostile reaction to it, fell apart. He had a brother who had also had mental health problems, though their sister, Bronislava, a noted choreographer in her own right, was spared her brothers' inherited problems.

Despite the attentions of the best available doctors, and a trip to the ballet arranged by Diaghilev in the hope of jolting Nijinsky back into reality through the doorway of dance, nothing was able to rescue him from the private mental world that he retreated into. Diaghilev had been accompanied on the ballet visit, rather tactlessly, by his latest lover and protégé, Serge Lifar, a panther-like dark-haired young dancer who was also, coincidentally, from Kiev.

Nijinsky was to die in England, in 1950. Buried here at first, he was eventually exhumed and reburied in Paris – largely thanks to pressure from Serge Lifar, whose own career was based in Paris from the 1920s until his retirement.

Though his body is no longer here, his spirit is strongly felt at both the Royal Opera House and the Coliseum – and indeed wherever dance, especially the ballets he choreographed or starred in, are performed. The Alhambra Theatre, where the Ballets Russes danced in 1919 (without Nijinsky in person, but with his spirit very much present) is commemorated by a small dark plaque on Charing Cross Road, where a Barclays Bank now stands. Diaghilev, who radiated opulence but who often lived hand to mouth, his fur-collared overcoat held together with safety pins, would, given his constant struggle to raise cash to keep his ballet company alive, have appreciated the irony.

The impresario's final hotel bill, from the Grand Hotel des Bains (the setting for Visconti's film *Death in Venice*) is among the memorabilia carefully preserved in the Theatre Museum's archives. Diaghilev had the superstition common to his generation of upper class Russians, and was terrified of a fortune teller's prediction that he would die on water. This was a major factor in his not accompanying Nijinsky on the ocean liner to South America, thus enabling Romola de Pulsky to get him into bed and up the aisle in Buenos Aires.

Diaghilev's favourite holiday destination was Venice, where he died, of complications from diabetes, in 1929. Though he had avoided ships whenever possible, the fortune teller had been right. Staying in Venice, of all cities, he had indeed died on water.

The most poignant reminder of the association between Diaghilev and Nijinsky, and of the impact that the Ballets Russes made on London and continental audiences before the First World War, is not a piece of paper bearing a hotel bill, but row after row, carefully hung up and protected by tissue paper, of the costumes from *The Rite of Spring*.

The most striking thing about them is their vibrancy. Designed to represent primitive peasant costumes, they are splashed with colour in geometric shapes. The intensity and energy of the design, as they hang, motionless, gives a very faint idea of how exciting they must have looked on stage. A century after they were first worn, they look as if they were finished yesterday, and are in tissue paper waiting to be transported in a van to the opera house where a company of young and talented dancers are waiting for them.

Curators have a duty to protect the items in their care, and human sweat is eventually damaging to fabric, but it would be wonderful if these costumes could be freed from Olympia, brought back into the West End, and danced in, even if only for a brief 10- or 15-minute excerpt, when they could come to life again. We would no longer be shocked, of course, but we would certainly be awed, to see just how perfectly the costume design expressed Stravinsky and Nijinsky's radical vision of dance could be.

Whether the Theatre Museum itself can ever be released from West London and brought back into the West End is an even trickier question. Having lost its base in Covent Garden – a building that was, admittedly, a strangely constructed and difficult space in which to store and display the Museum's treasures – it seems, especially in the current economic climate, highly unlikely that the money will be found to pay for a new site.

Yet given that Theatreland has itself moved, over the centuries, across the river and ever westwards, and that many important theatres spiritually, if not geographically, a part of Theatreland are to be found from the City of London to Hammersmith, and from Islington to Southwark, could the Theatre Museum itself not be represented in several sites?

The Covent Garden building had a room called the Paintings Gallery, which, as well as displaying the sort of work that its name implied, doubled as a cabaret space, and by the time of its closure was one of the most interesting small venues in central London, attracting a stylish young crowd for cabaret, burlesque, showbiz concerts and singer-songwriter recitals. Whether the space (which had its own entrance from the street) could be rescued as a separate entity from the rest of the site is unclear, but if it is too late to save the Paintings Gallery there must be other spaces that could be similarly converted.

One of the issues the Theatre Museum has always had to face is that theatre, opera and ballet are all transitory. They are fleeting performances that rely entirely on the energy and expectation that live performances generate. Each performance depends on how performers and audience interact, which is why no two performances are ever exactly the same. For the Theatre Museum to be responsible for hosting and promoting live performances, of a type that deserves more support than it gets in London, and for which there is an audience, would be a major step in making the work of the Museum better known and would publicize its other role – on other sites – of preserving Theatreland's heritage.

That the heritage can be preserved, and in unusual ways, at relatively little cost, is amply demonstrated by the Mander and Mitchenson Theatre Collection. This is the legacy of two nice old men who loved the theatre – and each other – and not only went to virtually every first night in the West End, but also gradually collected a massive amount of theatrical memorabilia, which came to fill their house.

A charitable trust was established to preserve the collection (hence its name) and it was for a number of years based in a decaying mansion in the middle of Beckenham Golf Club in Kent, about 40 minutes by train from central London. This was a picturesque location that, once you eventually reached it, had something of the air of a film set about it, with its faded gentility, crunchy gravel on the path and pigeons seemingly nesting inside the roof.

It has now relocated to the smarter but equally historic Trinity College of Music in Greenwich, where it occupies a suite of upstairs rooms. Taking the river boat to Greenwich a is more attractive journey (despite the prosperous charm of Kent) than going by train into Beckenham. There is something holiday-like about getting on a boat, however modern, and the various companies that run river services on the Thames provide some very smart vessels.

Travelling along the river from the Embankment or the South Bank takes you past many historic sights including three theatres: the Playhouse (visible if you look hard), the National and of course Shakespeare's Globe. You also pass St Paul's Cathedral, one of the most recognizable symbols of London. On the north side of the river is Execution Dock, where pirates, captured by the Royal Navy, were hanged.

These days we don't have capital punishment in England, let alone the very public deaths that were a major street entertainment until the late nineteenth century. Yet in one of those continual time loops in which parts of London always seem to return – even after an interval of several centuries – to their original use, just inland from the site of Execution Dock stands a large police station. This part of the north shore of the Thames is clearly destined to be a place of law and order, however administered.

A public hanging meant that the culprit was to be hanged by the neck until dead: a far slower demise in the seventeenth and eighteenth centuries than it was in Victorian times, when the art of a quick drop that broke the victim's neck was perfected, as an act of humanity. Pirates would, like land-locked criminals, have to choke to death, twitching and thrashing helplessly at the end of a rope.

At popular execution sites like Tyburn (whose site is by today's Marble Arch, and is commemorated by a nearby Catholic convent), friends or sympathizers of the criminals hanged in this way would break through the line of troops or other officials keeping order and pull on the doomed men's legs, to cut short their sufferings. Once the authorities believed the men were well and truly dead, the bodies would be cut down and might then be dissected by surgeons who had no other legal means of cutting up and exploring human bodies. This was an ignominious end, but not as unpleasant as that which befell pirates.

Their bodies, hanged from the dock at low tide, were left to be covered completely by three high tides before being retrieved. Piracy was a curse that was eventually swept from the high seas, largely thanks to the efforts of the Royal Navy. It is ironic that, when the only time the London public would normally hear about pirates is when listening to a commentary on board a boat from Westminster to Greenwich and passing an ancient place of execution, we should once again be hearing tales of pirate attacks on innocent shipping – this time not in the Caribbean but off the coast of Somalia.

Leaving the ghosts of eighteenth-century pirates behind, the ferry eventually arrives at Greenwich, where another maritime ghost seems to rise out of the ground to greet you. This is the *Cutty Sark*, a famously fast ship that was employed by tea traders to bring their products across the oceans to a British public that could never get enough tea to drink.

The *Cutty Sark* was badly damaged by a fire in May 2007 while undergoing extensive restoration and is, at the end of 2008, under wraps, as efforts are made by experts to salvage something from the wreckage. The fire is thought to have been started maliciously – an unbelievable act of vandalism against an elegant and historic example of the shipwright's art.

Passing what is left of the *Cutty Sark*, instead of heading into the centre of Greenwich, you make your way to the riverside collection of buildings that are Trinity's home. A visitor with a less focused agenda could also take in the National Maritime Museum, or the Queen's House (built for Queen Anne) or the Observatory, where they could see the Greenwich Meridian – the line from which all distance, and time, across the world is measured.

The theatre lover, however, would plough on to the Mander and Mitchenson collection. Here the small staff are headed by Richard Mangan, who has been a generous helper in preparing the illustrations for this book. Mangan is less well known than his daughter Lucy, a journalist with a popular regular column in *The Guardian*. While this reflects well on her journalism, Mangan *père* deserves more recognition for the work he and his team have done in maintaining the collection.

This is an entirely private organization with no government support. It relies for its continued existence not only on the home that Trinity College provides, but also on selling its services. This comes in the form of supplying (and charging for) research material, including illustrations, from its archive.

Given that the archive was established by two private individuals, Raymond Mander and Joe Mitchenson, neither of whom was particularly rich, the range of the material is astonishing. In a smaller, cosier style than the Theatre Museum at Olympia, Richard Mangan, like his opposite number, Geoff Marsh, displays row after row of boxes, in which programmes and press cuttings of a staggering number of plays and musicals have been carefully preserved.

Mangan takes great pride in his role as a curator but he is also a published scholar, who edited and introduced an official selection of the letters of Sir John Gielgud, published after Gielgud's death, and following Sheridan Morley's official biography of Sir John.

The Mander and Mitchenson is rightly proud of its independence but it would be an improvement if it had the funding to make its work more widely known and its collection more used. While it would be wrong for it to be in any way subsumed by the Theatre Museum, given that the Mander and Mitchenson is promoting theatre history, in a different part of London and one more easily accessed than Olympia by those living or working or studying south of the river and east of the City, might it not make sense for some sort of tie-in between the two?

Both organizations open their archives to research, with the Theatre Museum receiving many enquiries spurred by an interest in family history rather than purely academic or historical questions. If a family member believes their great-grandfather once worked with Ralph Richardson, or danced in the chorus behind Dorothy Dickson in a Drury Lane musical, then the study room at Olympia is the ideal place to go and find out – as indeed is the establishment at Greenwich.

The continued independence of the Mander and Mitchenson collection would be vital as the Theatre Museum is in itself a case of one museum being swallowed by another. To be fair, there was a historical reason for this, in the way that it was set up in the first place.

The Theatre Museum's collection is based on that of a wealthy theatregoer, Gabrielle Eindhoven, who left it to the nation. There being no Theatre Museum at the time – and given that part of the collection was costumes and other fabric – it was decided to give her bequest to the Victoria and Albert Museum, which specializes in fine art. Even after the establishment of a Theatre Museum as such, it remained – and remains – a part of the Victoria and Albert Museum.

The V&A, as it is universally known, is a world-class fine art collection with an unrivalled range of experts on its staff, but there is a strong body of opinion that believes that it is not – for all its commitment and care – the ideal repository for the nation's premier collection of theatrical memorabilia. So much so, indeed, that there was a campaign by some concerned theatre experts to press for the Theatre Museum collection to be taken away from the V&A and given its independence. This foundered, not least because the theatre community and its supporters were not able or willing to actually stump up the cash necessary for such an independence to be established.

While this was understandably disappointing, there was some logic to it. Theatre producers may make a lot of money on some productions but they lose a lot on others and in any case their business is in presenting live shows, not storing relics of long-dead ones. Sir Cameron Mackintosh, whose philanthropy within Theatreland has been extraordinary, supported the Theatre Museum by buying the historic archive of H.M. Tennent and donating it to the museum. Supporting and donating are entirely different from buying and running such an institution, so it is not surprising that the independence campaign finally came to an end, like the building it had tried to save.

25

Films on Stage

Cinema and the theatre have often been seen as rivals, especially when theatres like the Coliseum were taken over and used for showing films, a fate that overtook huge numbers of theatres across the country from as long ago as the 1920s and which accelerated in the years after the Second World War. This process saw Leicester Square, which was very much a theatre area with playhouses like Daly's and the Alhambra, morph into the most prestigious collection of London's cinemas. Despite this, the two industries have often benefited from each other and, as the first decade of the twenty-first century approaches its end, this mutual advantage seems even clearer.

Cinema, when it was a new industry, had no option but to take stage actors, as there were no others. By the mid-1920s the silent movies had reached a level of sophistication and artistry that deserves far greater recognition. That has been denied because they were so comprehensively replaced by talkies, and have ever since been seen as somehow primitive or second rate, when in reality they had and still retain a magic all of their own. A cinema that shows only silent movies would be a wonderful ambassador that could demonstrate this artistry to a generation of film fans who are unaware of their heritage.

The relationship between Theatreland and the young British film industry meant that in the 1920s writers like Ivor Novello and Edgar Wallace could have a stage success with a film one year and then issue a cinema release of the film version 12 months later – which in Novello's case he also starred in. This clearly benefited stage and screen alike.

Between then and now the main connection between the two art forms has been the hiring of movie stars by theatre producers to add some popular sex appeal or at least name recognition to theatre casts. The pale shadow of this is seen in posters for panto, which raids the BBC and ITV rather than Warner Brothers for its performers. With all due respect to television, this sometimes leads to the use of 'celebrities' with virtually no name recognition – hence the need to literally spell out on the poster which role they have played and in which TV series.

A new development in this relationship, and one which has been gathering momentum over the last decade, is for theatre not just to take film stars to sex up West End productions, but to adapt entire films for the stage.

Andrew Lloyd Webber's *Sunset Boulevard* is a classic example of this and it has returned to Theatreland in the form of a small-scale version in which most of the actors also play musical instruments, thus providing the band as well as the cast. This is a contrast with the original production, which opened at the Adelphi Theatre with a show-stopping (moveable) staircase as its centrepiece.

The central role of Norma Desmond, the ageing ex-silent movie star who is madly attempting a return to the screen in her own adaptation of the story of Salome, was played by Patti LuPone and then a number of other musical theatre stars including Elaine Paige and Petula Clarke.

Lloyd Webber's stage version has some of his best songs, including 'With One Look' which brilliantly sums up the visual rather than verbal skills that silent movie stars brought to their profession. The show itself had the advantage that international audiences were familiar with the original film, which starred a real-life silent movie star, Gloria Swanson.

A more difficult feat to pull off is making a stage musical from a British film. An example of how this can be done is given by Stephen Daldry's stage adaptation, at the Victoria Palace, of *Billy Elliot*. Daldry took his much-loved film and turned it, with suitable alterations, into a musical that no only won over Theatreland audiences, but also has transferred to Broadway where, despite its very (northern) British references it has melted the pens of even the toughest New York critics. This was a brave act by Daldry who, had it not worked so well, could have been accused of spoiling the memory of the film. Daldry was helped by his enlisting of Sir Elton John in the creative team to write the songs.

Sir Elton's contribution to the theatre, in Disney's *The Lion King* as well as in *Billy Elliot*, has given an already talented and wealthy musician a further string to his composing piano as well as providing a fresh injection of talent into Theatreland – and Broadway – at the very highest level. Some eyebrows were raised when he first became involved in musical theatre rather than pop, but Serge Diaghliev would not have hesitated to use him.

Other examples of films that have transferred to theatre are *The 39 Steps* and *Brief Encounter*. The latter was itself based on Noël Coward's stage play *Still Life* (1936), but although that play has been revived since then, it is the film that everyone knows and loves, and given that so much of its appeal is cinematic – the shots of the steam trains, the sense of period detail in the cinema and the restaur-ant that the lovers visit – it counts as an original work of art in its own right.

The physical theatre company Kneehigh Theatre's recent stage version of *Brief Encounter*, produced by David Pugh, made the most of the cinematic background to the stage piece – even to the extent of being performed in a cinema in the Haymarket – where the original film had been shown.

The production was a major success, even though some audience purists were not keen on Kneehigh's reworking of the structure and style of the piece, giving far greater prominence to the working-class characters who, in the film, were there just to provide some comic relief from the central story.

Despite this, the overwhelming opinion was that this was an ingenious and unexpectedly musical reworking of the film. As well as the inevitable excerpts from Rachmaninov, the company included some period songs: mainly by Coward but including, at one of the most poignant moments in the show, the singing, by two soldiers on leave, of the Boer War song 'Goodbye Dolly Gray'.

The stage version used film as a part of the story-telling, in a way that blended in with the action on stage rather than usurping it. This is hard to do, as the Royal Ballet found when, in a programme in tribute to Rudolf Nureyev they had dancers from the current company performing on stage while newsreel and other film footage of Nureyev, necessarily blown up vastly larger than life so that it could be seen, was projected on a screen above and behind them. Given his charisma, even when filmed simply walking into a room, this didn't so much dwarf the dancers as make them almost irrelevant – one just wanted the screen to expand, fill the stage, and give us all more of Nureyev.

Kneehigh's *Brief Encounter* avoided this, making the use of film a clever effect, sometimes comic, sometimes just surprising, sometimes highly romantic. The convention of showing waves crashing against the shore to denote passion is used in this *Brief Encounter*, but in such a way as to provide a recognizable shorthand and a way of emphasizing emotion rather than comically distracting from it.

One of the few other recent West End productions to have benefited from the use of film or video effects rather than suffer from the jolt that they can bring to a theatre audience's imagination is Lindsay Posner's production of *Carousel* at the Savoy, where William Dudley's designs are delightful – especially in the sequence where Billy, plus an attendant angel sent to get him, travel up to Heaven.

The 39 Steps at the Criterion, unlike *Brief Encounter*, is resolutely low-tech – the nearest it comes to cinema is the use of a white sheet onto which are projected the silhouettes of cut-out shapes representing Richard Hannay running through the Scottish Highlands – watched briefly by a cut-out of Alfred Hitchcock.

This is just one of many clever references to Hitchcock and his other films (in all of which he liked to make a fleeting anonymous appearance) by the adaptor Patrick Barlow. The reason for including the references is that, as previously mentioned, the stage show is based on Hitchcock's 1935 movie rather than John Buchan's 1915 novel which, despite being centred on the central character Richard Hannay's adventures on the trail of a German spy ring, had a very different plot.

In the novel, Hannay is back in England from the colonies and bored by city life. Like all Buchan's heroes he much prefers to be striding across windswept moors in a battered tweed or hanging on grimly to the side of a mountain – Buchan took his bride mountaineering on their honeymoon.

Hannay becomes involved in the German plot to steal Britain's naval secrets prior to launching an aggressive war, and his efforts are complicated by the fact that the police think he murdered the stranger who revealed the basics of the plot to him. The book is essentially a chase story, with Hannay dodging the police while trying to foil the Germans.

Hitchcock's film took the essential premise then radically changed the plot. He introduced scenes in a music hall and instead of the 39 steps being the staircase that leads from the spies' hideout to a beach, from which they plan to row out to a waiting German warship, Hitchcock made the name of the spy ring itself 'The 39 Steps'.

Barlow's play succeeds primarily because though it is a comic spoof of the movie it is highly theatrical, using a minimum of props and backdrops and thus involving the audience's imagination more than usual, drawing them further into the fast-paced action on stage. It is an affectionate spoof, not a mocking one, and as the actors, though clearly enjoying their over-the-top roles with an infectious gusto, perform with real conviction, the production works.

It has also proved to work with New York audiences who, given America's cinematic culture, know the film and are familiar with the rest of Hitchcock's *oeuvre*. Its extreme Britishness is also part of its appeal to Broadway audiences. John Buchan was similarly enamoured of America – he had an American as one of Richard Hannay's closest friends and allies in the series of thrillers that he wrote as a follow-up to *The 39 Steps* and he became a closer friend and indeed neighbour of the country when in 1935 he was given a peerage (as Lord Tweedsmuir) and appointed Governor General of Canada: a post he was still in when he died of a brain haemorrhage in 1940.

Both John and Robert Kennedy admired Buchan's various writings (he was a historian as well as a novelist and public servant) and Robert quoted from Buchan – referring to his belief in the potential nobility of a career in politics – in one of his last comments to the press before his assassination in Los Angeles.

Buchan has been credited as the father of the modern adventure story, and certainly of the genre that sees plucky English gentlemen saving the Empire or indeed the world (like James Bond) from super villains. He was, however, preceded by a writer whose most famous work was swiftly translated from page to stage, and who gave the English language a new word: Ruritanian.

The word came from the imaginary European country Ruritania, in which the adventures of the Englishman hero take place. The author was Anthony Hope Hawkins, known to the world now by his *nom de plume* of Anthony Hope.

Hope's father, the Rev E. C. Hawkins, was rector of St Bride's, Fleet Street, and was himself something of an author, writing, in 1905, a short history of the church and the surrounding area. The history was more of a pamphlet than a book, and was printed by students working in the technical classes at the neighbouring St Bride Institute, in whose basement the Bridewell Theatre is located.

It was the rector's son who was to become a world-famous writer, his greatest success being written while he was living in his father's rectory, in Bridewell Place. The street, an L shape that is a mirror image of the L of Bride Lane, runs south of the St Bride Institute and marks the northernmost boundary of HenryVIII's Bridewell Palace. The rectory, which was purpose-built for the rector in 1885, is now a set of offices that back onto the Institute, their walls touching each other. The modern, post-war rectory of St Bride's backs not onto the Institute but onto the church itself, on its south-west side, and has one of the few private gardens in the City.

Hope was a barrister by training, but with literary ambitions – hardly surprising for a creative artist living in the Bridewell precinct, an area so rich with literary history. As he walked from his father's house to work in the Temple, he began to create in his mind the adventure story that, written down each night, was to be published as *The Prisoner of Zenda* in 1894 and become an international bestseller.

The story has an English gentleman, Rudolf Rassendyll, mistaken, when travelling abroad, for the new King Rudolf V of Ruritania, a Central European nation with a volatile and colourful political situation and whose real King has been kidnapped.

Rudolf V, a hard-drinking wastrel, is unpopular with the masses, who seem to prefer his half-brother, Duke Michael – known as Black Michael for his colouring, in contrast to the redheaded Rudolf (and Rassendyll). Rassendyll, who turns out to be distantly related to the rightful – if reprobate – monarch is persuaded to impersonate the King, and, being an English gentleman, he turns out to be very good at ordering foreigners about and saving them from themselves, while also earning the heart of the beautiful Flavia, a Ruritanian princess.

The book's sense of dash and daring appealed to staid Englishmen living in suburban homes. It offered not just a romantic adventure but also a tantalizing sense that such an adventure might happen to anyone, if only they chose to venture across the English Channel and into the heart of Europe.

By the late 1890s it was relatively easy to cross Europe by train. Passports were not required until the First World War – another way in which that conflict wrecked a gentler and more civilized Europe – and much of the continent was still what we would today, thanks to Hope, refer to as Ruritanian. Germany may have become a militaristic empire by this time, but it was an empire that was a confederation of kingdoms, principalities and dukedoms where an aristocratic young Englishman might indeed have the sort of adventure that the *Prisoner of Zenda* brought so enjoyably to life.

While the book was very much of its time – in its assumption that monarchy was demonstrably the best and most natural form of government; that an English aristocrat was, by his very nature, the best man in a crisis (especially if he happens to look like a King); and that duty must invariably come before pleasure – *The Prisoner of Zenda* is nevertheless timeless in its sense that abroad is somewhere where anything can happen.

It is also as potent today as it was over a century ago, in its fascination with the rich and glamorous, and in the vicarious pleasure readers get from an adventure which they can fantasize could (improbably but just about possibly) happen to them, taking them from their humdrum lives in the City or civil service and raising them, however briefly, from their desks to a throne.

The combination of glamour, drama, cavalry uniforms and coups, set against a background of picturesque castles, made *The Prisoner of Zenda* perfect material for the stage, and it was performed as a play at the St James's Theatre in 1896. As was the pattern in the early twentieth century, the West End play went on to become a popular film – or rather films, as cinema went on to produce six versions of Hope's story (1913, 1915, 1922, 1937, 1952 and 1979), of which the 1937 is perhaps the definitive, starring as it does Ronald Colman, Madeleine Carroll (of Hitchcock's *The 39 Steps*), C. Aubrey Smith, Raymond Massey, Mary Astor, David Niven and that epitome of Ruritanian swagger, Douglas Fairbanks, Jr.

The Prisoner of Zenda was Anthony Hope's first and greatest success, though he was to produce a sequel, *Rupert of Hentzau* (1898) that did well too, and he also published *The Dolly Dialogues*, a collection of stories about London society.

Hope was knighted for his services as a writer (working on propaganda material) in the First World War, and wrote his memoirs, *Memories and Notes* in 1927. Having suffered from depression for many years, he died of cancer in 1933.

Hope's Ruritanian legacy was to inspire Ivor Novello, whose first and last major musicals (*Glamorous Night* and *King's Rhapsody*) were both set in Ruritanian countries – Krasnia and Murania, respectively. Today the story would seem wildly politically incorrect and would probably only receive a West End showing if it were presented in a comic version – like Barlow's *The 39 Steps* at the Criterion. This would be a shame as the story would work well, provided the production had the courage of its convictions, as the original author and cast would have done. The nearest equivalent in Theatreland today is the dashing Hispanic story of *Zorro*, directed by Christopher Renshaw, where Matt Rawle has brought the eponymous hero from screen to stage. As Zorro he swashbuckles gallantly six nights a week at the Garrick, proving that Theatreland still loves a good-looking swordsman.

26

The Savoy: From Theatre to Hotel

The Savoy Theatre is an art deco masterpiece. It is approached by Savoy Court, off the Strand. This stretch of road is the forecourt to the Savoy Hotel, whose frontage is also in the art deco style of the hotel's heyday between the wars. On the right, as you approach the hotel, and situated right next to it, is the theatre.

Given that the Savoy is one of the most famous hotels in the world, it is often assumed that the theatre must have been built to cash in on the availability of wealthy and theatre-loving guests, who would barely have to leave their oasis of luxury in order to reach the comfort of the stalls.

It is certainly true that the Savoy's guests have always been pampered, and that for the convenience of their chauffeurs and taxi drivers, Savoy Court is the only road in England where cars must legally drive on the right hand side rather than the left. However, the hotel came after the theatre and not before.

Built by the splendidly named impresario Richard D'Oyly Carte, it was designed to showcase the musicals of Gilbert and Sullivan, the most popular musical theatre lyricist-and-composer team in Victorian England. When it opened, with the duo's *Patience* in 1881, the theatre had a unique feature: it was the first public building in London designed to be lit entirely by electricity.

Such was the success of the theatre that, eight years later in 1889, D'Oyly Carte decided to use the profits to build a luxury hotel next door – for the convenience of patrons who would not then have to travel home after the show.

Patience featured a poet called Bunthorne, who was loosely modelled on Oscar Wilde, though he was also a wider satire of the then fashionable group of aesthetes of whom Wilde was the most instantly recognizable. Wilde was also a regular at the Savoy Hotel, though his fluctuating fortunes meant that his stay there could be shorter than he would have wished. As he wrote on one such occasion: 'My bill here is £49 for the week. I fear I must leave – no money, no credit and a heart of lead.'

Wilde would stay at the Savoy with his lover Lord Alfred Douglas, and would buy in rent boys with whom Douglas rather than Wilde cavorted. Wilde used to describe encounters with such youths – whether having sex with them or just watching Douglas doing so – as 'feasting with panthers'. The panthers had claws, and their testimony at his trial (he suffered two separate ones after his own initial prosecution of Lord Alfred's father, the Marquess of Queensberry, collapsed) was to bring him down.

Wilde's penchant for hotels was not just the practicality of having somewhere to have sex, safely away from his wife and two children in their family home in Tite Street, Chelsea. It was also the contrast between the grandeur and superficial respectability of such places, despite their sometimes exotic clientele, and the loucheness of the sex that took place in their hotel rooms, as well as the potential availability for sex of some of the male staff.

It was entirely in keeping with the way he lived this double life of politeness and panthers that Wilde chose to await the inevitable arrest, after the libel case against Queensberry failed, in a hotel. He had been urged to take a boat train and escape to France. There was a deliberate pause on the part of the authorities to allow him to do just that, but he chose to stay, waiting for the police at the Cadogan Hotel, in an incident that inspired Sir John Betjeman's poem of that name.

The Victorian interior to the Savoy that Wilde was familiar with was completely remodelled in the art deco style in a radical make-over of the building in 1929. The hotel had, in the meantime, come to be regarded as the natural home for visiting theatricals. Noël Coward made it his London base after he sold his flat in Belgravia and divided his time between homes in Switzerland and Jamaica, largely to avoid the ruinously high levels of British income tax. It was at the Savoy that he was honoured with a birthday lunch when he turned 70, at which the guest speakers were Lord Louis Mountbatten and Sir Laurence Olivier.

In the course of his speech to the assembled guests, 'The Master', as he was known in the profession, announced that he had had two great loves in his life. The dignitaries' faces around him froze in anticipation of his naming, in public, the two men who had been his principal lovers. Would he choose this occasion, of all times, to 'come out'?

There was a visible relaxing of clenched jaws when Coward blithely announced that these loves were, of course, the theatre and the sea, and he was delighted that these were present that afternoon in the form of Mountbatten, an Admiral, and Olivier, England's greatest living actor.

Coward passed on his other love, of the Savoy, to one of his later leading ladies, the American whirlwind of energy, Elaine Stritch. Miss Stritch based herself at the hotel during the run of the Coward musical *Sail Away*, in which she starred, and she used the hotel as her London home whenever she was in town on subsequent visits. She was at the Savoy, for example, during the run of her one-woman show at the Old Vic in 2002, and held the first-night party in the hotel's Thames Foyer – the area that during the day is used for the Savoy's afternoon teas, among the best in London.

Sir Hugh Wontner, one of the Savoy's best-known managers claimed that 'Acting and running a hotel are both exercises of the imagination', and hotels have exerted their influence on the imagination in a number of plays and musicals. These include the stage musical *Grand Hotel*, which was produced at the vast Dominion Theatre in the 1990s and on a very different scale at the Donmar Warehouse some ten years later.

Noël Coward set his last stage work, *Suite in Three Keys*, in a hotel in Switzerland, while Terence Rattigan's *Separate Tables* is set in a small hotel in Bournemouth. Alan Ayckbourn's *Communicating Doors* is set in a hotel which doubles as a mysterious time machine. The possibilities hotels offer for both comic and tragic situations are shown in Neil Simon's comedy *California Suite* and Arthur Miller's *Death of a Salesman*, whose most powerful scene takes place in a hotel room.

The Savoy, thanks to its general location in Theatreland and the proximity of the theatre that funded its construction, remains the pre-eminent theatre hotel. Despite this, The Covent Garden Hotel runs in a close second given its popularity with visiting American stars and some home-grown ones. Its restaurant and bar are also popular with the better-off West End actors: Kenneth Branagh was seen there during the recent run of *Ivanov*, as was Michael Sheen when he was playing *Caligula* at the Donmar in 2003. The Dorchester is more of a movie-star hotel, while the newly refurbished and re-opened St James's Hotel, one of the most beautifully decorated boutique hotels in London, offers a fresh choice to theatregoers who have already stayed at the usual suspects like Le Meridien and the Trafalgar.

During the Savoy's refurbishment the Savoy Theatre has remained open. The 'new' art deco theatre, having prospered for over 80 years, suffered a catastrophic fire that gutted the auditorium in 1990. Fortunately it didn't wreck the structure of the building, or spread to the adjacent hotel.

The theatre recovered from the fire after more than a year's painstaking restoration work, and was re-opened by Princess Diana in 1993 – an event commemorated by a plaque on the theatre's outside wall. Since then it has been the venue for one-man shows (including Simon Callow's *The Importance of Being*

Oscar); for Lorna Luft's gutsy and roof-raising evening of showbiz songs inspired by Judy Garland, *Songs My Mother Taught Me*; for a short-lived season of operas; and for plays by Noël Coward. It is a classy theatre, but a curiously cold one, in that all that art deco metalwork, though impressive, is a little too mechanical for the theatre.

Coldness was an obvious theme of the play *Antarctica* at the Savoy in 2001. The drama, which deserved a longer run that it managed, was based on a real-life incident, before the First World War, when a group of English explorers found themselves trapped in their tents for an Antarctic winter – six months in which howling gales swept over the desolate landscape and during which the sun never rose.

This was a gripping play with a real sense of danger. The men's ordeal – huddled together, often unable to leave their quarters even to answer the call of nature and unable to bathe for six months, desperately eking out their meagre rations – seemed even worse after the curtain call, when the audience emerged from the theatre into Savoy Court and the sight of the blazing lights of the Savoy, whose luxuries were the antithesis of everything the Edwardian explorers had had to endure.

The theatre's front-of-house area is on many levels, each separated by stairs – which greet you as soon as you come into the small foyer from Savoy Court – and a visit can seem like a practice run for a mountaineering weekend rather than a night in the West End. The dress circle bar is attractive, though as small as the rest of the public areas, and it makes good use of mirrors. This is an ideal place to stand if you want to surreptitiously people-watch in the mirrors while appearing to pay complete attention, glass in hand, to whoever is talking to you. Given the theatre's location, history and beauty it is always in demand as a venue so the mirrors are likely to remain packed with theatregoers, while the hotel's foyers will no doubt be as busy as ever once the Savoy re-opens.

27

The Road Goes On

The title of this final chapter is that of one of the songs from *The Lord of the Rings*, which opened at Drury Lane in 2007 and closed the following year, but which has a future life in Germany and on tour in the UK.

It appeals, as a title, for several reasons. First, because the song itself was an attractive one, sung by the hobbits as they overcame various obstacles on their way out of the comfort zone of the Shire and on towards Mordor.

Second, because Theatreland is bigger than any one production – even one that cost over £12 million to stage. After the hobbits left, the Theatre Royal dusted itself down, welcomed Dawn French and Jennifer Saunders for a brief run and then sang 'Consider yourself . . . at home' to Rupert Goold's production of *Oliver!*

Third, because just as every show takes the characters on stage and the audience watching them on an emotional journey, so the story of Theatreland itself is a journey, from one bank of the Thames to another, then westwards through a cityscape that the building of theatres was instrumental in creating and then populating.

Fourth, and lastly, because, as on a road, the view changes as you move forward. Theatreland, for all its love of the past and its continued connection, through people, plays, wood, bricks and mortar, with the people and playhouses that literally made it what it is today, is a constantly evolving part of London and an art form that, like the buildings in which it is performed, recognizes and reflects the changes in the society in which it exists

As an art and an industry theatre has survived for five centuries, adapting to wars, recessions, radical changes in public taste and major shifts in patterns of work and socializing. However dire political or economic circumstances may have been, people have always turned to the theatre, whether as an embodiment and exploration of their current woes in the form of serious plays, or as an escape from them, in the shape of big brassy musicals.

Ironically, one of the challenges that society as a whole faces throughout Western Europe – that of an ageing population – is something that should benefit theatre. For decades commentators have been bemoaning the fact that theatre audiences tend to be middle-aged or elderly (even more so for opera), as if this were self-limiting and entirely negative.

Yet audiences have always tended to fall in this age bracket, though they have also always (whatever the doom-mongers may say) included large numbers of young people and, increasingly, women, who now (according to the Society of London Theatre) regularly make up a majority of theatre audiences, just as they always have at the ballet.

No one says of gardening, a multi-million pound industry enjoyed by a large number of the general public, that because gardeners tend to be middle-aged and elderly the gardening industry will be doomed when they die. As young people get older they unsurprisingly tend to start to take an interest in things that traditionally appeal to older people. As with gardening – and golf – so with theatre.

It is as absurd to say that theatre is in trouble if it can't attract the young as it would be to say that the billion-pound baby-care industry is doomed because the babies it caters for will outgrow their need for its products in a few years' time.

Theatreland is itself partly to blame for this sense of panic about age. Directors of the subsidized theatres and companies are under pressure to tick the politically correct boxes and to show that they are desperately keen to encourage (among other groups) the young. How often have we heard the director of the National (whoever was actually filling the position at the time) say that he wanted to see more young people in his theatre?

By contrast, how often have we heard the director of the National, or the Royal Shakespeare Company, or the Royal Opera, say that he wants to see more *old* people in his theatre or opera house? Yet the one statement is as absurd, in its way, as the other. What are the young, whom directors love to see streaming into their playhouses, to do when they finally, after a couple of decades of enthusiastic theatregoing, turn 40? Shoot themselves?

Theatres need audiences. Different shows will appeal to different audiences. So long as the audiences turn up, their age – or race, or bank balance – should be irrelevant and of no cause for concern or triumphalism on the part of those responsible for staging the plays in the first place. If we are to look at the question of age, however, then the fact that theatre has tended to attract older audiences means that the undeniable ageing of Britain should be a goldmine for producers who can provide what the public wants to see.

Another trend that theatre can profit from is the increased enjoyment that audiences of all ages are taking in live performance. This has been shown very clearly in the pop industry – whose equivalent of the Oscars, incidentally, is the Ivors: the Ivor Novello Awards, named after the composer whose own music could not be further removed from that of today's winners.

Until recently, pop bands gave concerts to help sell their albums. Now the dynamic is the opposite: with internet downloads affecting the sales of traditional recordings, it has become the case that recordings are forms of advertisement for live concerts.

In an internet age where too many people seem to be sucked into an alternative reality that denies them actual human contact and relationships, and where even meetings with bank managers and shop assistants have been replaced by online banking and shopping, the pleasures of being part of a group of real people, watching other people performing on stage have become all the more tangible.

As this is very much a trend that younger people are part of, it bodes well for the theatre, though as mentioned in Chapter 17, young people are very much the target demographic for theatre producers in any case.

One of Theatreland's strengths in attracting different audiences is the sheer range of shows that it can offer, given the number of playhouses available. There is room for gritty dramas alongside musical fables like *The Lion King*. Revivals of classics have space to appear alongside new political plays, while favourite operas can co-exist with new chamber pieces. A revival of the farce *Boeing Boeing* can be supported by one audience at the Comedy, while another ensures a long run (in rep) for *War Horse* at the National. At the Royal Ballet, Wayne MacGregor's modern dance can be enjoyed one night and Marius Petipa's classical choreography the next.

The survival of so many theatres, and the adapting of other spaces to create new, 'fringe' venues, has been a success story and though the economics of the use of space in central London means that we are unlikely to see a purpose-built new commercial theatre there (though there has been talk of a Sondheim Theatre perched above Shaftesbury Avenue, between the Gielgud and the Queen's), the work of the Theatres Trust and the ingenuity of current and would-be theatre owners means that not only will our existing theatre stock survive, we will also see at some point soon the next Donmar Warehouse created out of a non-theatrical building, following a tradition that dates back to Shakespearean London and the Blackfriars Theatre.

Less positively, the future of Theatreland is not just in the hands of the theatre industry, but also of local and national government. The Society of London Theatre's 2004 West End theatre audience survey found that the great majority (over 80 per cent) of theatregoers use public transport to visit a theatre. Much as the Society can lobby the relevant authorities – principally the Mayor – it has no control over this vital aspect of theatregoing.

There is also only so much that theatre owners can do in terms of the urban landscape in which they operate. Dislike of crowds, noise and litter, and fear of knife crime or just generally thuggish behaviour are factors that put off many people from visiting Theatreland – especially the elderly who have always been a core constituency. Theatre owners may liaise with Westminster and Camden councils but they cannot influence policing policy for the capital.

Yet although the frequency and late running (or otherwise) of London's overstretched public transport system and the safety and cleanliness of its streets are real issues of concern, it remains a fact that early twenty-first-century theatre is in very strong shape.

As well as the range of theatres and shows on offer, there is a huge talent pool to draw on, in terms of directors and designers as well as actors. The increasing worldwide domination of the English language (due as much to today's internet as to last century's Empire) gives Theatreland another huge advantage.

For, as Europe's place in the world – militarily, politically, financially – continues to decline vis-à-vis the developing world's new superpowers, it is the case that the citizens of these nations, of China and especially India (which will be as important on the world's stage) will want to visit London, will increasingly be able to afford to do so and will want to go to the theatre when they do. This will be a sort of cultural imperialism in reverse: just as Europeans have always visited the Middle East and further abroad to look at quaint remnants of earlier civilizations, so Asian tourists will still want to visit our theatres, to see Shakespeare and Ayckbourn, Rattigan, Pinter, Terry Johnson and Ronald Harwood, long after they have given up buying our cars, washing machines and financial packages.

This is just as well, for we will not, however much the globe warms up, be able to attract people for our weather. Our financial services industry may be following our manufacturing base into some post-industrial twilight, but we will always (unless the government decides to reintroduce censorship of plays, presumably on the grounds of national security or community cohesion) have our theatre.

Our national genius, if one can still use that word, lies not in parliament, palace or cathedral, though all of those have contributed to it, but in our play-houses, whether the wooden O of Shakespeare's Globe, the ornate beauty of the Theatre Royal, Haymarket, the massive complex that is the National Theatre or little jewels like the Apollo, the Fortune or the Vaudeville.

With players as talented as Derek Jacobi, Judi Dench, Penelope Wilton, Samuel

West, Ralph Fiennes, Frances de la Tour and Siân Philips, to name but a few of the hundreds of recognizably great actors any producer and director can call on, Theatreland's lifeblood is running as strongly as ever it has and the five-century journey that this book has only had the space to hint at continues to be the most exciting one that any theatre, in any part of the world, has to offer. The Thames still flows through the heart of Theatreland – and the road goes on.

Index